TRACKING THE WILD COOMBA

ROBERT COCUZZO

TRACKING THE WILD COOMBA

THE LIFE OF LEGENDARY SKIER DOUG COOMBS

MOUNTAINEERS BOOKS

MOUNTAINEERS BOOKS

Mountaineers Books is the publishing division of The Mountaineers, an organization founded in 1906 and dedicated to the exploration, preservation, and enjoyment of outdoor and wilderness areas.

1001 SW Klickitat Way, Suite 201, Seattle, WA 98134
800.553.4453, www.mountaineersbooks.org

Printed in the United States of America
Distributed in the United Kingdom by Cordee, www.cordee.co.uk
19 18 17 16 1 2 3 4 5

Copy editor: Kirsten Colton, The Friendly Red Pen
Cover and book design: Jen Grable
Cover photograph: *At Mike Wiegele Helicopter Skiing in Blue River, British Columbia.* © Larry Prosor
Frontispiece: *Doug Coombs catching air in the Chugach.* Photo by Wade McKoy—Focus Productions

Library of Congress Cataloging-in-Publication Data
Names: Cocuzzo, Robert, author.
Title: Tracking the wild Coomba : the life of legendary skier Doug Coombs / by Robert Cocuzzo.
Description: Seattle, WA : Mountaineers Books, [2016]
Identifiers: LCCN 2016005120| ISBN 9781680510447 (trade paper) | ISBN 9781680510454 (ebook)
Subjects: LCSH: Coombs, Doug, 1957-2006. | Skiers—United States—Biography. | Ski mountaineering.
Classification: LCC GV854.2.C66 .C63 2016 | DDC 796.93092 [B] —dc23
LC record available at https://lccn.loc.gov/2016005120

Mountaineers Books titles may be purchased for corporate, educational, or other promotional sales, and our authors are available for a wide range of events. For information on special discounts or booking an author, contact our customer service at 800-553-4453 or mbooks@mountaineersbooks.org.

Printed on recycled paper

ISBN (paperback): 978-1-68051-044-7
ISBN (ebook): 978-1-68051-045-4

For David,
so the son may know the father

CONTENTS

AUTHOR'S NOTE

A tremendous debt of gratitude goes to writer-director Mark Obenhaus and The Documentary Group for giving voice to Doug Coombs in the pages of this book. The majority of quotes attributed to Doug Coombs were sourced from two interviews conducted by Jordan Kronick on August 21, 2005, in Jackson Hole, Wyoming, and by Mark Obenhaus on March 6, 2006, in La Grave, France, for the 2007 production *Steep*. Some of these quotations have been condensed and edited for grammar and syntax. Any quotes sourced from books, magazines, or documentaries are indicated accordingly. All other quotations were taken directly from interviews I conducted either in person, over the phone, or via email from January 2012 to December 2015.

I have made every effort in this book to provide an accurate account of the people, places, and events relating to Doug Coombs's life and to my experiences following in his footsteps. I have relied on the memories of Coombs's family, friends, and fellow skiers as well as on interviews, media reports, and extensive notes. Any factual misrepresentations are mine alone and purely accidental.

INTRODUCTION

Jackson Hole, Wyoming, 2013

I'm not exactly certain when I first learned of Doug Coombs, but when I sift through my memory a video clip emerges. The footage is shot from a helicopter hovering alongside a mountaintop buried in brilliant white snow. The camera zooms in on a tiny dot trickling down from the highest peak, and then a skier comes into focus. He's barreling down the mountain on two long skis, each of his turns sending snow cascading down around him like whitewater. The slope is so steep that I can gauge its severity only by the skier's uphill shoulder as it brushes the mountain behind him. He looks like a surfer deep in the belly of a giant wave, the mountain looming over him and falling out from beneath his feet. And yet amid the chaos, the skier descends the mountain with fluidity that transcends athleticism. Doug Coombs looks like a genius at work.

Well over a decade after I first watched that video clip, I sat in Doug Coombs's home office in Jackson Hole, Wyoming. Set at my feet was Coombs's backpack. Although I'd never seen this backpack in person before, I recognized it immediately. I remembered seeing this backpack in the *New York Times* in 2006. In the photo, you can't see Coombs's face, just this backpack. He is perched in the snow, watching another skier navigate a steep slope below him. It was the last photograph ever taken of both men.

If there was ever a shrine to Doug Coombs, it was here in this room. Shelves and cupboards and closets were stacked high with three-ring binders full of photos and negatives from his adventures in mountains around the world. Other binders brimmed with newspaper clippings and magazine articles and postcards and pamphlets telling of his many exploits and guiding operations. An upper shelf was devoted to VHS tapes, some still wrapped in plastic, with titles like *World Extreme Skiing Championships 1991*. Other labels were scrawled on by hand in black Sharpie: *Alaska guiding footage '95*. A string of climbing gear hung from a light fixture; jackets and skis and boots bulged from a closet; and an assortment of framed pictures, memorabilia, and ski passes covered every surface. I never met Doug Coombs, but here in this room, surrounded by seemingly every piece of evidence from his forty-eight years on earth, I might have been as close as I would ever get.

Doug Coombs and his wife, Emily, bought this home outside of the town of Jackson, Wyoming, right before the accident that claimed his life. Coombs himself never had the chance to live in it. The four-bedroom post and beam was set in a sprawling valley. Mountains crowded the sky around it. Two horses trotted around the property, often coming to the living room window for an apple or a carrot. This was truly western living out here, and the home possessed all the warm, rustic charm that you might hope for in a cabin in the mountains.

Coombs's nine-year-old son, David, sat at a downstairs computer with a headset on. He was two years old at the time of the accident, perhaps too young to feel the full pain of his father's loss and yet old enough to feel the void today. Emily told me that wherever David would go in Jackson Hole, there would always be someone telling him how great his father was, how amazing a skier he was, how fearless he was, how strong he was, and how modest he was. It's difficult to imagine being surrounded by so many memories of your father, while at the same time having so few memories of your own with him. The only thing that David might have heard more than old stories of his dad was that the apple doesn't fall far from the tree.

Doug Coombs might have been the greatest skier to ever slide down snow. I say "might have been" because there is no objective way to qualify that claim. One can't tally up Coombs's medals or records to understand the true brilliance of his skiing career. Yes, he won contests and races, but the arena of play where he excelled was big remote mountains, outside the race circuit, away from the resorts and audiences, beyond the boundaries, on slopes where only a fortunate few witnessed his prowess. In many ways Coombs's rightful place as the world's greatest adventure skier is a matter of opinion, an opinion that many in the world of skiing share.

Outside of skiing, however, Doug Coombs is as obscure as many other athletes and adventurers whose renown was forged in the realm of extreme. His legacy resides among those of climbers like Alex Lowe or surfers like Eddie Aikau. Yet based on athleticism alone, Coombs should be considered alongside more familiar names. Like Michael Jordan's jump shot, Doug Coombs's ski turn was more than sport. As the late Jackson Hole ski legend Howie Henderson once put it so perfectly, "The fluidity, the grace, the style, the effortless routefinding, the incredible angles, the easy athleticism . . . the man is simply so damn good that seeing him ski changes your whole life." From that point forward, a skier's relationship with the mountains was delineated as "Before Coombs" and "After Coombs."

When I moved to Jackson Hole in the winter of 2011 to pursue my childhood dream of living in a western ski town, Doug Coombs was little more than a series of video clips to me. I'd never met him and knew next to nothing about his life or the circumstances of his tragic death. From videos I'd watched in my parents' basement growing up, Doug Coombs existed fantastically in my mind as a man raised in the wilds of the mountains by wolves. His skiing exuded such a deep kinship with snow that I dreamed his childhood must have been in a place rugged and untamed, where skiing was as second nature to him as a game of catch.

Only when I moved to Jackson Hole did I learn that Doug Coombs's background was nearly identical to my own. Like me, he grew up in a suburb outside of Boston. Not only that, but he also learned to ski on the same 240-foot hill as I did. The year I was born, he rolled into Jackson Hole after finishing college, just as I did twenty-five years later. The parallels of our lives compelled me to want to learn more about the man behind the legend. How had Doug Coombs gone from skiing a molehill in Massachusetts to conquering the most extreme mountains in the world? Was he fundamentally different from me? Did he possess a unique mental capacity to manage fear and weigh risk? Or was he just an adrenaline junkie killed doing what he loved?

So began my four-year quest tracking the life of Doug Coombs around the world, meeting his family and friends, skiing some of the runs he skied, and living in the mountain towns where he lived. Along the way, nearly everyone I spoke to said the same thing: "He changed my life." The reality was that after hundreds of hours of interviews, thousands of dollars spent on travel, and countless nights lying awake pondering his life, I would never be able to know Doug Coombs like they did. I began to fear that Coombs would forever remain a story told to me, an article clipping, a scene I watched on a scratchy videotape. Then one day, as I boarded a flight to the remote French village of La Grave, where he spent the last days of his life, I realized that through some cosmic energy, Doug Coombs had taken me on the greatest adventure of my life.

A LIFETIME OF LINES

Valdez, Alaska, 1992

The helicopter's blades pounded through the cold Alaskan air like a jackhammer, loud and relentless, but they couldn't hear them. A tape cassette of Jim Morrison was screaming through their headsets: *Break on through to the other side! Break on through to the other side!* At the helm of the chopper was a Vietnam veteran named Chet Simmons. Back in 'Nam, the pilot had been shot down thirteen times flying gunships in and out of the shit, but now he and his Bell Jet Ranger were dropping off an elite troop of skiers onto unexplored peaks in America's last frontier. These mountains had never been climbed, never been skied. Most of them didn't even have names—at least not yet.

Break on through!
Break on through!
Break on through!

Wearing shorts, sunglasses, and a mustache, Chet Simmons epitomized Alaska's lawless spirit. Better yet, he reveled in it. "With gas and guns, we can do anything," he liked to mutter to himself. A pistol dangled from his hip, and if anyone held their skis upright when he came in for a landing—running the risk of hitting his helicopter's spinning blades—Simmons drew his weapon and fired shots at their feet. "You put your skis in the air and I'll shoot you dead," he'd say. "Because you know what? I don't care about you. I only care about my helicopter. Now get in!"

The helicopter cut through the sky, rolling over one mind-blowing mountain after the next. Take the Tetons, the Rockies, and the Sierra, shuffle them up, and stick them in the middle of nowhere, and you get Alaska's Chugach Mountains, an utterly vast range that once set the record for most annual snowfall—nearly one thousand inches—in the United States. Apocalyptic storms churned in warm from the Gulf of Alaska, dumping heavy wet snow that coated the steepest slopes like thick syrup. Frigid cold fronts then swept down from the Alaskan interior, sucking moisture from the snow and turning that syrup into powdered sugar. It was this deep, weightless snow that made ski bums quit their jobs, sleep in snow caves, and live in virtual squalor. Skiing this powder was better than sex, more addictive than drugs, and worth every penny they scrounged together to travel to this fringe of the United States where the living was rough and the air was thick with a wild energy that made everything seem possible.

Chet Simmons believed he could land on any of those peaks. "I'm not scared at all," he'd scoff, zeroing in on a landing zone the size of a picnic table. "Nobody's shooting at me." He made a habit of maxing out his helicopter on each landing, squeezing every bit of power and torque out of his machine to stick the helicopter's chin into the side of the mountain and give the skiers enough time to climb out. The danger was that if something went wrong on his approach, a gust of wind for example, Simmons didn't have enough power in his aircraft to right his course. Instead, he would nosedive over the other edge of the peak. Milliseconds before crashing, he'd regain airspeed and pull up. Simmons was happy to remind everyone on board that if they were going down, no one could crash-land a helicopter better than he.

He wore a bracelet made from the twisted metal of one of his downed choppers to prove it.

Crammed in the cabin of Simmons's helicopter, the four skiers waited anxiously to see where they would be landing and what they would be skiing. Simmons had an eye for picking out first descents, runs that had never been skied before, and here in Alaska there were seemingly infinite to choose from. With Simmons at the helm, the skiers had amassed hundreds of first descents, giving them names like Python, Pyramid, and Stairway to Heaven. These skiers were pioneers in every sense of the word. "They were double-A alpha guys," Simmons remembered. "They were just intense, especially when we were out on the hunt. And I fed off of that. It was just like going out on an ambush at night. It was dead fucking serious."

Intense as they were, there was one mountain in the Chugach range that the skiers had not dared step foot upon, and now Simmons was headed straight for it. Although it was one of closest mountains in eyeshot of the landing strip, Dimond Peak had never been skied, and for good reason: it was terrifying. Dimond stood out from all the other giant peaks in the Chugach, and no matter where you stared at it from, the foreboding mountain looked impossibly steep. The fact that snow even clung to its face was baffling. It reached into the crisp, cold sky, snow billowing off its summit like a smokestack. Only in Alaska could Dimond exist, and only in Alaska could you find a pilot crazy enough to land on it—and a group of skiers brave enough to ski it.

Simmons stuck his skids into the shoulder of Dimond, and the skiers popped open the door and climbed out into the blizzard of the rotor wash. The din of the helicopter's blades was deafening. They pulled their skis from the basket mounted to the skids, huddled together, and then gave Simmons the thumbs-up. The pilot lifted straight up before arching down the valley floor like he was napalming an enemy village. And then there was absolute silence. In every direction, the Chugach Mountains stretched into the horizon like the crests of countless waves breaking violently into the sea. "It looks like a lifetime to ski," said Doug Coombs.

THIRTY-FIVE-YEAR-OLD DOUG COOMBS WAS BORN to be in these mountains. Many considered him the greatest extreme skier alive, but he would never identify himself as such. Beyond the sheer immodesty of the claim, Coombs cringed at the term "extreme skiing." He thought that to popular culture, extreme skiing conjured images of reckless maniacs hurling their carcasses off cliffs and playing Russian roulette with the mountain. But that's not what he was doing here in the Chugach. No, Coombs was an elite ski mountaineer performing at the highest level of his sport. Skiing these mountains required pinpoint decision making, incredible athleticism, and superhuman aplomb in the face of peril. All of which he had in spades.

A big, toothy grin cracked across Coombs's face as he studied the mountains sprawling around him. The smile barely fit on his face. As long as he had been able to stand in ski boots, all he had ever wanted to do was make turns through snow. His passion for skiing and for being in these mountains radiated from his lanky, six-foot-two-inch frame like a force field, and whoever came into his presence got sucked right in by his charisma, infectious optimism, and undeniable talent. To see him navigate down a mountain was to witness perfection in motion, to watch a man fulfill his very purpose on this earth.

Coombs stood on the shoulder of Dimond Peak next to one of his all-time favorite ski partners, Jon Hunt. Soft spoken, Hunt was as modest as they came. Even after he won contests and sponsors begged him to sign with them, he turned them down. He flat-out refused to be interviewed or photographed. He didn't want be in movies or magazines. Hunt skied purely because he loved it, and yet even he had to admit, "I didn't think there was anybody that loved to ski more than I did, but then I met Coombs."

The two had come a long way from Jackson Hole, where they were renegades when they skied together, sneaking outside the boundaries of the ski resort to brave avalanche terrain and explore the wilds of Wyoming's backcountry. Alaska was Jackson Hole on steroids. There were no lifts, no boundaries, no ski patrol threatening to take away their passes. Everything was backcountry in Alaska, and they had these mountains all to themselves.

Hunt and Coombs had logged hundreds of days driving each other harder and deeper into the mountains. They possessed a unique ability to slow down time when they skied. Just as Hall of Fame hitters can read the seams of a fastball or a changeup, Coombs and Hunt could size up a situation on the mountain so fast while they were skiing that their bodies reacted before their minds even fully digested their thoughts. It was a superpower that had kept them alive and made skiing Dimond Peak actually possible.

As they stared down into the abyss, the only question left between them was who was going first. Like kids in a school yard, Coombs and Hunt bucked up for a match of Rochambeau to decide who would take the honors. Hunt won—or lost, depending on how you looked at it. Below their feet, two chutes ran down the length of Dimond Peak like a double-barrel shotgun. The mountain was so steep that they could see for only about thirty feet until the slope seemingly fell off the side of the earth. Beyond that was the valley floor. They called that the NBA effect: so steep that it was like looking down at a basketball and trying to see the bottom of it. Any number of things could be down there waiting to kill them. Massive cliffs. Bottomless crevasses. Avalanches so powerful that they could crush and contort a body beyond recognition.

Hunt pushed off and began making big turns down the right chute. It had been snowing for three straight weeks, and every one of Hunt's turns broke off chunks of sluff that cascaded down the face. He soon fell out of Coombs's view. Perched on Dimond, Coombs might as well have been standing on the moon. How had he gotten here? These were the mountains that he had dreamed about as kid while sitting in the library and staring at blank spots on the map. Now he was here filling in the map, giving these mountains names.

Coombs returned his focus to the apron at the bottom of the mountain, waiting to see his friend scorch out onto the snow below like he'd watched him do so many times before. A minute went by. Two minutes. Three minutes. No sign of Hunt. Suddenly the slope came alive. A wall of white ripped down across the valley below. "Oh no," Coombs gasped. Hunt had woken the dragon.

02

BREAKING TRAIL

Waitsfield, Vermont, 2013

Hulking snowflakes careened from the opaque sky and struck my windshield as silently as paws padding across a carpet. I sat behind the wheel of my car, the heat blasting my eyes dry as I watched the windshield wipers cut across the glass again and again. I had just driven two hundred white-knuckle miles through a blizzard from Boston, and now I was idling in Nancy Coombs's driveway in Waitsfield, Vermont, trying to muster the courage to kill the engine and make my way for her front door. *Why am I here?* The question was still tumbling through my mind like tennis balls in a dryer: *Why am I about to knock on Nancy Coombs's door on a Sunday to ask her questions about her late brother?*

I supposed the answer traced back to my childhood. Skiing was my first taste of real freedom when I was growing up in Massachusetts in the early nineties. Every Wednesday after school in the winter, my mom dropped me off at the ice rink down the street from our house with a set of secondhand skis and pair of her old ski boots. I schlepped the gear onto an idling school bus destined for Nashoba Valley, a 240-foot hill west of Boston that served as my introduction to skiing. With its windows fogged and kids cramped and restless, the bus pulled up to this rinky-dink ski resort, and the driver swung open the doors, setting us free to explore the hill.

I vividly remember marveling at how free and independent I felt. There were no parents holding my hand or teachers telling me where to go. For the very first time, I was in charge of my own life. The sense of empowerment only increased when I slid off the chairlift. Speeding down the slope, the wind pulling tears out of my eyes, I was wholly aware that I was going to ski for the rest of my life. Skiing became the gravity guiding me.

This same gravity drew me to a man who I had never met and never would. Doug Coombs existed in the scenes of skiing movies that I watched obsessively as a kid. Many nights were spent hunkered in my parents' basement with my buddies, watching and rewatching clips of Coombs ski. He was a superhero in my eyes, skiing mountains that I never thought I'd see for myself.

But beyond the skiing scenes, I was fascinated by the movies' brief interviews with Coombs. His magnetism buzzed off the screen. He came across as so lighthearted and fun, a perfect encapsulation of the joy I found skiing at Nashoba. Coombs had skied all over the world, won contests, appeared in magazines, starred in movies, and yet I could just tell from hearing him talk that he was driven by the same sensation of freedom, that same gravity, that grabbed me.

I was now sitting in his sister's driveway to find out if that was true. I wanted to know how he became one of the greatest skiers to ever live. Was there something from his childhood that made him predisposed to fearlessness? Or was fearlessness the wrong defining attribute? In this age of X Games and Red Bull, adventure athletes were often lumped together in some adrenaline-junkie class, but Coombs never came across as wild or out of control in the movies. He struck me more as akin to the great explorers, driven by a burning curiosity to see what was around the next ridge.

In seeking to understand the life of Doug Coombs, I was also seeking adventure for my own life. I was twenty-six years old and trying to break into a career as a writer. The majority of my buddies from college had pursued corporate jobs in the city and were gradually piecing together the semblances of stability and adulthood—but I wanted little to do with that.

The people who I admired most were the ones with the stories. The ones who could tell you what the dirt smells like at a bullfight. People who measured their education by the stamps in their passports rather than by the diplomas on their walls. I wanted a story to tell, and the life of Doug Coombs had seized my imagination.

But it wasn't enough for me just to do the research and interview his friends over the phone. I wanted to know what it felt like to look down a slope that was truly steep. I wanted to know how the helicopter blades sounded when they chopped through thin mountain air. I wanted to be gripped with fear, drenched in adrenaline, and overcome by the exhilaration that I saw in Coombs in all those movies I watched growing up.

So I set out to follow in his footsteps and ski in his tracks. I wasn't a professional skier—far from it—but I was determined to develop the skills and knowledge required to track down his story and live to tell it. I was now trying to take the first step of the journey.

"Glad you made it," Nancy Coombs said, smiling in her doorway. "Nasty storm." She was still wearing her ski pants from earlier in the day and her face was flushed.

"Thank you for having me."

Her home was big and airy with tall windows that let crisp natural light pour in, even as the storm raged outside. In her fifties, Nancy herself radiated a sort of youthfulness that was immediate to me when she opened the door.

"How was it out there today?" I asked, handing her my jacket.

"Beautiful. We got about five inches overnight. Great conditions."

As we made our way into her kitchen, I noticed a hobble in Nancy's gait and wondered if she'd taken a fall earlier in the day. "Sore?" I asked.

"My back's fused," she said bluntly, pulling out a chair at the dining room table.

"How did that happen?"

"I was in a car accident in 1980, but that was more neck. I spent a month in the hospital with that. And then I was an avid runner. I was one of those nuts that went out twice a day."

"Oh yeah?"

"Then I got into running, biking, running." She chuckled. "I would be in a race every weekend. I think it's something in our family. We get obsessed, you know?"

I nodded with a smile. "I do. I'm cut from the same cloth."

"I ran when I probably shouldn't have," she continued. "Then I started blowing out disks. I had herniated disks all the time, and it got to the point where I needed to have surgery. I couldn't function. And then—well, the problem was that after the first surgery I felt good, so I started running again, and I shouldn't have. Running year round. I pushed myself further than I should have. I should've listened to my body, which I regret . . . but I'm still able to ski."

I nodded again in mild disbelief. Skiing seemed like the last activity a doctor might recommend for a fused back.

"I still have to be careful," she assured me. "I have rods in my back, screws and stuff, but surprisingly skiing doesn't really bother me. I may ache afterward, but it doesn't seem to hinder my skiing. I think it's because I've been skiing my whole life."

She got up from the table and fetched a mug off the counter. "You want a cup of tea or something?"

"No, thank you."

"Anyway, Doug and I always talked a lot about our boo-boos," she said, returning to the table. "I mean, when Doug injured his neck—it was severe. I think he always ached. I don't think he was ever comfortable."

"Did people know about it?"

"He tried to hide it from his professional skiing life especially. I mean, he was pretty clear with all of us: he didn't want anybody to know. So he never talked about it."

She took a sip of her tea and looked off. "My mother can tell you more about the accident than I can," she said. "I was at school at the time."

"I would love the opportunity to speak with her."

"Sure, I can take you over there," she said, taking another sip of her tea. "Did you ever meet Doug?"

I shook my head.

"Okay, you never met him," Nancy said. "So it's hard to imagine—I mean, if he walked in this room right now, the whole room would light up. He was always the life of the room. He had so much energy. He was such a great brother. He was always making me feel like I was a young person when I was around him."

"Did you and Doug get along growing up?"

"Doug and I played a lot as kids," Nancy said. "It seemed like Doug had fifty lives. He was always getting hurt, and I always seemed to be there. I was sort of like his little protector."

"Was he reckless?"

"He wasn't really reckless. He was just busy. Always doing something. I still have visions of him as a little guy," she said. "When we were really young, he would always wear this Superman costume around. I can still picture him with his cape on, bare chested, and he would yell out, 'I'm going to places where nobody else has gone before!'" Nancy paused and smiled warmly. "And he did."

NANCY COOMBS COULD SKI. Boy, oh boy, could she ski. She picked a point down the slope, drew an imaginary line to it with her eyes, and then diced crisp, clean turns over the East Coast hardpack. It made one fact abundantly clear to me as I watched her from above: the Coombs family had skiing in their blood, blood that apparently got only thicker as they got older.

It was a classic New England ski day at Sugarbush, Nancy Coombs's home mountain. The snow that had fallen while we were talking in her kitchen yesterday had since been pushed around, revealing hard blue patches of ice in some spots. I was holding my own with Nancy, but I made sure to stay a turn or two behind her in case I caught an edge or hit some ice that would send me flailing down the slope in an embarrassing heap. I kept thinking to myself that this was Doug Coombs's sister, and how well—or poorly—I skied might say more about me than anything I had mumbled across her kitchen table.

"Did you and Doug ski a lot together growing up?" I asked Nancy after we plopped back on the chairlift.

"My brother Steve and I skied equally with Doug throughout his childhood," Nancy said. "Being the oldest, Steve was first to drive our parents' station wagon to the mountain, usually with Doug cheering him on to pass cars to get there sooner." She laughed. "We would drive into the huge parking lot of these ski resorts and be the only ones there. We'd be there way too early. The lodge wouldn't even be unlocked yet. Of course, that didn't make me too happy with my brothers."

"What was Doug's relationship with Steve like?"

"Steve and Doug were just as tight, but at different times in Doug's life," Nancy said. "Steve was six years older, so they spent more time together when Doug was out of college. Steve is also a fabulous skier. Doug often attributed his skiing to Steve."

As the chairlift continued to creep up through the cold, Nancy and I watched a young gang of skiers rip down the mountain below our skis.

"Doug was fearless when we were kids," she said. "We were up at our parents' cabin in Maine one summer. My dad built a place up there. Doug must have been seven or eight, and we were riding around on these mini bikes and a big black bear came out in front of us on the trail. Doug dropped this candy, a chocolate bar or something, that he was holding. He dropped it right in front of the bear." She laughed. "So he jumps off his bike, runs in front of the bear, and grabs the chocolate. My poor parents. My mother never thought he'd make it past high school. But she'll tell you all about that."

Later that afternoon, Nancy took me over to visit her mother. Janet Coombs lived in an assisted living center not far from Nancy's home. Only a year or so earlier, she had been on her own back in Bedford, Massachusetts, in the same house where she raised her three kids. "My dad died shortly after Doug," Nancy explained in the car ride over to visit her eighty-eight-year-old mother. "He was a healthy guy, but I think my dad really suffered when Doug died. I think it was really hard for him. He almost became obsessed with learning as much as he could about all of Doug's adventures, and it was slowly killing him." Nancy described how overwhelming the memorial services had been for her parents. As hundreds gathered to remember his life, Janet and her husband, Gordon, realized for the first time the full impact their son had had on so many people.

"I think my father was blown away by it. He was shocked by everything Doug did in his life and all the people he impacted," Nancy said. "I think my dad would have absolutely loved living Doug's life. He would say, 'Boy, if I were younger, I would love to do those things.'" Nancy explained that after attending the memorial services in Massachusetts and Jackson Hole, her parents wanted to get away from the condolence phone calls and sympathy visits. They found respite up at their cabin in Maine. It was there that Gordon suffered an aneurism and died, just three months after his son, now some six years ago.

"You're going to have to be careful when you talk to my mother. You just can't go there with her," Nancy said, referring to her brother's death. "She enjoys talking about Doug as a kid, you know—it gets pretty comical, some really funny stories—but you just can't talk about the accident."

I nodded emphatically.

"See, my mother and Doug had a special bond," Nancy continued. "Steve and I were older and had moved out, and my father traveled a lot, so Doug was home with her. He used to call her mumzy. She adored it." Nancy paused. "But I think when Doug died, that mumzy light went out."

Janet Coombs greeted us at the door of her small apartment. We sat in her carpeted living room, Nancy and me on the couch and Janet in her own chair. A cat slinked out of her bedroom. Much like her daughter, Janet Coombs exuded an immediate warmth and tenderness. She had soft, elegant features and sat in her chair with poise and an air of genteel refinement.

"So, tell me," Janet began in a faintly Boston accent, "do you want to know about Doug as a skier or as . . . ?

"I'd like to know about who he was as a person," I said.

"Oh, I'd like that," she said with a soft smile. "He did things like anybody, you know; he wasn't an angel."

I smiled. "Who is, right?"

"Like when he was a little kid, maybe in the third grade, the minute he'd walk in the door, he'd say, 'Do you want to hear about the good stuff or the bad stuff first?'" Janet laughed. "And I'd say, 'Oh Doug, give me the good stuff first.'"

"Yes, he couldn't keep a secret," Nancy added. "He couldn't live with himself if he did something wrong. He'd have to tell you what he did or it would just eat at him."

"After telling me what he'd done, whatever it was, skipping school or something, he'd say, 'Oh, I feel better now,'" Janet said. "And I'd say, 'Oh jeez, that teacher is going to be calling me.'"

"Did he get in trouble in school?" I asked.

"Well, his teachers used to say that when the snow started falling down, forget it, he was gone." She laughed. "Although he was a decent student. He was a good B student. He didn't really study hard, but he was a B student."

"What was he like at home?"

"He was always busy. If I found him asleep on the couch at five o'clock, I would say, 'Oh, he's sick.' Sometimes I'd say, 'Oh good, he's sick; now he'll be quiet for once!'" Janet looked over to Nancy. "He made everything fun," she continued. "He was nice. He had a nice disposition. He didn't get mad easy."

"No," Nancy agreed.

"Not like his sister could." Janet smiled. "Every morning, he'd wake up and tell us about his dreams. Oh, Nancy would get so mad. She'd say, 'Not again!' Doug was such a dreamer. He loved talking about his dreams."

"When Doug was traveling—when he was overseas in search of new places to ski—do you remember a lot of that time?" Nancy asked. "Like when he went to Antarctica?"

"We tried to stay in touch with him," Janet said.

"I know you did, yeah," Nancy said.

"They had some really scary trips where they had terrible weather. Where was it? In Russia they couldn't get out. I didn't like that. They were grounded with the weather."

"What was it like knowing that Doug was off skiing all these big mountains around the world?" I asked.

"If I had worried about what Doug was doing, I would have had white hair at thirty," she said. "My husband and I used to laugh because Doug was forty years old, but he wasn't really forty . . . is that alright to say?" Janet looked to Nancy.

"When Doug was forty, you're saying?"

"Even when he was forty, he was still a big kid in many ways," Janet said. "When he'd come home, he'd come in and pick me up and say, 'Hi, Mumzy!' and he'd come and give me a big kiss. He was very effervescent. He wasn't a phony. He would light up a room. That was Doug."

AFTER LEAVING JANET COOMBS, Nancy and I returned to her home, where she pulled out all the magazines, press clippings, and photo albums that she had collected of her younger brother over the years. "America's Best Skier," read the cutline on one magazine with Coombs on the cover. There were photos of him skiing down frozen waterfalls, outrunning avalanches, and navigating down insanely steep faces. Amid all the glossy magazines and images, a thick stack of computer paper stuck out. I pulled it from the fray and into the light. It was a printout of an online message board that was started immediately after Coombs's death in 2006. Nearly two hundred pages long, the printout was filled with memories shared by family, friends, clients, and peers, young and old, men, women, and children. "He was somehow on a higher frequency than the rest of us," wrote one childhood friend. "If you knew him, you were better for it. What an extraordinary human being."

The messages came from across the country and around the world, nearly every continent. "The Russian mountain skiers grieve together with you," wrote one. "Death Doug Coombs—heavy loss for mountain-skiing extreme world." Many of the notes began the same way: "I never met Doug, but . . ." People wrote at length about how they had been inspired by Coombs just from seeing him in movies and reading about his adventures in magazines. I could certainly relate to that. They wrote about him as if they were close friends, thanking him graciously for inspiring them. I sat late into the night completely engrossed in this black-and-white document. Reading story after story, I began to see more clearly that Doug Coombs was so much more than a star skier.

03

FIRST TRACKS

Bedford, Massachusetts, 1970s

Bedford, Massachusetts, in the midseventies was a vortex of freedom for a kid like Doug Coombs. Coming off the swinging sixties, hip young teachers were experimenting with new methods of education that were a far cry from the authoritarian style of the fifties. They introduced an open-door policy at Bedford High School, allowing juniors and seniors to come and go as they pleased like it was a college campus. Teachers figured if they treated students like adults, they'd act like adults. The experiment didn't work out quite as they planned, especially when it came to Coombs.

Coombs skipped school on more than one occasion, leading his buddies on wild adventures throughout New England. From their neighborhood in Bedford, they bushwhacked through the woods down to the interstate, where they hitchhiked north to New Hampshire and spent the day hiking in the White Mountains and snorkeling in the Pemigewasset River. It was in these mountains that Coombs felt most alive. He had a habit of stripping off all his clothes and running barefoot through the woods at top speed under the moonlight. He'd jump into the rapids of the Kancamagus River and bound off boulders downstream as if he were skiing moguls. "He was just unstoppable and awesome in the mountains," remembered one of his childhood friends. "He seemed like a natural mountain creature, like a bull elk, born to roam the mountain ridges."

Everything was possible in Coombs's mind, and he did it all in his own way. If he and his buddies couldn't hitch a ride up to the mountains, they hopped on to their bikes and pedaled a hundred miles or more to spend the night under the stars. They embarked on long endurance hikes from Vermont, marching thirty miles a day until they reached northern Maine. After reading about winter camping in a magazine, Coombs went off with a friend and hiked Mount Washington in subzero temperatures, wearing blue jeans and beat-up boots. "What fun he was to be around," remembered another childhood friend. "He had this wild energy like nobody else I'd ever met."

This wild energy spilled into everything. He had a freak ability to nap whenever the mood struck, and it wasn't uncommon in Bedford to find Coombs's bike pulled to the side of the road with him fast asleep alongside it in the grass, as carefree as Tom Sawyer. Once, when a state trooper conducted a field sobriety test on him, Coombs leaped onto his hands and walked thirty feet down the yellow line and back again. Springing back to his feet like a gymnast, Coombs flashed his big grin as if to say "ta-da!" The trooper just shook his head and let him go.

Doug Coombs's fun energy came off him in intoxicating waves that drew a devoted tribe of friends with him wherever he went. Many vied for his attention, but if he knew anything about his popularity, he never let on. He was modest and had friends in all circles. No one fell outside Coombs's boundaries because he simply didn't seem to have any. There was a glow about him, and as he got older, it became blinding, mesmerizing people like moths in a porch light.

AT SIXTEEN YEARS OLD, DOUG Coombs stood over six feet tall and had a long, rectangular head that his body was still catching up to. He had a square jaw and a tree trunk for a neck, and his auburn hair was long and straight. When he parted it at the corner of his brow, he was a handsome young man. Coombs liked to say that he was 160 pounds with each of his legs weighing 50 apiece. These powerful legs could end school-yard brawls by squeezing his opponents into submission. A snowball fired from his arm came in like a comet and sent kids scattering for cover. "If he got in a fight, he'd be all elbows and knees," remembered one of his lifelong best friends, Frank Silva. "You didn't want to mess with him."

Yet as a physical specimen, Coombs did have his flaws. His vision was atrocious, requiring him to wear thick Coke-bottle glasses, and he suffered from severe childhood asthma, which he eventually outgrew. Despite these ailments, Coombs ran the hundred-yard dash in eleven seconds. He kicked a soccer ball like a mule. When he played halfback on the football field, his might was unmatched—and all the coaches in Bedford seemed to know it. If the Bedford Buccaneers were on the goal line, they handed the ball off to Coombs for the touchdown.

One day, he walked into his home on Wilson Road to find his mother sitting across the kitchen table from Bedford High School's football coach. The coach wanted Coombs to focus strictly on football and was hoping his mother would convince him to give up his other sports. Whatever case the coach made apparently wasn't persuasive enough, as Coombs ended up quitting football entirely after his sophomore year to play soccer. There was a rigidity to football and the way it was coached that didn't line up with Coombs's freewheeling sensibility. Too much "yes sir, no sir." Football was a fun game, but that's what it was to him: just a game. Soccer, too, was just a game. Skiing, though—skiing was so much more. Skiing was like breathing to Doug Coombs. He couldn't live without it.

"In the middle of summer I used to sit there and stare at books in the library that had snow-covered peaks, thinking, *Oh man, I got six more months till winter?*" Coombs remembered. "And that was when I was ten years old. There was obviously something ingrained in me about snow." Indeed, for the quote in his 1975 high school yearbook, Coombs wrote, "There's no such thing as too much SNOW."

THE COOMBSES WERE A SKI family, and within their middle-class neighborhood it wasn't an uncommon thing to be. But if each family in Bedford kept a tally of the days they logged on the mountain during each season, the Coombses were most definitely in a league of their own. "After he'd ski for the weekend, Doug would get on the bus Monday and we'd all listen to his ski stories," remembered Frank Silva. "He'd just be so excited, sort of foaming and frothing at the mouth; his clothes would be all twisted and wrinkled, and he'd entertain us with his stories of how much fun he had skiing that weekend."

Many kids in the neighborhood had Coombs's parents, Janet and Gordon, to thank for teaching them how to ski. When the Coombs's station wagon headed up north each weekend to New Hampshire, Maine, or Vermont, friends of Coombs and his older siblings, Nancy and Steve, were usually in tow. "They did so much for me and had such an influence on me," said Silva. "Mr. Coombs would buy me lift tickets to the ski area; my parents didn't give me any money to get a lift ticket. He did. I didn't have any ski pants and he gave me some. He'd wax our skis and tune our skis. He provided us with a place to stay, and Mrs. Coombs would feed us. They would just say, 'Go out and have fun.'" The Coombses' door was always open. When trouble arose in other children's homes, whether it be a death in the family or an abusive parent, they found refuge at the Coombs's. They became family.

Skiing was the backdrop to Janet and Gordon's storybook marriage. Gordon Coombs had met his future wife, Janet Brown, in the second grade, when he used to dip her pigtails in the inkwell on his desk. The ink ran deep, and they had been together ever since. After he completed an engineering degree at Tufts University and a tour in World War II, Gordon joined Janet and other Bostonians in catching the Sunday Winter Snow Sports Train up to North Conway, New Hampshire. For $4.35 round-trip, they jammed into one of the twelve railcars leaving Boston to go ski in leather boots strapped to long wooden planks. When they married in January of 1950, Janet and Gordon celebrated their honeymoon by skiing in Stowe, Vermont. Seven years later, when Douglas Brown Coombs came into the world with ten fingers and ten toes, "future skier" might as well have been written on his birth certificate.

His love for skiing began by the time he could fit into ski boots. Many frigid nights of his early childhood were spent careening down a makeshift run he linked together through the backyards of his neighborhood in Bedford. "Even when I was a little tiny kid, I would try and ski every day," Coombs remembered. "Where I lived, I could even go skiing in my backyard. My parents would flip the light on and I'd ski at night." In the glow of porch lights, Coombs rushed down the icy slope, driving his legs to squeeze every bit of speed out of the three or four turns he could muster before grinding to a stop on the pebbled pavement of his driveway.

When the backyard lost its luster, Coombs graduated to skiing a steep stretch of woods across the street that the kids dubbed "Suicide Six." Most in the neighborhood braved Suicide Six on toboggans or Flexible Flyers, while Coombs took to the icy slope on skinny wooden skis with metal edges. When plows piled snow high along Wilson Road, Coombs climbed up onto the roof of his house and skied off into the snowbanks. He dazzled friends by performing fifteen-foot backflips off small jumps they built on the slope of a local dairy farm in Bedford, where the owner had installed a rope tow. "He didn't ski," one of his friends remembered. "He flowed. He floated. So smooth it was unreal."

When Coombs's older brother, Steve, got his license, he'd drive up to Wildcat Mountain every weekend with his friends and siblings. "We'd throw Doug, who was the youngest of all, in the back. He was sort of like the kid brother that had to go with you if you wanted the car," said Steve Coombs. "When you're in high school with your friends, and you have your little brother tagging along, that could be less than perfect, but it ended up being just fine." On the slopes, Coombs shadowed his brother and sister, following them off the trail and into the woods. What he lacked in experience, he made up for in sheer athleticism and gusto.

Coombs wielded his strength in astounding ways. Some years later, when Steve moved up to Vermont to work at Smugglers' Notch Ski Resort, his younger brother became a frequent visitor. During one of these visits, Coombs was skiing in deep snow outside of the resort when one of his friends blew out his knee. "Doug just said, 'Put him on my back,'" remembered Frank Silva, who was with him that day. "He skied him out. The guy must have weighed two hundred pounds."

As much as it was a feat of athleticism, Coombs's skiing was the result of a mental gift. He possessed a mathematical mind that computed terrain faster than he skied it, effectively slowing down time and extending his window to maneuver. His grandmother taught him at a young age to play chess, and even when she fell ill and was placed in a nursing home, Coombs would sneak in through her window after visiting hours to set up the pieces for a match. Pretty soon he became unbeatable. His skiing mimicked his chess play as he visualized many moves down the line and executed each turn like he had done it a hundred times before. Once Coombs skied a run, he never forgot it. He had a photographic memory for mountain terrain.

As captain of the Bedford High School ski team, Coombs was a complete racer. In those days, ski racers competed in both alpine and Nordic events. Coombs dominated the slalom at Nashoba Valley, winning nearly every race he entered. On the cross-country course, he competed on skis his father crafted from old alpine ones in his workshop, and Coombs finished near the top. By his junior year in 1974, he'd earned the hallowed Dual County Skimeister Award, recognizing him as the best all-around talent in ten towns.

AS COOMBS'S SKIING PROGRESSED, he was drawn farther away from the racecourse to the snow that fell outside the resorts' groomed corduroy. He'd shoot through the woods, snaking around trees, jumping off rocks, and skiing down riverbeds and frozen waterfalls. "No one ever said to me, 'Don't go off the trail,'" he recalled later. "We were off-piste skiing when I was seven, ten. I just didn't think of it as that. I just thought it was going through the trees."

It was ultimately his father who exposed Coombs to the full potential of skiing in the backcountry. Early one morning Gordon Coombs packed up the family's station wagon and drove his three kids to the base of Mount Washington. After pulling into the parking lot at Pinkham Notch, the four of them set off hiking with skis on their backs. "I didn't realize it was this two-hour slog through the forest . . . it was pretty miserable, really," Coombs said. "Then all of a sudden you pop out of the trees and there's this two-thousand-vertical, forty-five-degree face covered with snow. It was amazing."

Carved into the east face of Mount Washington, Tuckerman Ravine was as close to the Alps as a kid from Bedford could get on a tank of gas. Many ski historians point to Tuckerman as the birthplace of extreme skiing in the United States. While the steep glacial cirque saw its first ski track in 1913, it wasn't until the 1920s and '30s that Tuckerman Ravine became a wild proving ground for hundreds, sometimes thousands, of skiers during the spring season. Collegiate slalom races, Olympic tryouts, and grueling endurance races known as the American Inferno were held in the ravine's natural amphitheater. In April of 1939, Austrian-born skier Toni Matt dusted the American Inferno's eight-mile course in six minutes and twenty-nine seconds, hitting speeds of up to eighty-five miles per hour. Matt's straight-line descent became the stuff of legend, and Tuckerman emerged as the earliest theater for extreme skiing in North America.

After 2.4 miles of switchbacks, the trail from Pinkham Notch gave way to the sight of a magnificent bowl, so steep and snow filled that it looked designed for no other purpose than skiing. Due to Mount Washington's violent winter weather, most skiers waited for the spring to hike up to test themselves on Tuckerman's steeps. When the sky was clear and the sun was out, hundreds of people sprawled out on the Lunch Rocks at the bottom, sunbathing, drinking, and watching the skiers above.

This lightheartedness vanished once a skier reached the top of the ravine and looked down its headwall. Spectacular falls were common. Botch one turn, and gravity took care of the rest. Then there was the avalanche risk. Pitched at upward of sixty degrees in some spots, the slope could have a winter's worth of snow precariously clinging to it, like dynamite just waiting for a trigger. Massive slides carried skiers eight hundred feet to the bottom. Of course, this element of danger was part of the appeal, and not surprisingly, Coombs took to the ravine instantly.

"There's nobody out there with signs. There's no ropes. There's no patrolmen. There's nobody taking care of you on the slopes like all the ski areas," Coombs said of Tuckerman Ravine years later. "You're on your own. You have to make decisions on your own. And when you're sixteen years old, you make a lot of bad ones."

One of those bad decisions came when he and his buddy Frank Silva decided to ski Tuckerman one February. Although people do ski the ravine in the winter, it's attempted only in ideal weather conditions. Mount Washington is one of the deadliest mountains in the world due in large part to its ferocious, unpredictable weather. Winds can gust over two hundred miles per hour, while the temperature can drop to thirty below. As far as Tuckerman itself is concerned, avalanches are an especially violent killer.

"We were clueless on avalanches, we didn't know anything about the stuff," said Silva decades later. "We knew there were such things as avalanches, but we were never worried about it at all." It was snowing heavily as the two boys set out hiking up the ravine. When they were halfway up, Coombs and Silva dug a hole in the face and climbed inside to eat lunch. As they chewed on their sandwiches, snow began cascading over the opening of their snow cave, lightly at first, and then harder and harder. The two boys shot each other a look. Suddenly a massive avalanche ripped by the opening of their hole like a freight train.

When the snow settled, Coombs and Silva popped their heads out of the hole. Blocks of snow and debris were strewn all over the slope. Down at the base, people were frantically searching for them. They thought the two boys had been buried. "We pop out of this little hole and start hiking again," remembered Coombs, "and all of a sudden they start screaming at us, 'Get off the mountain! Get off the mountain!'"

Tuckerman Ravine became the backdrop for the inspired skiing of Coombs's adolescence. The chutes and steeps honed all his abilities as a racer, while his imagination allowed him to pioneer new routes that no one had ever considered. He and his buddies camped at the base of the ravine for days on end, spending hours hiking up and skiing down. One sunny afternoon in 1973, Coombs set off up the ravine by himself. "We're down at the Lunch Rocks having a snack, and we heard this ripple go through the crowd," said one of his buddies, Bill Stepchew. "People were yelling, 'Look! Look!'" Every set of eyes shot to the headwall at the summit to find a lone silhouette perched over a steep and narrow chute that cracked down the center of the rocks like a lightning bolt. "Oh my God . . . it's Coombs!" Stepchew yelled out.

Silence passed over the crowd of hundreds. Coombs plunged into the chute. The snow came up to his neck and immediately avalanched. From below, the crowd could make out only his arms punching out from the rushing river of white, his head bobbing side to side like a prizefighter's. He executed a number of precise turns in the chute before bombing out the bottom in an explosion of sluff. The crowd erupted. Their cheers reverberated off the snow walls and filled the ravine with an electric buzz that gave his buddies goose bumps. Pride burst through their chests. "Everybody is looking over at us and clapping," remembered Stepchew. "We couldn't have been more proud of him and ourselves for just being with him."

Entering the spring of his junior year of high school, Coombs was poised for a promising skiing career. His prowess on the racecourse would likely earn him the attention of college scouts, and then perhaps he'd point his skis on the professional race circuit. Coombs's future looked bright and boundless, but then the unthinkable happened.

04

TUCKERMAN RAVINE

Pinkham Notch, New Hampshire, 2013

The dense trees scattered puzzle pieces of light onto the trail as I tried to find a rhythm in my hiking. *Step up with my left, breathe, step with my right, exhale.* The rhythm was easy enough, but as rocks broke through the spring snow and my plastic ski boots began slipping in the slush and the mud, frustration brewed. The skis latched to my backpack were causing the straps to cut into my armpits, and my fingers had gone numb. I promised myself I would wait for at least another two switchbacks before asking the question out loud, but my growing fatigue forced it out of me all the same: "How much farther to the top?"

There was nobody around to answer. I was alone, playing hooky from work to hike up to Tuckerman Ravine and ski this backcountry zone where Coombs cut his teeth as a teenager. My only company was the occasional chipmunk that scampered out from the forest lining either side of the trail. Hiking to ski was entirely unlike my formative experiences in New Hampshire's White Mountains, which had consisted of riding chairlifts at nearby ski resorts such as Wildcat and Attitash.

Beyond some prerequisite reading on where to find the trailhead, my knowledge of skiing Tuckerman Ravine was mostly limited to a handful of videos I had watched online the night before in my motel room in North Conway. The clips of skiers cartwheeling uncontrollably down the ravine, losing gloves, goggles, and, in some cases, consciousness in spectacular fashion before a crowd of hundreds were impossible not to play over and over. Yet even after watching all those bone-breaking falls, my thought process now remained the same: *How crazy could this possibly be? I mean, this is New Hampshire, right?*

The truth is Mount Washington can be an absolute killer. Well over a hundred people have perished on this mountain since the early 1800s. Hit with the wrong weather at the wrong time, the 6,288-foot summit might as well be at the top of Everest. The wind can blow strong enough to flip a car like a poker chip and create blinding whiteout conditions. Above timberline, the temperature can drop so precipitously that frostbite gnaws instantly at any exposed skin. At Tuckerman Ravine, avalanches, falling ice, and gravity are the main killers in the spring. Given that New England had received a moderate amount of snowfall over the winter, I wasn't overly concerned about the avalanche risk, but tumbling down the side of the ravine and into the boulders at the bottom was another story entirely, one that I tried not to think about as I hiked.

After two hours, the trees opened up and the ravine finally came into view. It looked like the Colosseum plopped on the top of the mountain. Exposed rocks lined the left and right sides of the ravine, and a wall of white spanned the middle with rocks and ice scattered about. Whimsical clouds streaked across the blue sky directly above the bowl, making the landscape seem otherworldly.

I continued my way up the trail to the Appalachian Mountain Club's caretaker's cabin, where a young guy with dreadlocks was sweeping off its small porch.

"How's it going?" he asked, a smile poking through his scraggly beard. "Getting an early start, huh?"

"Yeah, man. How's the skiing been up there?"

"Good, real good. We had a couple bad crashes last weekend, but the skiing has been solid."

"How long have you been up here?" I asked, smelling the guy with my eyes.

He thought about it for a second, stroking one of his beaded dreadlocks. "A week or so, maybe. I'll be headed down on Friday."

I slung my backpack onto one of the picnic tables on the deck and pulled out a water bottle, then studied the ravine, which was still a mile or so up. I could now see the headwall where Coombs had made his legendary descent. Even from down here, with no real sense of its steepness, the line looked pretty gnarly. I stowed my water bottle and shouldered my pack.

"Any advice?" I asked the caretaker before leaving.

"Don't fall," he said with a grin.

By the time I reached the foot of the ravine, two other skiers had caught up with me. They were an attractive, athletic couple from Canada. Blond and handsome, the guy was carrying both sets of their skis, while his svelte girlfriend pranced up the trail behind him.

"Do you know anything about this place?" I asked the guy, feeling instantly stupid for posing a question about what was ostensibly my backyard to a Canadian.

"It looks like there's a boot pack there to the left," he said, pointing it out with his pole. "That must be Left Gully. And then I think you can go up here to the right and ski down from the headwall."

Of the two options, Left Gully struck me as the most manageable, perhaps because the route down was so obvious. The chute of snow doglegged down between rock walls. There was no getting lost up there.

"Great. Good luck, you two." With that, I strapped on my helmet and started hiking through the snow up into the ravine. The angle of the path steepened quickly until I was climbing on all fours, punching my ski boots into a staircase stomped into the snow by those who had come before me. It felt like climbing a ladder, and every twenty steps, I paused to consider what I was doing. This was steep—steeper than anything I'd ever skied. The slushy spring snow seeped through my gloves and down my jacket as I pressed up against the slope. To get a better view of how much farther I had to go, I pushed myself off the snow slightly, but then was gripped by that unnerving sensation you get when almost tipping back in a chair.

"Holy shit, this is steep," I yelped, flopping back against the slope.

My options were limited. There was nowhere to put my skis on here. I needed to either strap in at the top or start climbing back down. I stood there weighing my options. What would Doug Coombs do? The answer was obvious: "You don't know if you don't go."

At the top, I made quick work of clicking into my skis and dialing in my gear. I felt extremely vulnerable. The snow had that quick, slippery quality to it like sand on a shuffleboard, and I wondered when my skis had last been waxed. Hopefully not that recently; I wanted everything I could get to slow my descent.

From my perch at the top of Left Gully, I plotted my first turn. This looked to be the steepest bit. A fall from here would be nasty, undoubtedly leading to uncontrollable tomahawking, maybe into the rocks or all the way to the bottom. I now regretted watching all those videos the night before, as I knew a fall wouldn't necessarily kill me but could definitely cause enough pain for me to want to be dead.

Tuckerman was to be my first real lesson in steepness. Coombs thrived off steep skiing. He traveled around the world in search of slopes pitched between forty-five and sixty degrees, so steep that snow could barely cling to them. "He could eat his lunch of fifty degrees," one pro skier told me. But until you're on top of something truly steep, fifty degrees is only an abstract number. From what I had read the day before, the maximum pitch of Left Gully was forty-five degrees, with a sustained angle of thirty-five. Just looking down the face now filled my gut with vertigo.

Pushing into my first turn, I felt gravity hanging heavily on my shoulders as if I were wearing a soaking-wet trench coat. It wanted nothing more than for me to slip and fall into its complete control. I held my first turn, sliding down the steepest section cautiously and dragging my hand along the slope beside me to keep three points of contact with the mountain. In the minutes that ensued, I made every turn defensively, with intense concentration, not caring at all about the aesthetics of my form, but rather focusing entirely on getting down the face safely.

When I reached the Lunch Rocks at the bottom, other skiers had arrived and were scouting their own lines and beginning to hike. I came to a stop nearby and turned to face the ravine. Tracing my haphazard ski track with my eyes, I contemplated hiking back up for another run—but I really didn't want to go back up there. I was too afraid. The degree of difficulty wasn't what had me rattled, but rather the high risk of injury.

My fear of getting hurt went beyond most people's wont for self-preservation. When I was twelve years old, I nearly lost my leg to a rare staph infection. After I was misdiagnosed with a stress fracture for a year, a CAT scan revealed that a serious infection called osteomyelitis was eating away at my right tibia. I went into surgery the very next day to have the infection drilled out of my bone, which left a gaping hole that looked to be the size of a crayon on the X-ray.

The doctor said that the procedure left my tibia as fragile as an eggshell, and putting even the slightest bit of weight on it would cause the bone to break. So after a week in the hospital, I spent the summer sitting at the end of my driveway in a wheelchair with an IV pumping antibiotics directly into my heart. Nine months later, when the bone failed to regenerate on its own, I had a bone graft. During the two years it took for my leg to fully recover, I didn't think I would ever be able to ski again. How could my eggshell of a bone withstand the impact of skiing? I kept picturing myself making a hard turn and then having my leg snap in half at the boot.

But thankfully, the bone graft proved successful, and two years later, I was able to get back on my skis. The whole saga was now a distant and faded memory, but I hadn't forgotten how quickly skiing had been taken away from me. I'd since made a point of leading an active life and getting the most out of my healthy legs, but when it came to taking risks, I was also extremely cautious. I never wanted to be back in that wheelchair.

As I turned to hike back down to my car, feeling defeated for not having hiked up for another run, I thought about how my fear of injury was only going to become more pronounced as I journeyed to bigger, more dangerous mountains of Coombs's past. At some point I would need to quell the voice telling me to play it safe and just take a risk. Of all people, Doug Coombs knew what it was like to get hurt and have skiing ripped away from him. However, the circumstances of his injury were far more serious.

05

FALL LINE

Waterville Valley, New Hampshire, 1974

As a teenager, most mornings Coombs didn't so much sleep in as hibernate. He squeezed every last second out of his alarm clock's snooze button before dragging himself out of bed to chase the school bus down. His morning sluggishness wouldn't have been such a problem had he not been responsible for a daily newspaper route. Eventually Coombs devised a way to get the job done without missing a minute of his beauty sleep by bringing the papers onto the school bus and hurling them out the window as they drove by each house.

Despite his penchant for sleeping in, on the morning of April 13, 1974, Coombs was up before the roosters. It was the Saturday of Easter weekend, and Waterville Valley Resort had its chairlifts running earlier than usual to ferry people to a special service at the top of the mountain. Coombs and his buddies Bill Stepchew and David Underwood had no intention of attending the service, but they were happy to sneak onto an early chair.

With the sun peering down from a cloudless sky, Waterville Valley had full-on spring skiing conditions. Coombs wore blue jeans, a baggy gray sweatshirt, and a white bandana wrapped around his head that gave him look of a kamikaze pilot when he barreled down the slopes.

By ten thirty, the temperature peaked at seventy degrees and rivulets of meltwater ran down the mountain and across the trails. The snow was as wet and slushy as it could be when the three boys pulled up to the top of the World Cup T-Bar. Stretching 1,500 feet below, Tommy's World Cup Run pitched and rolled down some three hundred vertical feet. The trail was named after Waterville's founder Tom Corcoran, who opened the resort in 1966, and it would later be made famous by Coombs's ski racing heroes, US Olympians Phil Mahre and Steve Mahre. Coombs was more familiar with this run than any other on the hill. That winter he had spent weekends competing on the resort's ski team, and this was their training course.

The sixteen-year-old surveyed the course below, how it pitched steep, flattened out, and then steepened again. "Somebody had set up a camera tripod and was taking pictures on about the middle of the trail," remembered Bill Stepchew. "Cameras always made Doug do things that were camera worthy." Coombs spotted a crude jump built on the side of the trail. He nodded to the mound of snow and then shot Stepchew and Underwood his unmistakable grin: *Watch this.*

Shoving off, Coombs smeared his turns down the first steep. Even in the sluggish snow, he moved with effortless grace. His upper body remained perfectly balanced while his legs swooped below him in unison. His poles struck the snow purposefully, waving through the air like two magnificent scepters. With the jump in his crosshairs, Coombs straightened out his skis and dropped into a crouch. He gained speed and made a line for the jump. "He launched off this ramp and just went as high as I'd ever seen anybody go—like telephone-pole high," remembered Stepchew, who had skied down below the jump with Underwood to watch. "He flew so far that he was going to land on the flats."

But after takeoff, Coombs's body started rolling forward. His legs spread apart, and for an instant he looked like he'd just been bucked from a bronco. He flapped his arms, trying to right himself, but it was to no avail. Coombs's ski tips hit first, catching in the wet snow and catapulting him directly into the ground with punishing force. His face slammed into the snow with the violent snap of a rattrap.

Lights out.

Coombs lay unconscious in the snow. "He was just lying there like a rock, for maybe fifteen seconds," Stepchew said. He and Underwood were shocked. The fall wasn't a spectacular rag doll, but the force of it was nauseating to witness. Coombs had gone from poetry in motion to a heap of helpless body parts. "Doug never fell, and the sight of it just didn't register."

Coombs's eyes fluttered open. Wet snow was packed up his nose and in his ears and mouth. He pushed himself up to his feet, looked around for a second, and then blacked out again. His face slammed back into the snow. His friends began feverishly sidestepping up to come to his aid, but before they could reach him, Coombs shot awake for a second time. He was furious. He never fell, and now his inability to control his body added insult to injury. Coombs jumped to his feet, angrily clicked his boots into his skis, and bolted to the bottom without a word to his friends.

It took only a couple of turns for Coombs to realize that the crash had bruised more than just his pride. His back ached and he felt woozy. Reaching the lodge at the base, he clunked his way to the first-aid office, but no one was there. He rang the bell, but still nobody. Since it was Easter weekend, volunteers were running the resort's medical office and everyone was apparently out on a ski break. After a few minutes, Coombs decided there was nothing better to do than get back on the lift.

When he slid off the chairlift at the top of the mountain, Coombs felt dizzy and tired. Maybe he just needed to sleep it off, he thought, so he skied into the woods behind the mountaintop restaurant, popped off his skis, and fell asleep in the snow. Meanwhile, his friends had no idea where he was. Coombs's parents had rented a condo near the mountain that winter, and they were up for the Easter holiday. The boys concluded that Coombs must have met up with them. They never imagined he was passed out in the snow.

When Coombs awoke an hour or so later, he couldn't move. He tried to pick himself up from the snow, but the message from his mind didn't reach his muscles. He lay there motionless for a few more seconds and then tried again. This time he was able to get up, but he was met with excruciating pain. Something was most definitely wrong. He needed to find a doctor.

After stepping back into his skis, Coombs wasn't able to ski in his usual perfect form. Every turn sent agonizing pain down his spine and deep into the marrow of his bones. Instead of snowplowing down the mountain like a beginner and running the risk of being hit by a reckless skier, Coombs ducked the ropes to a trail called Bobby's Run, a steep black diamond named after Bobby Kennedy that had been closed due to bad conditions. He painfully picked his way down through exposed rocks and grass, falling a few times before he finally reached the bottom.

When Coombs's mother entered the lodge, she found her son sitting unnaturally upright on the floor with his head and back pressed up against the wall. The look of distant worry in her son's eyes was unmistakable. Again Coombs tried to pick himself up off the floor, but his body was frozen. Janet had to help her son to his feet.

"We took him over to the first-aid station. That particular Easter weekend, there was voluntary patrol, and this big Dr. Pierce from Mass General was on duty," Janet Coombs remembered. "They took him right in for X-rays, and I was sitting there thinking that he just sprained his neck. But then the doctor came out and put his arm around me. When they do that, you know it's not good."

When Dr. Donald Pierce raised Coombs's X-ray to the light, he couldn't hide the shock on his face even after all his years working as an orthopedist. "It looked like you put a couple glass bottles in a plastic bag and smashed them all up. It was just shattered pieces all over the place," described Bill Stepchew, who saw the X-ray later. "Nobody could understand how he could walk, let alone ski, with all those broken bones floating around."

Coombs's cervical vertebrae were fractured from C4 to C7, essentially from his Adam's apple to his sternum. The X-ray revealed that one shard of bone, about the size and shape of a razor blade, pointed dangerously close to his spinal column. Dr. Pierce said that only Coombs's thick, muscular neck was keeping all the bones in place, preventing paralysis. They immediately strapped him to a backboard and loaded him into an ambulance, which got lost on the way to Massachusetts General Hospital.

When Coombs finally arrived at the hospital, doctors discovered that he was also coming down with pneumonia. His broken neck desperately needed to be fused, but they couldn't perform the surgery while he was sick. Coombs was strapped to a bed for a week until he recovered. "My folks lived at Mass General," Coombs's sister Nancy recalled. "My mom told me there were many dark days prior to his surgery. They didn't know if he would even be able to walk again while they were waiting for the swelling and pneumonia to go away."

Once Coombs overcame the pneumonia, Dr. Pierce took him directly into surgery. "The operation, I remember, was all day long, seemed like," Janet Coombs said. "It was a nightmare." Dr. Pierce made an eight-inch incision in the back of Coombs's neck and then carefully spread each vertebra, removing the damaged disks and shaving away any bone spurs. He put the puzzle back together using steel rods and screws.

After the surgery, Coombs needed to be put in a halo brace to keep his head stationary and allow his fused vertebrae to heal. According to Janet Coombs, Dr. Pierce was the only physician at Mass General who could perform the halo brace procedure at the time, which had come into practice in 1959. Prior to that, spinal injuries were typically treated with bed traction, where the patient was strapped tightly to a bed for months on end. Horrible bedsores and muscle wasting led doctors to come up with a better treatment. Enter the halo brace. Four titanium pins were drilled into the patient's skull, two in the front and two in the back. The pins were then connected to a metal halo that circled the patient's head and was linked to a fleece-lined chest brace. The whole rig looked like a torture device. Depending on the severity of the break, the patient remained in this uncomfortable contraption for a couple of weeks up to a couple of months. Although the halo brace was more humane than bed traction, the procedure itself seemed far more barbaric.

"They told Gordon and me to go as far away as we could because they were going to put this halo on Doug, which is horribly painful and you have to do it without [general] anesthesia," Janet Coombs remembered. "They didn't want us to see him or hear him screaming."

Dr. Pierce entered the room and, after a local anesthetic was administered, began by wrapping a measuring tape around Coombs's head. He then made two marks with a felt-tip pen on his forehead. After Dr. Pierce did the same to the back of his scalp, Coombs was placed in the chest brace that he'd be stuck in for the next two months. They positioned the halo around his head. Picking up a surgical screwdriver, Dr. Pierce looked down at Coombs and told him to think of every curse word he knew.

When his parents entered his room after the procedure, Coombs was staring blankly up at the ceiling through the cage now screwed into his skull. It must have looked freakish to Janet and Gordon Coombs seeing it for the first time. With his head still throbbing from the screws and the vest pressing snuggly around his shoulders and chest, Coombs must have been feeling the full gravity of his situation setting in. The invincible Doug Coombs had been broken. The star athlete couldn't run through the woods. He couldn't climb trees. Worst of all, he couldn't ski. Coombs turned to his father and told him to go home and burn his skis.

COOMBS SPENT THREE WEEKS AT Mass General recovering after his surgeries. "He was a terribly sick guy for about a week," his mother remembered. "We hired special nurses to be with him around the clock for days. He was too sick to see anybody. All the kids from high school came and I couldn't let them in." The pain medication had its way with his system, and Coombs floated in and out of fever.

Once he pulled through, though, his boundless optimism fueled his recovery. First came sitting up in bed, and then standing a day or two later. "One morning we went in, and there he was on one of those exercise bikes in the hall," his mother said.

"Did you burn my skis?" Coombs asked his father. Gordon shook his head.

"Oh good!"

Coombs became the darling of every nurse on his floor and a favorite among his fellow patients, including his much-older roommate, who found him endlessly entertaining. He was a model patient, rarely complaining and always smiling through the metal cage.

As far as the doctors were concerned, Coombs was something of a miracle. "There were about twenty people in the severe neck ward, and he was the only one who had any chance of ever walking again," Bill Stepchew said. "A lot of doctors wanted to come in and take a look at him because it was sort of astonishing that he survived the injury, let alone was able to function like that."

After he was released from the hospital, Coombs was asked to return for more than just his regular checkups. As his mother remembered, "The doctor called and said, 'Would you mind if Doug came in and talked to a lady who's going to have the [halo procedure] done to her? Because she's petrified.' So Doug went in and held her hand and calmed her right down. He said, 'Look at me, I'm walking around with the thing!'"

Back home on Wilson Road, Gordon Coombs fashioned a wooden ramp at the head of his son's bed for the halo to lean against so he could sleep. The metal contraption made even the simplest task a complete hassle. People stared at him wherever he went. "It was really tough because he wore that halo into the summer," remembered his sister. "The halo was attached to a heavy vest, and he was sweating all the time."

If Coombs was a big man on his high school campus before the crash, he was a giant after it. His metal halo loomed high over the rest of the student body like the exposed beams of a new skyscraper. He regaled his buddies with grisly play-by-play details of his accident, each telling more graphic and elaborate than the last.

"Doug was the king of exaggeration," remembered Frank Silva. "We called it the Coombs factor." By the time Coombs got done telling a tale, inches of snow magically turned into feet, mile walks became marathons. The story of his broken neck was no different. One version included him popping a bottle of champagne with the ambulance driver on the way to the hospital. In another, Coombs claimed to have knocked out a pesky medical intern who kept pricking his legs with needles to make sure he wasn't paralyzed. When the screws in his halo came loose one day, Coombs walked out of school and into the office of a local doctor. The doctor peered for a while at the contraption, then fetched his toolbox and a screwdriver from the trunk of his car. The last story, Janet Coombs confirmed, was true. Fact or fiction, it didn't matter to his buddies. They lapped it up all the same.

It didn't take long for skiing to reenter Coombs's mind. "Even when he had the halo on, he used to stand in the living room with his skis on," said Nancy Coombs. "He missed his skiing so much." Coombs did everything he could to maintain the strength in his legs, walking everywhere and performing wall squats for five minutes at a time. When he devised a way to slip a backpack over the halo, he returned to the White Mountains and hiked the days away.

When the halo finally came off, the mobility in Coombs's neck was extremely limited. Dr. Pierce had effectively turned four of his cervical vertebra into one long bone held together by screws and steel rods. To look in any direction, Coombs had to shift his entire upper body. He couldn't tilt his head to look up. This severe immobility would remain with him for rest of his life.

The more serious prognosis was that another bad fall might not just paralyze Coombs—it could kill him. The jostling associated with skiing could dislodge the hardware and cause damage to his spinal column. Worst of all, the location of the fusion rendered him extremely vulnerable. The major danger zone wasn't necessarily his fused vertebrae, but rather the C3 vertebra, which hadn't been broken in the crash but was now sandwiched between the steel and his skull. The slightest fall could snap it.

At sixteen years old, Doug Coombs had a decision to make. He could follow the doctor's orders and live a safe and sedentary life, one that would keep his fused neck intact and keep him alive. Or he could choose to follow his passion and ski again, even if that meant running the risk of being killed by the slightest fall. For Coombs the answer was obvious. As one of his childhood friends recalled, "I asked him once that year, his junior year of high school, 'Doug, do you think this will slow you down some?' He said, 'No way, I'll be the same.' I said, 'How do you know that?' And he said, 'Because I'm Doug Coombs.'"

06

I'M GOING TO JACKSON

Jackson Hole, Wyoming, 2013

My chest was on fire. I was sprinting through Denver International Airport trying to catch my connecting flight to Jackson, Wyoming, and the altitude had my sea-level lungs in a death grip. "Last boarding call for . . ." My name echoed out over the intercom. Wheezing and lightheaded, I handed my crumpled-up boarding pass to the ticket clerk and then stumbled down the ramp, out onto the tarmac, and into the twenty-seat plane idling in the Colorado cold. I was sucking wind too hard to care about all the scowls directed my way from fellow passengers as I collapsed in the last remaining seat in the plane.

"Made it," I huffed to myself. "I made it."

Jackson Hole was the next stop in my quest to track the life of Doug Coombs. After attending college in Montana, Coombs moved to Jackson Hole, where he became one of the most dominant skiers in town. His legacy had since grown to folkloric proportions, and I needed to connect with some crucial people from his past who were still living there in order to find out who the man behind the myth was.

This wasn't the first time I'd been to Jackson Hole. Three years earlier, I, too, had moved to Jackson after college to fulfill my childhood dream of living in a western ski town. I had always imagined what Coombs's life might have been like off the mountain when the cameras weren't rolling. What I had quickly discovered—beyond the magical powder days and carefree après parties—was that living in Jackson Hole required a lot of personal sacrifice. Jobs were tough to come by and housing was expensive. To pay for my $1,875 ski pass my first season, I worked at a meat shop, scribbling down phone orders and occasionally packing slabs of wild game on dry ice that burned my skin to handle. Grizzled hunters would pull up with freshly shot elk bleeding away in the back of their pickups, and I'd help haul in the carcasses to be butchered. With putrid hindquarters in my hand, my college diploma felt caught squarely in the back of my throat like a potato chip.

But it was all worth it once I got to the ski area. Jackson Hole Mountain Resort dwarfed the mountains of my youth. There were seven lifts, a gondola, and the state-of-the-art Aerial Tram, nicknamed "the big red heli" because it flew skiers over four thousand vertical feet to the top of the Rendezvous Mountain in just nine minutes. The diversity of the terrain was astounding: 2,500 acres of open bowls, glades, groomers, couloirs, and cliffs spread out over two mountains. When Paul McCollister opened Jackson Hole Mountain Resort in 1965, he pledged to make Jackson Hole an international ski destination, America's version of Chamonix. Luckily for him, he was working with the right kind of mountains to bring his vision into reality.

Positioned along the western border of Wyoming, Jackson Hole is fortified by hulking mountains: the Teton Range to the west, the Gros Ventre Range to the east. Yet of all the surrounding peaks, the Tetons unquestionably reign supreme. At the core of the range is the Cathedral Group, five granite peaks clawing at the Wyoming skyline, the tallest of which is the 13,779-foot Grand Teton. Gazing upon their western faces in the late 1800s, a pack of French trappers—who were apparently missing the warmth of women—named the massif Les Trois Tétons: the three tits. Some years later, when Teddy Roosevelt rolled into Jackson Hole, he was rumored to have taken one look at those beauties and declared, "That's how mountains should look."

Yet what struck me most when I first moved to Jackson was the level of commitment these mountains inspired in people. Every morning at dawn, hundreds collected at the base of the resort and formed a line at the tram dock that stretched into the parking lot by eight o'clock. A hierarchy existed within this steaming line of Gore-Tex-clad humanity. At the back of the line were the "gapers," vacationers with their paper tickets flapping off their one-piece ski suits and their skis splayed in their arms like flailing babies. Next up were the college grads who were ski bumming for a season before they got "real jobs." Then there were the converts who came planning to stay for one winter but now couldn't find a good enough reason to leave. It went on like this until you reached the front of the line, where an elite group of lifers could be found, hardcore locals who might as well have had 'JH' branded on their hides like prized ponies. Shuffling stoically in place, gnawing on breakfast burritos and sipping coffee from thermoses, they wore avalanche beacons and backpacks and shouldered bazooka-like powder skis that made me feel strangely inadequate. If you looked closely enough, you could just make out the patch sewn to the back of their jackets: JHAF.

When Coombs moved to Jackson Hole after college in the winter of 1984, he also spotted this gang of elite skiers at the front of the tram line and did everything he could to keep up with them. Like an excited golden retriever, Coombs chased them as they bombed down the mountain's four thousand vertical feet with grueling endurance. Never stopping to talk, never stopping to catch their breath, they were skiing machines. When the men reached the base of the mountain, they popped out of their skis and ran directly back on to the tram with military efficiency. "I chased them nonstop," Coombs remembered.

"They did it again and again and again. By number six, I was worked. I watched them go and I just thought, 'Okay, these guys are nuts . . . but in a good way.'"

The guys belonged to a hardcore ski fraternity in town called the Jackson Hole Air Force. Like Hells Angels with goggle tans, Air Forcers were brash, brave, and completely unapologetic. Or, as one put it, "We were flagrant, against authority, and felt like we could do whatever the hell we wanted." As long as there was snow to ski, the Air Force laid siege to Jackson Hole Mountain Resort, launching off cliffs, lapping the tram ten times a day, and mercilessly tracking every square inch of powder wherever it fell.

The Air Force was the brainchild of one of the most legendary ski bums in the American West. Benny Wilson grew up at the base of Jackson Hole Mountain Resort after his father bought a plot of land in Teton Village and erected a hostel dedicated to ski bums. Romping around the resort in the sixties and seventies, Wilson raised hell with a gang of kids nicknamed the Teton Village Mafia. He learned to ski race under Olympian Pepi Stiegler, and later led pro skiers and filmmakers to his secret stashes around the mountain. But when Wilson had a run-in with the law, the police gave him two options: join the army or do jail time. "So instead of becoming a criminal, I became a paid assassin," Wilson joked. Returning home from his tour of duty as a Marine three years later, Wilson devoted himself to skiing. He had three central pursuits: skiing deep powder, catching air off big cliffs, and exploring the dark and forbidden corners of Rendezvous Mountain.

As Jackson Hole Mountain Resort became more popular in the mideighties, finding untracked snow within the resort became increasingly difficult for Wilson and his cronies. They went to extremes to find virgin powder, even skiing down the roofs of the resort hotels. But soon their hunt for fresh tracks led them to secretly duck under the closed-area ropes set by the Jackson Hole Ski Patrol and enter the backcountry.

Skiing the backcountry was forbidden by the ski patrol, so Wilson and his gang had to be as stealthy as assassins when ducking below the boundary ropes. Their motto was "Swift. Silent. Deep." *Swiftly* duck the ropes, be *silent* about where you skied, and go after the *deepest* snow possible, even if that meant going out of bounds. Wilson designed a patch bearing a skull and crossbones to be sewn onto the jacket of each member. Induction to the club was quiet and without ceremony. If you proved yourself to be a hard-charging skier devoted to Jackson Hole, Wilson tapped you on the shoulder in the lift line and handed you a patch. That was it—you were in. You were now a made man.

It didn't take long for Coombs to catch the attention of Benny Wilson and the rest of the Jackson Hole Air Force. "We were skiing off the tram, lapping and lapping, and I was coming out the bottom and there was this guy right on my tail," Wilson remembered. Wilson was one of the fastest skiers in town, and yet this guy had stuck to him like a shadow. When Wilson got into the tram line with the rest of his crew, he spotted the stranger standing by himself with a huge grin on his face. "Who are you?" Wilson blurted out. "You're keeping right up with us. Who are you?"

Of all the elite skiers initiated into the ranks of the Jackson Hole Air Force, Coombs became the most iconic. His name was uttered in lift lines and barrooms with reverence and awe. His reputation as the greatest skier to ever come out of Jackson Hole was discussed not so much as a matter of opinion, but as a matter of fact. There were many other brilliant skiers carving their own legacies in Jackson Hole, but the legend of Doug Coombs still ran the deepest.

AFTER NINE HOURS OF TRAVEL from the East Coast, I was happy to be back in Jackson. Moseying around Town Square, I took in the lights of the Million Dollar Cowboy Bar, the creaky wooden walkways between the shops and restaurants, and the view of Snow King Mountain looming down Cache Street. Jackson still felt delightfully western.

Of course, what had brought me back was not this honky-tonk town, but rather the ski area located twenty minutes away in what is known as Teton Village.

Early the next morning, I boarded a shuttle from my hotel to Jackson Hole Mountain Resort to meet up with an old-timer named Bill Maloney. Now in his midseventies, Maloney was an honorary member of the Jackson Hole Air Force who still logged over a hundred days of skiing every season. He was an elder statesman around the resort, the kind of guy who knew most people by their first names, knew their kids' names, knew where they worked and where they skied on their lunch breaks. I knew Maloney because we graduated from the same college some fifty years apart, and I had made a point of introducing myself when I first moved to town in 2010. Now I was hoping he could help me navigate the inner circles of the Jackson Hole ski community and connect me with some key people from Coombs's life.

Despite having lived and worked in Jackson Hole before, I was worried that I didn't have enough "street cred" to gain access to the hardcore local ski community, which Coombs once belonged to. Local skiers in Jackson Hole could be territorial. Tourism had made the resort more crowded, the lines longer, and the après beers more expensive. As a result, when new people showed up in the tram line, locals could be tightlipped, if not downright standoffish. By their standards, I was still very much a "gaper" in these parts. I couldn't just walk up to someone wearing a Jackson Hole Air Force patch and expect them to enter into a conversation with me about Coombs, their most venerated member. Without someone like Bill Maloney vouching for me and making the introductions, I didn't think they would give me the time of day.

Maloney and I met in his small makeshift office at the base of the resort. After some profitable business conquests earlier in his life, Maloney had moved to Jackson Hole, where he now ran his ventures out of two broom closets located in the tram dock. His office walls were covered with photos and news clippings, one of which, a photo of Coombs, caught my eye.

"I used to have so much fun skiing with him," Maloney said, gesturing to the photo of Coombs. "Without question, there wasn't another skier—I don't think ever, maybe never again—who will be what he was to big mountain free skiing." He pulled the photo off the wall and then handed it to me. "This one particular day, my friend and I went skiing with Doug. My friend had hired Dave Miller as a guide for three weeks every winter, but Miller had broken his shoulder the week before, so Doug was going to guide us for the day. In any event, we're on the tram dock and Doug comes in with that grin of his; he said, 'Well, I called Dave Miller last night, and he told me I could take you guys anywhere.'"

Maloney leaned back in his squeaky office chair and cleared his throat. He was clearly amused by recounting the memory. "So Coombs takes us up the tram, and we ski across Rendezvous and then out the gates into the backcountry," he continued. "We're hiking up Cody Peak, about halfway up, and Doug says to us, 'Well, boys, I'm taking you to Once Is Enough today.'" Maloney paused for dramatic effect. Located on an iconic peak in the backcountry, Once Is Enough was exactly how it sounded: ski the line once, and that was enough for a lifetime. A childlike smile stretched across the old man's face. "I was sixty-eight years old at the time," Maloney said. "I never thought I'd ski Once Is Enough, but I said to myself, *If I'm ever going do it, I'm going to do it with Doug Coombs.*"

He perked up in his chair, reenacting the story. "So Doug pulls out a rope, makes a snow anchor, and says, 'Okay, boys, who wants to go first?'" Maloney volunteered. Coombs tied the rope around his waist and instructed him to lean over the edge so that he could lower Maloney down the first steep section to where he could actually get his skis in the snow. "I am so stoked up, you can't imagine the adrenaline pumping," Maloney said, his eyes wide. "I hit the snow and it was almost thigh-deep powder. I was so pumped up that I forgot I had the rope on, and I just started skiing. I totally forgot Coombs was on the other end of the rope." Maloney broke into a flutter of laughter. "Doug is up there, and I can't hear him, but he's yelling, 'The rope! The rope!' I get to the end of the rope, and I was like a dog at the end of the leash." He threw his head back comically to demonstrate how the rope stopped him in his tracks. We both laughed.

Catching his breath, Maloney continued. "A couple of weeks later, Doug was headed to La Grave for the final time. He bumped into me outside the Village Cafe and he said, 'Well, Bill, now that you've done Once Is Enough, next year I'm going to take you up the Grand Teton and we're going to ski it together.'" The old man beamed with pride. Then his eyes welled up slightly, and he sighed. "I never saw him again."

Maloney and I spent the morning making laps on groomed trails. After each run, we took the gondola back up the mountain and he'd tell me more stories about Coombs. Occasionally, a ski patroller he knew or a fellow member of the Jackson Hole Air Force would join us in the gondola, and he'd prod them for their own Coombs stories. I learned that when Coombs first moved to town, he got a job tuning skis at Teton Village Sports, a ski shop at the base of the mountain. A friend there eventually introduced him to the owners of High Mountain Heli-Skiing in Jackson Hole, and Coombs became a heli-guide, learning the mountain skills that he would cultivate for the rest of his career. To get a free season pass during those early years, Coombs worked as a ski host for the resort, greeting people coming off the chairlift and answering tourists' questions. "Of course, Coombsie probably did more skiing than hosting," joked one patroller. When a film crew came to the resort in the early eighties and its ski stars couldn't handle the local terrain, one of Coombs's friends, Bill Lewkowitz, who worked in the resort's marketing department, said he had the perfect guy for them to film. So began Coombs's early career as a professional skier.

"You know," Maloney said when we were alone again in the gondola, "you really need to speak with Emily."

Emily was Emily Coombs, Doug Coombs's widow. As far as the hierarchy of the Jackson Hole ski world went, Emily Coombs was royalty in my mind. I was painfully anxious to meet her. Without Emily's blessing to pursue her husband's story, my journey would be over before it really got started.

"Would you mind introducing me to her?" I asked Maloney.

"Sure," he said. "Tell you what, let's go down and grab some lunch, and then I'll ring her from my office."

Fifteen minutes later Maloney and I were studying the sandwich board down at the Village Cafe when I noticed someone striding over to us. She walked across the room through the crowd of skiers, and then tapped Maloney on the shoulder.

"Hi, Bill!" she said gleefully.

Maloney turned to her and his mouth dropped open. "I can't believe you're here right now," he exclaimed. "I was just about to call you."

He threw his arms around her.

"Emily, you have to meet this guy," Maloney continued. "We've been talking about Doug all day."

I'd rehearsed this moment countless times, but the fact that Emily Coombs had just unknowingly waltzed into my life—minutes after I asked Maloney for an introduction—left me dumbfounded. The best my mind could cough up was a meek hello.

"Hi," she responded uneasily. Her blue eyes were wide and curious; a braid of red hair fell over her shoulder. She was shorter than I'd imagined.

"I'd love to talk to you," was the next thing I heard myself say.

"Well, I'm about to get on the tram and go skiing with some friends . . ." she said.

"Oh okay. That's cool. But, you know, later—maybe we could grab coffee or something?"

"Yeah," Emily said hesitantly. "Well, do you want to just come skiing with us?"

I was hungry, cold, and sore from skiing with Maloney all morning, but every fiber of my body knew the answer to Emily's question. I raced out the door, grabbed my skis, and followed her up the stairs to the tram. Minutes later I was wedged in the corner of the tram inches away from this woman who, unbeknownst to her, I'd just traveled thousands of miles to meet. My mind raced through my mental index of questions I wanted to ask her, but I kept coming to the same conclusion: *Holy shit, I'm about to go skiing with Emily Coombs.*

She seemed entirely wary of my company, which I couldn't fault her for, as she'd just been forced to ski a run with some stranger. Meanwhile, I filled every second of uncomfortable silence as best I could, describing how I grew up watching movies of her husband, how he inspired me to move to Jackson Hole, and so on. She nodded politely but didn't seem overly impressed. I imagined that my story was not unlike the stories of many others in the tram right now, and she'd heard it all before.

"I grew up skiing at Nashoba Valley," I finally offered, arriving at the bottom of my story's barrel.

"Oh wow, Nashoba, huh?" Emily responded with genuine enthusiasm. "Can you believe Doug came from there?"

"Yeah, that's what really got me thinking. I mean, how does a guy go from skiing at Nashoba to doing what he did?"

"I'm from Massachusetts too, you know?" she said. "Wellesley."

I hadn't known that but was encouraged to have made some connection.

When the tram doors finally opened, Emily turned and asked over her shoulder, "Hobacks good with you?" It hadn't snowed in weeks and the only feasible skiing, in my mind anyway, was on the groomed runs; Emily wanted to head off-trail into God knows what kind of gnarly, ice-chunked terrain.

"Sounds great," I gulped.

From the moment we set off, I was doing everything in my power to keep up with her. The slope was strewn with frozen moguls the size of Volkswagen Beetles, which Emily weaved deftly. While fighting to stay on my feet, I marveled at her impeccable skiing. In the tram, she struck me as just another middle-aged woman, but now watching her dominate the mountain, she was the Emily Coombs I had read about: world extreme skiing champion, heli-skiing pioneer, the love of Doug Coombs's life.

All of a sudden a mogul appeared in front of me. It had been shrouded in the flat light, and I had no time to slow down. Instead, I launched off it at full speed. The ground dropped away and I was soaring through the air, my arms flapping frantically, like a chicken shot out of a cannon. My worst fears were coming true. I was about to explode water balloon–style in a sorry heap of skis, poles, and broken body parts. Emily would probably have to stop and hike back up the slope to peel my carcass off the snow. How embarrassing.

Miraculously, when the backs of my skis met the snow, I was somehow able to keep it all together. My butt hit the frozen ground and then I popped back on my feet. Before I could even register what had just happened, Emily came to a stop ahead of me in the middle of the run. I pulled up alongside her, my heart still rattling around in my rib cage. Emily stared down the slope.

"Doug and I used to ski this every day," she said. "We'd ski this nonstop, top to bottom, to get our legs ready for Alaska."

"You ski amazing," I blurted between breaths, not sure what else to say but truly meaning the compliment.

"Oh no." She shrugged, looking back at me with a coy smile. "This is my first day back. I haven't been at the resort all season."

EMILY AND I MET FOR coffee a week or so later at 43 North, a restaurant located at the base of Snow King Mountain in downtown Jackson.

Emily ski-raced at the resort a few days a week. We sat in big leather chairs, watching Snow King's old lift crawl up the steep face. When the coffee started to kick in, Emily began revealing bits and pieces of her former life with her husband.

"When my brain goes back there," she said, cupping her mug, "I just think, *Whoa, I can't believe I lived that life.*"

Emily told her stories of her husband like she was picking up photos that had fallen out of an album and now lay in a collage on the floor, mixing timelines, characters, and places. She wasn't scatterbrained—her memories were exquisitely detailed—but rather her life with Coombs had been so full and action-packed that her stories seemed to burst at the seams. "If we were going to get in the car for the day, I needed to know what sport we were doing," Emily said. "Doug, do I need my bicycle? Do I need my skis? Do I need my crampons?"

They spent their winters skiing in Jackson Hole, springs heli-guiding in Alaska, and summers windsurfing in Hood River, with adventures in Europe, South America, Greenland, and other far-flung places sprinkled throughout. Eventually, Emily and Coombs traded their winters in Jackson Hole for a quieter existence in France. Up to that point, a year in their life would put most people's bucket lists to shame. "Our values were the same," she said. "Our dreams were the same. Life plan was the same. Our passions were the same."

"Was he aware of the risks of that life?" I asked.

"He sort of thrived on danger and technical skiing combined," Emily explained. "But I don't think he saw it as dangerous. When I would say, 'If I fall, then I'm dead,' he would say, 'Why would you think that way? Why would you fall?' He just had a different head. He didn't acknowledge the danger."

"Beyond breaking his neck as a kid, did he have any injuries?"

"If you asked Doug if he'd ever been hurt, he'd say, 'No, I've never been hurt.' And I would say, 'Excuse me? Didn't you break your neck, break this arm, break that arm?' In his mind he never got hurt. Or he'd say, 'Oh, I've never been in a car accident.' But what about that time you were passing the semitruck and you flipped and went off the road? And he'd say, 'Oh, that wasn't my fault. It was raining, I couldn't see.'" Emily laughed.

"Did he have any big crashes skiing?"

"He knew he couldn't crash because of his broken neck," Emily explained. "Doug never took whippers because he was always afraid of his neck. He was very protective of that neck. He was never a big cliff jumper. He always knew that he couldn't have a crash."

I took a sip of my coffee, thinking about how it made sense that so many people praised Coombs as an immaculate skier who never seemed to fall. I wondered how many people knew that falling simply wasn't an option for him.

"That's just how Doug's mind worked," Emily continued. "Negative things just never stayed with him at all. But he did get Lyme disease, and that put him down."

"Oh, really?"

"It put him down bad," Emily said. "The doctor operated on him, thinking that he had torn cartilage in his knee. He opened him up and closed him up right away. He said something was weird in there. There was this discoloration. It was full-blown Lyme disease."

"How did Doug react?"

"He was so bummed out," Emily said. "He had intravenous drugs. He had to inject it twice a day for six weeks. That winter he was really tired. He'd ski and then fall asleep in the back of the car. It was bad. Every once in a while, even later in life, he'd say, 'I'm feeling kind of Lyme-y today.'"

"Did it slow him down?"

"A little bit at first, but he never wanted to acknowledge that anything was wrong," Emily explained. "It's like he couldn't deal with it because his life was about being able to do stuff. He was frantic about getting it all in before he couldn't anymore. Maybe it was something to do with when he was in the hospital with a broken neck when he was young. After that, he just wanted to get it all in."

Emily looked back out the window to see the lift crawling up Snow King. "You know, I still dream about him all the time," she said. "Like he's still here, but he's away. He's still with me. He's still my husband. He's still the guy of my dreams, literally."

07

RIDGE HIPPY ROMANCE

Bozeman, Montana, 1980s

When Emily Gladstone first met her future husband while she was studying photography at Montana State University, Doug Coombs was hardly the picture of a prince. His beard grew in brown tufts that just begged for a razor. He bathed irregularly. His hair was long and shaggy. His tattered clothes grew mold and he wore thick, often smudged glasses. His giant quads barely fit into his seventies-style jeans, and when the seams gave way, he replaced the rips with colorful patches. Friends came to call him "Doug the Slug."

Coombs's overall dishevelment was matched with a carefree, fun-loving attitude. He was in his own world, absentmindedly parking in handicapped spots and dabbling in his fair share of the psychedelic drugs of the time. He showed up to the mountain late, often forgetting a glove, a boot, or even his skis. To save money one year, he lived in an unheated porch, where he slept even in the frigid months of winter. When Mount St. Helens erupted in 1980 and people in Bozeman were ordered to stay indoors due to all the volcanic ash falling in town, he wrapped a scarf around his face and went outside on his merry way.

Coombs wasn't much for following the rules, and his friends loved him for it.

"Everyone wanted to do these things with Doug because he was just so downright fun to be with," wrote one of his college buddies. "Whether he was blazing trail through the bathroom window at Gallatin Gateway to sneak in and listen to Hunter Thompson, or skiing the stairs at the farmhouse, or making fake name tags so we could ski free at the Bridger Bowl instructor's tryouts, Doug made you feel alive and invincible, much like the fidgety child set free on the first day of summer vacation."

Coombs enrolled at Montana State University (MSU) in the fall of 1977 to race on its Division I ski team and continue the geology degree he had started back East at New England College. An obscure university outside of Bozeman, MSU was transitioning from a honky-tonk campus of ranchers to a mountaineering mecca for skiers and climbers when Coombs arrived. "It was still a western town back then—ranching and all," commented one of his MSU ski buddies, Jim Conway, who would ski with Coombs for the next two decades. "The year before I got there, the locals shaved half of some hippy's head. It was definitely still cowboy culture."

Coombs went to MSU to ski-race, but he was quickly distracted by a backcountry zone in the Bridger Bowl Ski Area known simply as the Ridge. Accessible only by hiking, the Ridge was defined by a series of narrow chutes running down its steep, rocky face. Given names like Cream Jeans, the Orgasms, and Cuckoos, the chutes required tight, technical skiing between rocks, off cliffs, and down steep drops that often avalanched. "It was like a laboratory," Coombs said. The Ridge was Tuckerman Ravine on steroids, and Coombs was hooked.

Before long he was skipping race practice to go ski on the Ridge. Even on race days, Coombs hiked up to the Ridge with a pair of binoculars and his racing bib tucked into his pocket. When he spotted his number coming up on the scoreboard through the binoculars, he scorched down, catching air off cliffs and jumps, before skiing right into the starting gates, covered in snow and his veins coursing with adrenaline. "We would then wipe ourselves down and bolt out of the gate," he remembered. "The coaches hated it."

Coombs found that the strictness of racing conflicted with his love of skiing. "When you get to that level, racing NCAA Division I, you're racing against guys that are maybe one step off the World Cup; some of them even came from the World Cup," explained one of Coombs's MSU teammates, Rusty Squire. "It's really competitive and all consuming, and it puts you in one small arena. I don't think Doug wanted to be caged up in one small arena. He wanted the whole mountain range to be his arena." By the end of his junior year, Coombs quit the race team entirely.

Instead, he joined a different kind of team, a motley gang of mostly East Coast skiers that the Bridger Bowl Ski Patrol nicknamed the Ridge Hippies. The Ridge Hippies didn't hold practice. There were no races. There were no rules. They were just a talented group of backcountry skiers hiking up the Ridge and pioneering new routes down. The Ridge Hippies bombed down chutes, launched off cliffs, and outran avalanches. They spoke their own language, using code names so no one could discover their secret powder stashes on the Ridge. Like Benny Wilson and the Jackson Hole Air Force, Coombs and the Ridge Hippies emerged as some of the most dominant skiers on the mountain.

"It was fate that those guys met and pushed each other," remembered Jim Conway. "We had very similar motivations and energy levels. We just drove each other to do something that put our little crew as one of the more innovative and experienced groups of skiers out there."

For Coombs and the rest of the Ridge Hippies, there were no such things as sponsorships, no roles in ski films, no contests, no fame, no fortune, and no free skis. They all assumed they would eventually need to get real jobs and submit to their parents' wishes of starting retirement accounts. Coombs figured he would end up working as a geologist on an oil rig, hopefully somewhere near the mountains. Until that time, however, he and his ragtag gang pushed deeper and deeper into the backcountry, bagging peaks and evading avalanches purely for the love of skiing.

By the early eighties, the Ridge had become a hotbed for the future of mountaineers and skiers, gaining the attention of even *Rolling Stone* magazine. As Tim Cahill wrote for *Rolling Stone*, "They're up there now, on the ridge above Bridger Bowl Ski Area, risking their lives, catching clean air, running the avalanches and the Orgasms, banging chutes, kicking the snow loose, packing it down, controlling the danger, stabilizing the slope. They embrace the concept of terminal wipeout and broken bones, of the face wash . . . not to mention the possibility of being buried alive under several tons of snow—like voracious lovers."

Joining Coombs on the Ridge were future pro skiers Tom Jungst, Jim Conway, and Scot Schmidt, all of whom would later star in ski films. Emil Tanner and Rusty Squire both became professional cyclists. There was climbing prodigy Alex Lowe and future avalanche expert Bruce Tremper. They were architects, geologists, scientists, engineers, photographers, and artists—all drawn to the Ridge like bees to honey. And then there was Emily Gladstone.

EMILY GLADSTONE GREW UP IN the well-to-do suburb of Wellesley, Massachusetts. Her father worked for one of the country's top publishers and her mother taught at Wellesley College. The Gladstones opened their doors to kids from Boston's inner-city projects so they could benefit from the school system in their town, and like an exchange program, Emily then went into the inner-city classrooms and gave nature presentations. As this little white girl with screaming red hair presented the finer points of tree frogs, the students hung onto her every word.

But Emily never quite fit in around Wellesley. Despite her girl-next-door beauty, she was shy and had little luck with boys. She struggled in school and couldn't settle into a group of friends. Instead, she found refuge working at a horse stable in a nearby town, where she fell in love with a dangerous mare named Honey.

Honey violently bucked Emily to the ground over and over, breaking her collarbone, and then her femur. But she kept dusting herself off and climbing back on to the wild horse until Honey finally warmed up to her. Unfortunately, the Gladstones hadn't warmed up to the idea of Emily working at the horse stable. They had had quite enough of the trips to the hospital and forbade their daughter from working there anymore. But Emily refused to leave Honey. After much pleading on Emily's part, the Gladstones agreed to buy her the horse, and the two became inseparable.

The year before college, Emily moved up to Vermont with Honey and became a summer trail guide at Stratton Mountain Ski Resort. During the winter, she worked on the ski patrol there. When she moved to Bozeman the following year to study photography at Montana State University, Emily tearfully gave Honey away to a school for children with autism. Honey became sweet as a puppy dog in the hands of the children.

As a skier in Montana, Emily was the only girl who could keep up with the Ridge Hippies. "I was riding the chairlift at Bridger Bowl," remembered Bruce Tremper, "when—and this vision is permanently burned into my deep neurons—a beautiful, shapely woman skied by under the lift with her long red hair flying, carving perfect turns on the hard spring ice. She may have been the best female skier I had ever seen at Bridger Bowl."

Although she grew up only thirty minutes away from Coombs in Massachusetts, Emily didn't meet him until he launched off a cliff and landed right at her feet in Montana. "He was a total goof," she said. "His whole presence was goofy. He had all this hair and this beard. He talked funny. He sort of said hello, and then he just skied off." The two became friends and skied together, but no romantic sparks flew.

A year later, Emily pulled into the chairlift line at Bridger Bowl to find Coombs standing right beside her. She barely recognized him. Coombs was applying for jobs as a geologist and had cleaned up a bit. "He got a haircut for one thing, which helped. Probably had a bath too," she remembered. "We were just standing in the lift line, and I looked at him and thought, *Wow, he's kind of cute.* All of a sudden my feelings changed." A year after that, they started dating, and Emily fell deeply in love with Coombs. She had found another Honey.

When Coombs moved to Jackson Hole, he and Emily broke up and dated other people. Professionally, he earned a modest income tuning skis and heli-guiding during the winters, while he spent his summers working as a geologist on oil rigs in Wyoming. Despite his parents' wishes that he secure a full-time position as a geologist, Coombs was entirely disenchanted with the career. He'd entered the field out of a love for nature, but now he found himself on the tip of the spear tearing it apart. Moreover, Coombs wasn't much for a nine-to-five existence. He just wanted to ski.

After Emily left MSU, she moved around, spending a year in New Mexico and three winters in Utah. She eventually landed in Verbier, Switzerland, in the winter of 1988, and to earn enough money to ski there each season, spent her summers working at Glacier National Park in Montana.

Coombs and Emily were apart for six years. During this time, they'd occasionally bump into one another at ski areas and a short-lived romance would ensue, but it never lasted. "We did a good job breaking each other's hearts a few times," Emily remembered. "When Doug came back into my life, I had just been dumped by some guy and I had sworn off men. All they did was hurt you, I thought." In 1989, Coombs landed in St. Anton, Austria, to star in his first ski film. He asked Emily to come visit. She drove as fast as she could from Switzerland, and the two spent three days skiing together, sleeping each night in a car in the parking lot. "It was so much fun, but I thought, 'Okay, that was just another one of those flings with Doug," Emily recalled. "I said bye and went back to Verbier."

But the two stayed in touch and visited each other when Emily returned to Montana that summer to work at Glacier National Park. When it came time to return to Verbier that fall, Emily asked Coombs to come back with her. "He didn't want to go," she said. "He liked his job at the ski shop in Jackson. He didn't want to leave. He was a homebody. He had his friends there, his home there." So even though she thought the quality of the skiing in Jackson was a step down compared to Verbier, Emily moved to Jackson Hole to be with Coombs.

Four years later, while they were vacationing in Hood River, Oregon, Coombs rowed Emily out onto middle of the White Salmon River. It was the night before Halloween, and a full moon glowed in the sky. He handed her a bottle of cabernet sauvignon and told her to read the label.

Emily,
Will you marry me?
Love,
Doug

TWO MONTHS LATER, ON JANUARY 27, 1993, Coombs and Emily were married in a low-key ceremony on the banks of the Kelly Warm Spring in Jackson Hole. The two had a yin-and-yang type of relationship that worked. Coombs was loud, gregarious, and outgoing; Emily was quiet, shy, and reserved. "They were the definition of opposites attracting," said one of their mutual friends. The couple drew strength from their differences and believed fully in one another. That was especially the case when it came to supporting Coombs's career as a professional skier. "This is what he was born to do," Emily recalled thinking. "And I was going to do everything I could to make it happen for him."

Emily convinced Coombs to travel back East and tell his parents that he was going to become a professional skier. "Why don't you tell them who you really are?" she said to him. "You're not this geologist who's going to go back to your geology career. This is who you want to be. This is what you want to do. Someday you might be dead and they would never have known who their son was." Despite his good intentions, Coombs's parents "freaked," Emily recalled. "Doug came back and said, 'That was really bad advice.'"

Janet and Gordon Coombs had lived through the Depression. They believed in being financially stable, and the life of a professional skier was anything but. They tried to convince the young couple that they needed to start thinking about their futures. They needed to start retirement accounts. What were they going to do if they had a child? "We didn't know where Doug's interest in skiing would lead," said Coombs's brother Steve. "Dad was worried about what he would do as he got older or needed to make some money. Ski careers back then were ski instructing, ski shops, or working at ski areas." Coombs's sister Nancy remembered that "they were proud of him. I do think that, being a skier himself, my dad was especially interested in what he was doing, but they also worried about how he was going to make a living for himself and Emily. My mother worried about his safety. She didn't like looking at the pictures of him skiing the big mountains." Despite their protests, Coombs and Emily remained committed to the life they wanted to live, emboldened by their shared passion for being in the mountains.

Doug and Emily Coombs were the definition of a team, a true skiing power couple. Emily was a brilliant skier and fiercely athletic. In 1992, she was crowned the women's world extreme skiing champion. "Emily is still the steep skier in the family," Coombs said of his wife. "She's actually technically a better skier than I am. I'm just more daring."

Yet being Coombs's wife was not always easy. "In the house he drove me nuts," Emily said. "It was like living with a big dog in a small apartment. He was really hyperactive and muddy and loud." Coombs's nature made it impossible for them to go skiing in Jackson Hole without attracting flocks of people wanting to join them. Emily would have preferred to ski with her husband and a select group of friends, but "Doug always had his 'boyfriends,'" she said, "who followed him wherever he went."

Even more taxing was sharing a life with someone who lived on the edge day in and day out. "I don't know how Emily puts up with me," Coombs said. "I think my wife is super tolerant. She must think I'm a complete kook. I think she's the most tolerant person in the whole world because I haven't been slowing down very much. She knows me so well, and she knows that to make me stop doing something that I love is not possible." When she knew Coombs was out doing something especially treacherous, Emily would whisper into her wedding ring, which had once belonged to Coombs's beloved grandmother. Neither of them was particularly religious, but she believed in the energy of people and thought she and Coombs were connected on some higher level. "Even when we were apart, we would dream about each other," she said. "I think it was understood that we would always connect with one another in our dreams."

Once, while Coombs was out skiing, Emily whispered into the ring as she always did—when suddenly its stone fell out. When Coombs finally came in through the door, she was deeply relieved. Although he was safe for now, the memory of the stone falling out never left her.

08

TAKING OFF

Valdez, Alaska, 1989–91

In the spring of 1989, Valdez, Alaska became the site of the worst manmade environmental disaster in American history when the supertanker *Exxon Valdez* ran aground in Prince William Sound, spilling 10.8 million gallons of crude oil into the Gulf of Alaska. Sometime after eleven o'clock on March 24, captain Joseph J. Hazelwood handed over command of Exxon's 987-foot tanker to his third mate and left the helm. The decision proved cataclysmic.

Despite repeated warnings from the local lighthouse keeper, the *Exxon Valdez* veered out of the shipping lanes, picked up speed, and then slammed into Prince William Sound's Bligh Reef. As oil seeped from its cracked hull and spread over 1,300 miles of pristine Alaskan shoreline, the tanker's captain fled the scene of the accident. Hazelwood briefly became a fugitive of the law, before ultimately turning himself in to authorities. "These are misdemeanors of such magnitude that have never been equaled in this country," the judge declared. "This is a level of destruction we've not seen since Hiroshima."

The spill killed hundreds of thousands of birds, fish, and mammals; cost hundreds of millions of dollars to clean up; and devastated the fishing and tourist industry. Overnight, Valdez's population swelled from 3,500 people to 12,000. Cleanup crews booked every room in town. "If you could plug up your bathtub, you could rent it out for a hundred bucks a night," said one local taxi driver.

Yet even before they were forced to drag themselves out of the oil spill, the people of Valdez had a history of overcoming gargantuan challenges. Resilience ran down this port town's very roots. Back in 1898, when gold was discovered in the Alaskan interior, Valdes, as it was then spelled, became a launching pad for thousands of rugged gold rushers who forged a trail over miles of treacherous, crevasse-strewn glaciers. The gold rush turned Valdez into a lawless frontier town complete with saloons, gambling, and ladies of the night. In 1964, when a mega earthquake—the third largest in recorded history—rocked Alaska, an underwater landslide in Prince William Sound swallowed the town. The landslide triggered a forty-foot tsunami that crushed the unsuspecting waterfront, killing thirty people and injuring many others. A little more than ten years later, after relocating entirely, Valdez rolled up its sleeves once again to help build the most ambitious oil pipeline in American history. The Trans-Alaska Pipeline snaked eight hundred miles through Alaskan wilderness, ending in Valdez and turning it into a boomtown. The pipeline also brought in helicopters—lots of them. And with helicopters eventually came heli-skiing.

The first skiers and snowboarders in Valdez explored the surrounding Chugach Mountains by foot, hiking up from a stretch of Richardson Highway known as Thompson Pass with skis strapped to their backs. One of these early skiers was a smooth-talking Colorado native named Michael Cozad, who came to Valdez to fish commercially in 1984. "It was very local back then," Cozad remembered. "A dozen guys normally on the weekends. On the pass there, you might see thirty or forty or fifty people. Ten cars or something." One day while in town,

Cozad bumped into a friend who was hanging posters for a pilot advertising his services to skiers.

The pilot's name was Chuck McMahon, and he had aviation in his blood. As the son of a bush pilot, McMahon's earliest memories were of hunting wolves with a shotgun from the window of his father's Super Cub. When work on the pipeline brought him to Valdez, McMahon saw the skiing potential of these wild mountains and began shuttling skiers into the Chugach. Mike Cozad became one of his first passengers. "We would reach out to these vast distances," Cozad recalled. "You'd be sitting out there thirty miles from nowhere and wolverines would show up. After an hour and a half, you'd be wondering if this guy was ever coming back to get you."

Skiing these mountains that would take him days to reach by foot or dogsled was exhilarating, and Cozad began to envision Valdez as an international ski destination. He thought people would come from all over the world to experience this caliber of skiing in the Chugach. One day while flying with McMahon, Cozad leaned up to the pilot and yelled to him over the din of the plane, "I think we could do something with that place." At the end of his pointer finger was a beat-up old lodge that just so happened to be up for sale.

The Tsaina Lodge was a rundown roadhouse built on Thompson Pass in 1949 to accommodate weary travelers making their way on the dirt roads of Richardson Highway. The lodge changed hands a couple of times, before eventually being abandoned and falling into disrepair. Yet even in its sorry state, Cozad saw the potential of the Tsaina Lodge as the base for a heli-skiing operation. He convinced McMahon to join him in putting down some earnest money in 1988, and then they went to find a loan. When they ended up at the Small Business Administration, the only loan they could get was from the Vietnam Veterans Division. "And that's how old sweet Chet Simmons got involved," said Cozad.

After flying gunships in Vietnam, Chet Simmons returned to his native Alaska and flew choppers on the oil pipeline in Glennallen.

When work brought him up country to Valdez, Simmons was among the early skiers hiking up from Thompson Pass and later catching flights with McMahon. Simmons, too, saw the untapped potential of Valdez as a heli-skiing destination. He was quick to sign on to get the veterans division loan and buy the Tsaina Lodge with Cozad, McMahon, and a local carpenter they enlisted, Vin Tikigawa. Cozad hired a crew to help dig out the Tsaina and start what was going to be an extensive renovation of the dilapidated building. The first heli-skiing lodge in Valdez was about to take off, but then fate muddled Cozad's plans in the form of black gold.

Just three days after they began renovating the Tsaina, the *Exxon Valdez* ran aground. The spill prompted workers to flock to Valdez, where they could earn bundles of money on cleanup crews. Cozad's own crew quickly vanished, including his carpenter and the lodge's majority owner, Chet Simmons. It didn't take long for Chuck McMahon to get cold feet as well, and he bailed out too.

Over the next two years, Cozad painstakingly pieced the Tsaina Lodge back together himself, but it remained a financial nightmare. He needed something to jump-start his business, something to put heli-skiing in Valdez on the world stage. Mike Cozad needed to come up with something big, something that would grab headlines and shake up the ski world.

DOUG COOMBS DIDN'T KNOW WHAT to think when he first spotted Cozad's ad for the World Extreme Skiing Championship in *Powder* magazine in the winter of 1991. The ad was calling for expert skiers who wanted to compete against one another in Alaska's Chugach Mountains. Coombs had never heard of the place. Moreover, the idea of holding a competition for extreme skiing struck him as completely contradictory to the sport as he understood it. Extreme skiing existed mostly out of eyeshot of anyone, save a ski partner and maybe a camera. It was a deeply personal pursuit, one done away from ski resorts, away from racecourses and crowds, in remote mountains where exploration was the goal and survival the reward.

Coombs's view of extreme skiing had been shaped by following the career of his childhood hero, Patrick Vallençant. For nearly twenty years, Vallençant pioneered harrowing first descents in the French Alps and the Andes, climbing up impossibly steep mountains with crampons and ice axes and then skiing down. Of these extreme descents, Vallençant liked to say, *si tu tombes, tu meurs*—if you fall, you die.

"A thought flashes, an image appears," Vallençant wrote of one of his first descents in his 1979 book *Ski Extrême*, "that of a fall, those that one would leave, a wife, children. In a confused way, I perceive that drama of it, their pain, and I receive like a blow the emptiness of their future—but then a turn sweeps away these vague thoughts, pushes them aside so that I am free of my movements, that I don't consider them too important and that I don't stop and continue on foot."

Coombs was mesmerized by footage of Vallençant. "He just had that flamboyant French flair," Coombs remembered. "He just seemed like this cartoon [character] that was untouchable." With his bright-purple ski suits, ornate facial hair, and long headbands that flapped behind him as he skied, Vallençant looked like a comic book superhero to Coombs. His bravado glared off the magazine pages that Coombs ripped out and obsessed over while he was growing up. "You'd read about him and about his descents in Peru and in Chamonix, and he was picking them off right and left with a lot of flair," Coombs gushed. "We were madly infatuated with him. We all wanted to have headbands like him and purple clothing."

Vallençant had an unlikely rise to extreme skiing stardom. Born in Lyon, France, in the rubble of World War II, he fled the city as a boy to find adventures in the surrounding mountains. At eighteen years old, he enrolled in the elite High Mountain Military Academy in Chamonix but was kicked out after two years. Instead, Vallençant became a ski instructor in Switzerland with his girlfriend, who later became his wife and lifelong ski partner. Vallençant's dream was to become a mountain guide, a highly revered position that was reserved only for the most elite mountaineers. French mountain guides were born and groomed in the Alps, while Vallençant was a city rat from Lyon. When he enrolled in guiding school in Chamonix in 1970, they told him that he'd never pass, but three years later Vallençant proved them wrong.

As he became more famous in the late seventies and early eighties, Vallençant started an extreme skiing camp based in Chamonix called Stages Vallençant. When Coombs discovered this while in college, he traveled all the way to Chamonix to meet his hero. "I went there and banged on the door and said, 'I want to ski with Vallençant,'" Coombs recalled. "I don't have any money, but I'm willing to give what I have to ski with this guy because it would just be a dream." The man at the door wasn't impressed. "Everyone wants to ski with Vallençant," he told Coombs. "Get in line." Then he slammed the door in his face.

A few days later, while Coombs was tuning his skis outside the tramway, he spotted his hero walking across the parking lot with skis slung over his shoulder. "Here he comes marching by at a full stride like he's on a mission," Coombs remembered. "He jumps on the lift, and I jump on the lift behind him." At the top, Coombs raced behind Vallençant, chasing him over a fence and then down a steep, off-piste ski run. He skied high on the outside walls of the chute so as not to crowd his hero. When they reached the bottom of the run, Vallençant turned to Coombs. Face to face with the legend, the young skier froze. Finally Vallençant spoke: "You ski the walls well." And with that, he took off.

"To have Vallençant say that was the biggest compliment you could ever imagine," Coombs said. "All of a sudden we had this bond." The moment would echo throughout the rest of Coombs's life as an example of the skier he wanted to be: a revered ski mountaineer, a guide that could ski the steepest peaks in the world and take others with him—all the while doing it in style.

Now faced with Mike Cozad's ad for the first World Extreme Skiing Championship, Coombs must have wondered what Vallençant would have made of all this. Was this the direction Vallençant envisioned for extreme skiing? To be competitive? To be judged? To be turned into a media spectacle? But Coombs never had the opportunity to ask him because only two years earlier, Patrick Vallençant had fallen to his death in the mountains. Just as he had feared, Vallençant left behind a wife and a son.

"IF YOU DON'T WIN, YOU have to come back and paint the building," said the president of Lifelink after Coombs asked him if the company would pay for his flight to Valdez to compete in the World Extreme Skiing Championship. Lifelink was a small backcountry gear manufacturer based in Jackson Hole that had become one of Coombs's first sponsors. "I didn't realize they were just joking on that," Coombs said, "but I was thinking, *I don't want to paint that building.*"

As Coombs and his fellow competitors arrived from Anchorage in April of 1991, the town of Valdez rolled out the red carpet. Mike Cozad had managed to get everybody involved, not just the townspeople but also the Alyeska oil company, the National Guard, and the local government. In the gloom of early spring, when the only bit of entertainment came from the occasional shoot-out between herring fishermen, Cozad's World Extreme Skiing Championship—what people started referring to as WESC—injected a festive air of excitement into the sleepy port town. Half of Valdez's 3,500 people lent a hand in playing host to the skiers and their ragtag entourages. The mayor was in attendance, along with members of the city council. Even Miss Valdez made an appearance, sash and all.

As it turned out, Cozad's crazy idea for an extreme skiing contest didn't seem so crazy to a number of skiers like Coombs. More than a hundred skiers responded to the ad; thirty-seven were invited to participate. Among them were the who's who of the budding professional ski scene. "Their names read like the cast of an award-winning extreme skiing movie," wrote John Page for *Snow Country* magazine in 1991. "Dean (*Return to the Snow Zone*) Cummings, Christopher (*Steep and Deep*) Leveroni, Kim (*License To Thrill*) Reichhelm, and Kevin (*Extreme Skier*) Andrews." Rounding out the roster was Doug Coombs, a goofy-looking heli-skiing guide from Jackson Hole, Wyoming, who nobody had ever heard of.

As the townspeople and athletes mingled over smoked salmon and strong drinks at the local civic center, a curious cross section of American culture was on full display. On one hand there were the hardy yet courteous Valdezeans, and on the other a merry band of extreme skiers epitomized by the ever-flamboyant Glen Plake, who sported cowboy boots; fluorescent pants; a red, white, and blue leather jacket; and his trademark Mohawk. Plake was one of the contest's celebrity judges, along with pro skiers Mike Hattrup and Scot Schmidt. The three celebrity judges had become the most famous faces in extreme skiing after starring in *The Blizzard of Aahhh's*, a cult classic ski film that popped extreme skiing into VCRs around the country and landed Plake and Schmidt on *Good Morning America*. "Okay, if you thought skiing was skiing and there was a certain sameness to it all, I suggest you buckle your breakfast seatbelt," Bryant Gumbel told American viewers while flanked by Schmidt and Plake. "What we're about to show you is something called extreme skiing. It lacks only a disclaimer that you not try this on your own. We assume your sense of self-preservation will tell you that. Extreme skiing is virtually outlawed in this country . . . [and] out-of-bounds skiers don't have any sanctioned competitions." That was about to change.

Despite the convivial air of the opening ceremonies, questions and concerns lurked about how this competition would actually unfold. "Extreme skiing is a dangerous game to begin with," wrote Craig Medred in the *Anchorage Daily News*. "It becomes an insane game when someone begins promoting it as a competition, when points are given for coming the closest to death."

Even *Powder* magazine, which was a leading sponsor, had initial misgivings about Cozad's contest. "*What a lame idea,* I thought, as this guy, some guy, who knows what guy, really, just a voice on the phone saying he was calling from Valdez, Alaska, went on and on and on about some extreme contest he wanted to have," wrote *Powder* magazine's editor, Steve Casimiro, in 1991. "I mean, Alaska. Too far, too cold, too dark, too big, too crazy. I pictured this guy, Mike Cozad: too many Januarys bivouacked with that mean old bugger, Yukon Jack. Bright red snowmobile suit. Beard. *Looong* beard. A long, greasy beard. Spends the summer working on the herring fleet, the winter cleaning his guns. Until one day, when he says, 'Hey, Homer, I got me an idea . . .'"

Practically speaking, the organizers had wrestled with how to judge an extreme skiing competition. "It didn't sound very well organized," remembered judge Scot Schmidt. "It sounded quite dangerous, frankly: forcing competitors to take lines on a day that you wouldn't normally do it." After some heated deliberation, the judges agreed upon six measures of criteria, each bearing the same value. One, aggressiveness: How hard did the skier attack the run? Two, fluidity: Did he ski it in a smooth, seamless line, or piece it together choppily? Three, form: How was the skier's technique? Tight and precise, or loose and sloppy? Four, air: Did the skier jump off rocks or cliffs? If so, how much air did he catch? Five, degree of difficulty: Did the skier play it safe and pick an easy line down the mountain, or did he push the envelope and craft a challenging, creative descent? Six, recovery: If the skier started going out of control, how well did he pull himself back together? Once the competitors finally got a look at what they were skiing, however, survival was the main measure of criteria most of them were concerned about.

The contest was to take place on Thompson Pass, which ran into the heart of the Chugach Mountains. There would be no set racecourse—just three peaks, one for each day of the competition. If there was any doubt about whether Cozad's competition would actually be extreme, those doubts evaporated on the first day when a ski patrolman entered the competition's first run on 27 Mile Glacier and froze with fear. The thirty-seven competitors and 150 spectators were forced to wait for forty minutes until Coombs skied down to the terrified patrolman and tied him off to a rope to be rescued.

The first run was pitched at forty-five degrees, for 2,600 vertical feet. For the crowd below, appreciating the true steepness of the slope was impossible. It felt like skiing down a rollercoaster, so steep that the line between skiing and flying was nearly indistinguishable. "If any-one falls on the steep stuff, you can damn near pick them up at the bottom of the mountain," rescue coordinator Dave Decker told the *Anchorage Daily News*.

On the Chugach's forty- to fifty-five-degree slopes, studded with rocks and slick snow, falls were horrifically gruesome. When Garret Bartel caught an edge at the very beginning of his run in the 1992 WESC, he lost his balance and tumbled the length of the mountain. Bartell cartwheeled seventeen times over three rock bands before sliding helplessly on his back down the rest of the run. The thirty-seven-second crash was so spectacular that the whole town of Valdez crammed into the civic center that night just to watch the footage on the big screen. Miraculously, Bartel survived.

A year later, however, a Steamboat Springs skier named Wilbur Madsen would not be so lucky. While waiting for his run at the 1993 WESC, Madsen stepped out onto a cornice. "A piece just sheared off where he was standing, and he slid down a ways, his heels dug in, and it launched him out, and there was a rock band there," remembered a race organizer who had just helped Madsen out of the helicopter. "He did a header into the rock band and totaled his cranium and then slid down the hill headfirst on his back like a human rag doll. Even the next morning there was a frozen blood stripe down the mountain." Madsen was the first casualty at WESC. "This isn't sport; this is cra-ziness," wrote Craig Medred in the *Anchorage Daily News* after the accident. "What next, bungee-jumping competition where the goal is to see how close you can come to the ground without leaving your face smeared all over it?"

COOMBS PULLED HIS GOGGLES DOWN over his eyes and the world turned orange. The helicopter buzzed away like a dragonfly dwarfed by the Chugach. Stepping into his bindings, he envisioned his first run. He had studied it on the flight up, committing to memory how a steep chute ran down the gut, how rocks were strewn across its eastern face, and how he could piece together both sections to create a truly magnificent descent. Coombs treated this mental image like a chessboard, working his way though each of the moves in reverse, from the last turn all the way to where he was standing at the top. He hated when people stopped and started on a run, scoping out the next series of turns. The ultimate for Coombs was to ski the run in one swift, fluid descent without stopping.

Coombs dropped into the main chute and began making crisp, clean turns that sent snow running down around him. He snapped his skis with expert precision, keeping perfect time with his pole plants. Where most skiers made one turn, Coombs made three. There was no sliding, stuttering, or moments of indecision. He was a matador, deftly seducing this wild bull of a mountain into his control.

Coombs then veered to his left, exiting the main chute and entering the dangerous section of rocks. A fall here would be fast and ugly. Time slowed in his mind. Each rock came toward him in slow motion, allowing him to flow around it without ever taking his foot off the gas. Coombs moved across the steep face as if it were his home mountain—all the while talking to himself, commenting on a particularly good turn or identifying a crux ahead.

Coombs then straightened his skis onto a shoulder-width stretch of snow that reached high across the rocks like a catwalk. Jetting off the end of it, he launched into the air and soared through the sky. He landed back in the steep chute, made five giant turns, and then blazed out the bottom of the run at Mach speed. The crowd erupted. The judges were floored

"Who is this guy?" one gasped.

"Coombs," another replied, reading the name off the paper in his hands. "Doug Coombs."

They'd never seen anything like it. "He read the mountain the way a sailor reads the sea," one of the judges reported later. Steve Casimiro agreed: "Between rocks, around rocks, over rocks, he was the picture of control—all the while taking the most aggressive line of the day." After two runs on 27 Mile Glacier, Coombs led the competition by ten points with a total score of 73.1. "My strategy is always to ski something that no one else can ski and do it fast and smooth and fluid," Coombs explained later. "And I always try to make things that are really hard look easy."

Coombs's dominance continued on the second day as the skiers braved Odyssey, a 1,500-vertical-foot run buried in deep powder. Three hundred people made the five-and-a-half-hour haul from Anchorage to catch the action on Thompson Pass. Cars lined up on the shoulder of Richardson Highway. Families dug seats in the snow at the base and broke out barbecues to behold the spectacle. Once again, Coombs distinguished himself from the pack with his confidence, his form, and his sheer creativity. "Coombs blew away the field because he so clearly worked the mountain best," wrote Casimiro. Judge Mike Hattrup agreed. "I've skied with a ton of great skiers," he said, "but he was a level above everybody else."

While he seemed completely at ease in these wild mountains, most of the other competitors were utterly rattled. "I don't want to die," one skier from Colorado kept muttering to himself after the second day of the competition. "This is crazy. I don't want to die." Meanwhile, Coombs moseyed around the Tsaina Lodge regaling people with extreme skier jokes. "How many extreme skiers does it take to change a lightbulb?" he opened. "One hundred . . . One to change it and ninety-nine to say, 'I could do that!'" He'd then break out in his trademark giggle.

Despite his superhuman ability on the mountain, Coombs was like a kid, bounding with energy and flashing his big grin to everyone he passed. In a sport fueled by machismo and one-upmanship, Coombs seemed without ego. "I didn't think of it as a competition," he remembered. "I thought of it more as a festival where you had this core group of hardcore extreme skiers, or whatever you want to call them, together strutting their stuff." Competitors quickly came to admire this unknown skier from Jackson Hole, amazed by his knowledge and skill in these mountains. "He was so incredibly comfortable on steep faces," said fellow competitor Kim Reichhelm. "What Doug skied took the rest of us twice as much energy. He could ski anything."

When the third and final day of the competition was canceled due to bad weather, Coombs's title was confirmed. He had faced off against the best skiers in the country, braved some of the fiercest terrain in the world, and now joined the ranks of Patrick Vallençant as one of the greatest extreme skiers in the world. Movie roles, magazine covers, and sponsorship deals were all on his horizon, and whether he liked it or not, Doug Coombs would forever be synonymous with extreme skiing. He had officially arrived.

09

GUNS, DRUGS, AND FIRST DESCENTS

Valdez, Alaska, 1992–93

Jon Hunt had woken the dragon, and it looked furious. A wall of sluff rushed across the valley like a billow of flames spewed from the belly of the beast. Perched on the lower flanks of Dimond Peak, Coombs nervously scanned the snow collecting some five thousand vertical feet below him, trying to spot Hunt amid the debris. Coombs was joined by Jim Conway, Hunt's brother, Rick, and others in their crew who had been skiing on a nearby peak to the west. Minutes ticked by. "Then all of a sudden here comes this little bug out onto the glacier," Coombs remembered. The scale of the Chugach dwarfed everything, and now as Coombs narrowed his eyes at this speck in the snow, he realized it was a man. Hunt had survived. The men exploded in cheers. Dimond Peak was skiable.

Coombs didn't waste any time. The snow purred along his legs as he took off down the slope, his turns breaking off layers of sluff that chased him down the mountain. All combined, the sluff had the look, feel, and force of an avalanche. "It's like being on a giant wave at the ocean," Coombs thought. "The wave is about to crash on you, but if you keep skiing hard and you keep skiing the right way, it's going to be there, but it's never going to get you." He skied down onto the glacier and over to the helicopter, which was waiting for him in the snow. "That was the best run of my life," he yelled to Hunt and Simmons.

"Mine too," Hunt yelled back, grinning through his mustache and thrilled to be alive.

Their renegade pilot didn't miss a beat. "Why don't we make it the best two runs of your life?"

And just like that, they were back in the helicopter, ripping through the sky toward Dimond Peak for another run. "We were on a rush, as they say in poker," Hunt remembered, "getting dealt great hand after great hand." A powder-hungry feeding frenzy ensued, with Coombs and his crew working their way up and down Dimond. A few days later, Coombs, Conway, and the Hunt brothers sacked the summit. The first descent of Dimond Peak represented a tipping point in the Chugach. If this terrifying mountain could be skied, what else could Coombs and his friends carve lines down in this new frontier of skiing?

After getting just a taste of the Chugach at the first WESC, Coombs had returned to Thompson Pass in the spring of 1992 with Emily and some of his closest friends from Jackson Hole and Bozeman. "It was one of the great periods of ski history," said Jim Conway. "Somehow that contest exposed Alaska to the greatest skiers in the world, and the word quickly spread to the people who could handle it." Cozad's contest and Coombs's win had succeeded in putting Valdez on the radars of hardcore skiers around the world. They collected on the airstrip on Thompson Pass, where pilots were now offering flights into the mountains in helicopters and fixed-wing single-prop planes. A crude economy was emerging between the skiers and pilots. Helicopter flights cost thirty-five dollars and fixed-wing plane flights cost twenty-five dollars. Skiers bought black and green poker chips in town that they turned into the pilots on the airstrip like boarding passes.

A number of pilots were offering their services on the airstrip, but perhaps none were more memorable than Chet Simmons. "I am the master of my machine," he'd say while loading his sidearm. "If you come within the rotor blades, you're mine." Once Coombs and his friends entered the chopper with Simmons, they could land on anything they wanted. "No one could tell me where I could ski, what I could ski, when I could ski," Coombs said. "Any of those rules were thrown out the window. I could do whatever I wanted at any moment, at any time." So began a period of boundless exploration, skiing harrowing first descents on nearly every run, charting the blank spots of the Chugach, and giving the peaks names. "It was real. It was absolutely fucking real. And these guys loved it," Simmons said. "I had these energy bombs riding around the helicopter with me, and you just had sparks flying out of your ass at all times. It was as wild as things could get with masters of control."

The hunt for first descents fueled Coombs. He poured over topographical maps and charts each night, studying contour lines and imagining each descent. He had a photographic memory for ski runs and logged away the information that he would then mentally review on the helicopter ride up to the peak. "You have about five minutes to memorize a big line in the helicopter," Coombs explained. "I just start memorizing features and start clicking them off in my head over and over as I'm getting closer and closer." If the route was especially complex, Coombs pulled out a Polaroid camera and snapped a photo from the helicopter. Once he was standing on the summit, all he had to navigate by were the information in his mind and the four-by-four photo in his pocket. Coombs could see only a couple of turns down the run before the slope rolled completely out of view. If he misjudged his location or forgot the line, he could end up skiing off a cliff. The slopes were also riddled with bergschrunds, gaping cracks in glaciers that could swallow a skier whole. Avalanches were an ever-looming threat. There were just as many ways to die as there were peaks in the Chugach.

But Coombs didn't focus on the things that could kill him; rather, he obsessed over the unique variety of terrain and the potential lines he could ski. "A lot of the lines had an element of death," Emily said. "They were technical and dangerous, but he didn't dwell on that." Couloirs were always his terrain of choice, tracing back to his days at Bridger Bowl snapping turns down the tight chutes of the Ridge. There were spines and flutes that ran down the mountains like drapery folds. Most of all there was deep powder. "I just saw hundreds of runs from the highway and immediately fell in love with it," Coombs said of the Chugach. "You could actually ski harder and more intense than anywhere I'd ever been. Suddenly sixty degrees didn't seem that far-fetched." He could see lines that others couldn't, and after scratching one off the list, there was no fanfare; he just went on to the next. Coombs amassed so many first descents that he eventually ran out of names for them. "I got so burnt out from naming them," he recalled. "I'd just walk into the bar and say, alright, you guys name it because I can't come up with anything." By his own estimate, Coombs made around five hundred first descents during his tenure in Alaska.

Off the mountain, life was just as wild. Coombs, Emily, and their fellow skiers lived in virtual squalor. Some slept in caves dug into the forty-foot snowbanks along Richardson Highway, while others, like Doug and Emily, slept in trailers. One skier even slept under the helicopter every night. "It was pretty third world up there," Emily said. "There were no bathrooms, no showers. You'd open the door and the guys would just be peeing out back."

Skiers loitered around the airstrip wearing harnesses and beacons, carrying ropes and ice screws, ready to drop everything and jump into the helicopter. Their clothes were filthy from refueling helicopters and tinkering with snow machines. They scrounged their money to pay for flights. Some opted to work on the herring fleet during the summer, while another group of snowboarders calling themselves the Alaskan Mafia resorted to running drugs in cigarette boats on the Bering Strait.

When it came time for heli-ski season, they spent their huge bankrolls on hours of flight time and arsenals of firearms. "They started the whole gun thing," remembered Jeff Zell, an Air Forcer who followed Coombs from Jackson Hole. "They'd go and shoot the icefall down there on the highway, and I'd be ducking behind the wheel of the van and you could hear the bullets ricocheting around."

Every day brought a new story on the airstrip, like the time a skydiver landed in Simmons's helicopter blades. The machine was powering down on the airstrip, and one of the blades caught the skydiver in the stomach and hurled him into a snowbank. Before he could get his wits about him, Simmons launched out of his helicopter, pistol drawn, ready to berate the man.

When weather grounded the helicopters for days on end, depression set in. The adrenaline withdrawals from not skiing became so rampant that Coombs gave it a name: Val Disease. "The highs and lows in Valdez are huge," Coombs said. "You have the best powder day of your life, and the next day it snows all day and it's going to be high avalanche danger, and everyone's gloom and doom." If they couldn't ski, they partied—hard. It wasn't uncommon for three or four skiers to end up in the clink each night. "On any given night in town, it was total chaos at the bars," Jim Conway said. "You just bring that many alpha males together, give them a couple weather days, and they'll throw on a pretty good buzz." As far as the town of Valdez was concerned, the skiers fit right in. "The pipeline was crazy, crazy times here, so nobody was put out by a little party action," said one local Valdezean. "I mean, it's Alaska. It gets rough-and-tumble up here. People shoot at each other. You should see it during fishing season."

People did what they wanted, when they wanted in Valdez. "I remember the postman would come by and roll a big fat joint, smoke it, and then go on his way," Coombs remembered. "He didn't even think twice about it. And I think the guy was around seventy-five years old." When a woman from Jackson Hole drove up to Thompson Pass in a Winnebago, she converted it into a burger joint so people wouldn't have to leave the airstrip to eat. "It was the wild wild west up there," said photographer Ace Kvale. "Thompson Pass had this fantastic, healthy outlaw energy that seemed so far removed from the regulations of the States. It was surrounded by some of the best skiers in the world who could just look at a peak and then go ski it."

Ground zero on Thompson Pass was the Tsaina Lodge. There was a palpable energy at the old roadhouse. The Chugach loomed over the small cabin as if it were a stone plopped into the middle of a big, fluffy comforter. It felt like the center of the universe. "At the end of each day in the Tsaina Lodge, the vibe was so up," Coombs remembered. "The music would get louder and louder and louder, and the whole place would be flexing. It was always open to the last person. There is no closing at the Tsaina Lodge. There's no time there. Time stops."

Parties raged into the early morning hours. "It was like New Year's Eve in Las Vegas every night," remembered a former dishwasher at the Tsaina. When the party packed out the bar, it spilled into a massive snow cave built outside. Sixty people could fit in there, dancing the night away, while massive bonfires roared into the star-speckled sky.

Coombs thrived on Alaska's lawless spirit. It wasn't the partying that appealed to him, but rather the limitless potential of the surrounding mountains. "Between the northern lights going off every night, being up high in the mountains, and having those beautiful glacier faces out the front door, there's a lot of energy going on," he remembered. No matter what time of day—or night, for that matter—if the mood struck him, he could jump in the helicopter and ski. Living on the edge of adventure all the time propelled Coombs fully into the skier—the man—he was destined to be. "Maybe he didn't know it, but it was the place he was looking for his whole life," said Casimiro. "It was the right place, at the right time, and the right guy."

10

GETTING SCHOOLED

Jackson Hole, Wyoming, 2013

Avalanches are measured in many ways, but they might be understood most simply on a scale of destruction from one to five. A D1 avalanche slides for about thirty feet, moving less than a ton of snow and posing little risk to people. D2 avalanches rush the length of a football field and can bury people with enough force to strip them of their clothes and pack snow into every orifice, even under their eyelids. D3 avalanches make matchsticks of timber-frame houses, while D4s can crush locomotives like tin cans. The most destructive avalanche, a D5, is violent enough to rip up the very earth upon which it runs. The friction can cause the temperature of the snow to rise by a few degrees. But when avalanches settle, the snow turns from a churning sea to a block of cement. The weight of the snow can crush a buried skier to death. Otherwise, asphyxiation or blunt trauma can also do the job.

Coombs had a sixth sense for avalanches that traced back to his college days, when he had studied under the country's preeminent avalanche expert, Dr. John Montagne. During World War II, Montagne served in the US Army's Tenth Mountain Division, an elite troop trained in ski mountaineering. After returning from his tour in Europe, Montagne jumped right back into his geology and snow science studies, which he had begun at Dartmouth College before the war. He established the first search-and-rescue outfit in Grand Teton National Park a few years later, before taking a job in MSU's Department of Earth Sciences. Soft-spoken and wise, Montagne took Coombs and his fellow classmates up to major slide paths in the fall and spring, pointing out the signatures of avalanches and warning them of the deadly wrath of the white dragon.

Montagne's lessons stuck with Coombs for the rest of his life, but nothing had made a bigger impression on him than being caught in an avalanche himself just after graduating college. That day, it was snowing hard in Montana's Tobacco Root Mountains, and Coombs was skiing in the trees. He figured that the trees provided the greatest degree of stability to the snow, and, in theory, the greatest degree of safety for him. But the avalanche broke from above the timberline, sending the telltale *whumpf* through the snowpack. The slope stampeded toward him like a herd of furious elephants. The snow ripped all the way to the frozen ground and rushed through the trees in a torrent. Coombs's only option was to grab onto a tree and hang on for dear life.

When the snow settled, one of his skis was split in half and a handful of his fingers were broken, but his fused neck was miraculously intact. "He barely got out of that one alive," remembered one of Coombs's MSU ski partners, Emil Tanner. "That was the scariest thing I'd ever heard of—period—among my friends." His neck aside, had Coombs been buried, he wouldn't have been found until the spring, as there was no one around to dig him out. "That was it," wrote Bruce Tremper, another of Coombs's friends from MSU who later became one of the top avalanche experts in the country. "Doug suddenly got religion, and we spent endless hours talking about all the subtleties of depth hoar, surface hoar, and other lurking dragons, which he would quickly master if he was going to survive . . . Eventually Doug turned into one of the cagiest avalanche professionals I have ever known."

What made Coombs so competent, according to Tremper, was his eye for patterns. "Avalanches are all about pattern recognition," the avalanche expert explained. "Good chess players recognize patterns, and Doug was a very good chess player. He never lost a match. When it came to snow and skiing, he had very good pattern recognition. He was hyperaware and nothing escaped his perception."

Coombs's instincts were equally acute when he was responding to avalanche rescue situations. While he was a guide for High Mountain Heli-Skiing in the late eighties in Jackson Hole, Coombs rescued the owner of the guiding outfit on Wyoming's Wolf Mountain. He and Lud Kroner were waiting at the bottom of the run by the helicopter when the group above them triggered a massive avalanche that ripped down the entire length of the mountain. "I looked up and saw a big cloud of snow coming," remembered Kroner. "Unfortunately, I was in a depression in a valley, so I got slammed." Kroner was buried up to his neck. "I was just hoping a log wasn't going to come down and take my head off," he said. Instead, a second wave of snow came down and buried him completely. "When the snow stopped, things got real dark. You can't move—it's like concrete. Within three to five minutes, I was unconscious."

When the snow hit Coombs, he pounced out of it like a cat. He waded through the debris, scanning the giant blocks of snow and ice with his avalanche beacon to locate Kroner. By the time Coombs and his fellow guides dug Kroner out, he was unconscious and not breathing. He was given CPR and came to, nearly hypothermic but alive. Lud Kroner was lucky, but several of Coombs's colleagues would not be so. In the course of his career, Coombs would dig out a number of frozen corpses and retrieve bodies so mangled by blunt trauma that the very thought of them would silence even him years later. "If skiing didn't have avalanches, it'd be the greatest sport in the world," Coombs once told a ski magazine, "but then [skiing] wouldn't be what it is."

FOR ME TO EXPLORE THE MOUNTAINS that defined Doug Coombs's life beyond Jackson Hole, I couldn't just buy a plane ticket and book a hotel room. To experience the wild mountains of Alaska firsthand, I needed to learn how to survive them. I needed to understand snow science, what caused avalanches, and how to rescue people. At the very least, I needed to familiarize myself with being outside the relative safety of resorts, in the wilds of the backcountry.

Jackson Hole locals made it clear to me that it was completely asinine to ski the backcountry without the necessary gear, knowledge of the terrain, and most importantly an understanding of snow science and avalanche safety. Cautionary tales came out of the resort every year. The story that stuck with me was of a snowboarder who unknowingly entered Granite Canyon, a treacherous, north-facing backcountry zone just outside the boundaries of the resort. In a matter of ten turns, he was completely lost. When ski patrol finally found him later that evening, the snowboarder was attempting to set his shirt on fire to stay warm. The moral was that skiing the backcountry was a privilege, one you needed to earn and respect. If you didn't, the consequences could be deadly.

So I enrolled in a three-day Avalanche Level I, or AVY I, course conducted by Jackson Hole Mountain Guides (JHMG). Fifteen other skiers joined me for the course, which began in a makeshift classroom on the second floor of the guiding operation's satellite headquarters in downtown Jackson. After signing my life away in liability waivers, I was handed a questionnaire gauging my experience and conditioning in the mountains. "How would you rate your physical fitness?" the questionnaire asked. I had about thirty days of skiing under my belt that season, and my legs and lungs felt pretty strong. Looking around the room, I sized up my fellow students and circled eight out of a possible ten.

The first two days of the course were divided between classroom time in the morning and field time in the afternoon. Sitting on the carpeted floor with my fellow students, I tried to follow along as the instructors explained the various types of snow formations. Up to that point, I had been only loosely aware that snow wasn't just universally *snow*. I now understood more clearly that each geographic location had its own type of snow, which was then uniquely affected by weather systems. I learned terminology like "rime," "slabs," and "surface hoar," and how each played a role in whether a snowpack was stable or avalanche prone.

After lunch, the instructors took us to Teton Pass, the mountain pass connecting Wyoming and Idaho, where many backcountry enthusiasts spend their winters earning their turns by hiking up the mountains and then skiing down. We practiced beacon drills in the parking lot and then latched our skis to our backpacks and followed our instructors. They explained that Teton Pass was a good laboratory for studying avalanches. Massive slides were known to rip down these slopes, sometimes running over the highway and catching vehicles in their wrath.

After the laborious hour-long hike to the top of Glory Bowl, we dug snow pits, and the instructors showed us how to read the layers of snow like the rings of a tree trunk. The snowpack served as a historical record of the winter, and observing the relationship between the different layers told us about the snow's stability. I did my best to log all this information away in my mind for future reference, but I kept realizing that snow was way more confusing than I had originally thought. Clearly this AVY I course was just an introduction to a study that would last a lifetime.

On the third and a final day, the instructors took us to Albright Peak, in the backcountry of Grand Teton National Park, to put our new knowledge to the real-world test. On the map, Albright looked a far cry from the Grand Teton. If the Grand were the *Titanic*, Albright would be a tugboat. *How tough could this be?* I thought.

The trek into Grand Teton National Park was my first time skinning, sticking special fabric to the bottoms of my skis, and using heel-releasing bindings that allowed me to climb uphill without sliding backward. As we skinned along the densely wooded trail, I pigheadedly pushed my way to the front of the line until I was nipping at the heels of the lead guide. Matching his stride like a shadow, I regretted not circling ten when asked about my physical fitness. But then the trail began to steepen and switchback sharply. Exhaustion bled into my lungs and legs like the early crackling of a forest fire. Heat radiated up through the collar of my jacket. Sweat began dripping down my face and off my nose like a leaky faucet. My body began to whisper the truth that my mind didn't want to admit: *I'm going to crack. I'm going to crack. I'm going to crack.*

As I slowed to a crawl, every person who I had triumphantly hopscotched earlier now passed me without saying a word. I took to staring down at my skis both out of exhaustion and embarrassment. The next time I looked up, the pack of skiers was fifty feet ahead of me, with no one left behind me. I was now the caboose on this train chugging away into the backcountry, and I was about to go off the rails.

One of the guides dropped back to keep me company, but the situation only got worse when my skins started coming unstuck from the bottoms of my skis, causing me to slide backward with every step. Fatigue turned to frustration, which turned to despair and then finally full-blown panic. Even with the guide at my side, I honestly believed I wasn't going to have the energy to get to the top. If by some miracle I did make it, there would be nothing left in my legs to ski to the bottom. Then I thought about the reason we were out here to begin with: to practice backcountry safety. If there was an avalanche, I would be utterly useless to help in the rescue effort. Completely defeated, I took some morbid sense of comfort in knowing that if an avalanche did happen, I'd probably be the one caught in it. At least then I could rest.

I made it out of Grand Teton National Park by the skin of my teeth, thanks entirely to the Jackson Hole Mountain Guides. Compounding the embarrassment of my humiliating ascent to the top of

Albright, my legs on the ski down turned into two overcooked noodles that had forgotten how to turn. I was left chewing on a big fat hunk of humility by the whole experience. Beyond the beacon drills and shovel tests, the central lesson I took away from my AVY I course was that I was entirely unprepared to be in the backcountry. All the movies I'd watched of skiers gleefully bounding through chest-deep powder failed to prepare me for the reality of what it took to actually access that snow outside the resorts. It wasn't enough to ride the lifts and log thousands of vertical feet. I needed to hike to earn my backcountry conditioning and hone my knowledge. The experience put Doug Coombs's athleticism into greater clarity. As I suffered to breathe, the guide at my side could have been whistling "Dixie." I wanted to get that strong. So began months of training, hiking, and following others into the backcountry to prepare for the bigger peaks that were ahead.

"HE WAS DEFINITELY THE BEST steep, tight, icy couloir skier that I had ever met," said Dave Miller, stacking his leather gloves on the table along with his goggles and helmet. We were sitting in Corbet's Cabin, the legendary waffle hut at the top of Rendezvous Mountain at Jackson Hole Mountain Resort. "Dougie's skills were superb right from the start," Miller continued. "He had really fast feet and a superdynamic turn, a lot of pizzazz. It wasn't sliding—it was crisp and clean—"

The radio attached to Miller's chest crackled, prompting him to pull it up to his ear and hear if the call required his attention. Now nearly fifty-seven years old, Dave Miller was the head backcountry guide at Jackson Hole Mountain Resort, and his main responsibility was keeping tabs on the rest of the guides. He had the unmistakable air of a mountain man with a face that looked carved out of granite. Back in the eighties and nineties, Miller skied with Coombs almost every day as a member of the Jackson Hole Air Force before following him to Alaska.

"I skied with him probably fifteen years here. Then we went up to Alaska," Miller said. "He was definitely my mentor. To this day, if I get into something squeaky tight, I'll think of his turn."

"What was it that made him so good?"

"He had an uncanny way of knowing where his skis would be four or five turns down," Miller said. "It was a reflex thing with him. He could be going sixty and make it seem like he was going ten. That's how his mind worked. He could anticipate so much that he would slow the whole run down."

"Was he an adrenaline junkie?"

"Oh, definitely. He liked endorphins and adrenaline like nobody you've ever met," Miller said. "But at the same time, he had a really good head about it. I wouldn't call him reckless by any means. He wasn't reckless. He had the skills to back it up. Everything was calculated. He was good at calculating risk."

"From a guide's perspective, what made him such a good guide?" I asked.

"He's the best guide I ever worked with, and I've worked with a lot of guides," Miller said. "Number one was his ski ability—I mean, that's a given. Number two was his sixth sense for the snowpack and what was going on. He could just feel things that other people couldn't." Miller paused. "But I'd have to say that the best quality he had was his heart. He had a really big heart. He'd do anything to help somebody out."

"Do you recall a specific instance of him helping somebody?"

"When we were up in Alaska, he was always helping people," Miller said. "Like, he came down and helped me when I got hurt up there. He was there in a second."

"What happened?" I asked.

"I had mounted my own bindings, which was a big mistake. I didn't have the forward pressure set right. I jumped off the cornice on a run called Elephant, which is fifty degrees, probably. Anyway, I jumped in and both skis blew off, and I started tumbling down, headed for a five-hundred-foot cliff."

The cabin hushed to a murmur, and I realized that the group sitting at the table next to us was listening to the story too.

"I needed to self-arrest," Miller continued. "So I just jammed my foot in the snow as hard as I could, and I broke my heel and my ankle straight through my boot. I hit a rock and it slowed me down; I came to a stop just above the cliff.

"I remember Doug blasted right down. He helped me over to this rock outcrop, a rocky perch where a mountain lion would hang out if he lived up there. Dougie called in the helicopter. The plan was for the heli to come in, and I was just going to jump in the front seat. But when the helicopter came in, the pilot decided that the blades were just way too close to the rock band, and he flew off. So then we thought, 'Hell, I'll just jump into the ski basket on the skid.'"

Miller described how when the helicopter came in the second time, Coombs held Miller by his harness so that he could reach out and grab the basket. "The heli hovered in and got just close enough; I grabbed the ski basket and it just shocked the hell out of us," Miller said. The centrifugal force of the helicopter's spinning blades had generated a static electricity charge that shot through the basket, into Miller, and then into Coombs. "Dougie had a hold on my harness so that I wouldn't fall off into the abyss again, and I look back and he's just getting shocked," Miller laughed. "But he never let go." Miller released the skid and broke the circuit. On the second pass, he tapped the basket to ground the charge before he rolled in. "That was one instance of Dougie coming in to help someone," Miller said. "If a friend was down, he was there. It didn't matter if it was sixty degrees, seventy degrees; he'd still come in right after you."

11

VALDEZ HELI-SKI GUIDES

Valdez, Alaska, 1993–97

François von Hurter had never been so terrified. He had heli-skied all over the world with some of the top guiding outfits, but nothing like this. The helicopter pulled away, leaving the Swiss investment banker staring down a nauseatingly steep slope. It was beyond anything he'd ever seen in the Alps or in Canada. The Chugach Mountains were utterly vast. There were no trees, no exposed rocks—nothing to give any sense of scale to this alpine landscape. He couldn't even bring himself to stand up. "It's like no other up here, right?" Coombs said nonchalantly.

François had booked this skiing trip in 1995 to Valdez without ever having met Coombs. He'd only read about him in magazines, about how this two-time extreme skiing champion was actually guiding amateur skiers in Alaska. Some clients were even making first descents and naming the runs themselves. "Valdez . . . as Sick as It Gets" read the cover of *Powder* magazine. After thirty years of skiing in Verbier, François had wanted to see for himself what all the hubbub was about in Alaska, but now he regretted that decision.

Coombs could see the doubt building in François's face, but he refused to let his client get consumed by it. "François," he said, hanging the man's name out in the quiet. "Go big or go home!" He then flashed his trademark grin. "You can do this. No problem," he said, looking down the slope. "No problem at all."

François got to his feet and wobbled uneasily over to Coombs's side. With his pole, Coombs casually pointed out the route they would be taking down. François was used to dealing with Swiss guides, who were notorious for keeping their clients in the dark, making them feel small and dependent in the mountains, but Coombs made him feel empowered. He gave François a full understanding of the run, treating him like a peer, not a peon. The more Coombs talked, the more François warmed up to the idea of actually skiing the run. *If Doug thinks I can do it, then I must be able to do it,* François finally told himself. And he did—again and again.

Skiing with Coombs in the Chugach fundamentally changed François von Hurter's life. With Coombs leading the way, François was able to vanquish his fears and find new levels of confidence within himself that he couldn't source on his own. Coombs guided him down runs that he had seen only in movies and magazines, runs that he thought no guide would ever dare take a client down. The experience dramatically altered the course of François's life.

"After those two visits in Alaska and the sheer joy of being out there and the exposure to Coombs, I decided to stop my career," François explained. "There was a link. There was a trigger to seeking a different life. To do something different with one's life." François didn't take up the life of a ski bum, but upon returning home from Alaska, he abruptly quit his lucrative career in banking, went back to school, and then started a publishing company. He took up the life he'd always dreamed of. "I think it had something to do with the time spent with Doug," he explained. "Being with someone as optimistic and as eager and seeking out adventure put things into perspective. I realized the time I wasted in the corporate world. It was like a light went on. I saw the light of Doug's life, of his example."

SINCE HIS DAYS OF LEADING his buddies on adventures in the White Mountains, Coombs had been destined to be a guide. The profession offered him a way of making a living in the mountains that was more rewarding than simply skiing for the camera. "When you have a guy from Kansas skiing fifty degrees in perfect snow, there's nothing like it," Coombs said. "He'll never forget that for the rest of his life. I get to bring people into my world, and I see them getting all excited and pumped up like I used to ten or twenty years ago."

Coombs struck a balance between nonchalance and seriousness in the mountains. It was nothing for him to break out a box of cookies while perched on a fifty-degree slope and then explain the run to his clients in between bites. "No hero skiing" was Coombs code for "take this seriously." If the run was particularly dangerous, he might note that a fall here would result in a "closed-casket funeral." Above all, Coombs's unfaltering optimism had a way of rubbing off on his clients. If he said they could do it, they fully believed him. "I don't make the impossible possible," Coombs said. "I make what people *think* is impossible possible."

As with many things in Coombs's life, guiding in the Chugach had begun informally. Coombs trolled the airstrip offering up his knowledge in return for a paid seat in the helicopter. By the spring of 1993, he and Emily started seeing more and more people coming to the Chugach without the knowledge, experience, or ability to ski these mountains safely. "There was a transition period in Valdez where people needed to start hiring guides," Emily explained. "They were coming because of the media hype, as opposed to coming because their natural progression in the sport led them there." As more people arrived at the airstrip, Coombs and Emily recognized an opportunity. In 1994 they launched Valdez Heli-Ski Guides (VHSG).

Despite Coombs's boundless optimism, this idea was initially met with extreme skepticism. "We're guiding this stuff?" Mike Fischer said when he first arrived on Thompson Pass. "This is crazy." Fischer had more heli-guiding experience than anyone else on Thompson Pass and had seen his fair share of extreme terrain, but nothing like the Chugach. Fischer's concerns were confirmed on his very first run, when he was caught in a massive avalanche that nearly buried him in a crevasse. Almost exactly a year later, again on his first run of the season, Fischer triggered another avalanche that almost killed him.

"Almost everyone outside a small circle of friends was telling us it was suicidal and people were going to die," said Jerry Hance, who was one of the first guides Coombs hired. The fear echoed a concern over heli-skiing that was rampant in the United States in the midnineties. In 1994 two high-profile heli-skiing disasters sent shock waves through the industry. In Telluride, Colorado, a heli-skiing crash left supermodel Christie Brinkley and others in her helicopter stranded on a 12,800-foot peak for eight hours before they were rescued. Just a month later, the president of Walt Disney was killed along with six others in a heli-skiing crash in Nevada's Ruby Mountains. As a result, many aviation companies grounded their heli-skiing operations. There was a serious concern among pilots that another such crash could result in strict regulations and quite possibly the termination of heli-skiing in the United States entirely. Thus Coombs's idea to fly amateur skiers into some of the most remote mountains in the world, miles away from safety, raised obvious concerns.

But Coombs's unfaltering optimism pushed Valdez Heli-Ski Guides forward amid all the doubts and naysayers, and he and Emily began building the business out of nothing. "Our first week, we didn't have a cent to our names, and we just told people to send us a deposit," Coombs said. "That got us enough money to buy a couple of transceivers and shovels and a few knickknacks. We just started out really bare bones." The operation was so bare bones that Coombs didn't even have a car to drive to work. Every morning he hitchhiked to the airstrip, and more often than not, one of his clients picked him up on the side of the road in downtown Valdez.

Some of these early clients had experience with polished heli-skiing operations, complete with gourmet lunches and posh lodges, but they found none of that in Valdez. "It was a shithole," remembered one client. There was no lodge, no roaring fireplace to come home to. They weren't even given a bagged lunch. The operation was run out of a trailer on the airstrip, where the closest thing to an amenity was the outhouse. Instead, clients were rewarded with a group of talented guides who were bold enough to take them into the Chugach. "It's the total mecca," Coombs said. "I tell people whenever they've done all the skiing in the world, they've got to go there. Everybody needs to ski Valdez once; then you'll have fulfillment in your ski life."

When clients arrived, Coombs created groupings. From a two-minute conversation in the lodge, he could deduce their comfort levels, their goals, and perhaps even their abilities, without ever seeing them ski. He then created groupings that put like clients together, regardless of whether that meant splitting up friends and putting them with strangers. As the owner of the operation, Coombs cherry-picked his group, selecting only the most talented. If you were skilled enough to end up in Coombs's group, chances were good that you would ski sixty-degree first descents all day long. He taught them how to evade avalanches and outrun sluff slides, what he called "sluff management."

Conquering heavy doses of fear was central to the Doug Coombs skiing experience. Some clients occasionally became so terrified after skiing with him that they refused to come out of their hotel rooms the following day. "We had one client go missing," Emily remembered. "Doug found him hiding in the trunk of his car. He was just so freaked out." But overcoming that fear became addictive, bringing Coombs's clients back year after year. They scheduled their calendars around that annual trip to Alaska. They trained. They read ski magazines. And they all came to say the same thing: "Doug Coombs gave me the best day of my life."

While Coombs may have been the draw for clients, his team of guides was equally elite. "Doug collected a group of diverse, knowledgeable people to be in that company, people who he could trust," said Jim Conway, who became VHSG's operations manager. "We all had a common goal: let's make this the first and the best steep-skiing operation in the world, because nobody had ever done steep heli-ski guiding before." Coombs enlisted fellow Jackson Hole Air Force members like Dave Miller, Mike Fischer, and Jeff Zell, as well as Jerry Hance and Dave Swanwick, to be guides the first years of the operation. "I was looking for the safest people to take clients in steep terrain," Coombs said. He and Emily paid these guides handsomely. Dave Miller remembered earning $1,000 a week, plus tips and a bonus at the end of the two-month season.

But it wasn't enough just to have talented guides; they also needed talented pilots. The days of flying with Chet Simmons were over. Despite the bond he and Coombs shared, Simmons was too much of a cowboy for VHSG's paying clients. Not long thereafter, Simmons crashed his helicopter with two snowboarders and a film crew aboard. He maxed out that old Bell Jet Ranger one too many times, and when the wind shifted on him during the landing, Simmons didn't have the power reserve to right his course. Thankfully, thirteen crash landings in Vietnam had taught him how to put his aircraft down in a hurry. "For a helicopter wreck, it was one of the best I've seen," Simmons said. "I chopped part of my foot off, but that was no big deal." Doctors were able to reattach Simmons's severed foot, which happened to be wearing a pair of Coombs's sneakers, but his flying days were over.

To get VHSG up and running, the Coombses contracted their helicopters and pilots through Era Aviation. Enter Marcel Schubert. Born and raised in Switzerland, helicopter pilot Schubert grew up skiing and had flown for other heli-skiing outfits in the Ruby Mountains of

Nevada. By 1996, Schubert was Coombs's main pilot, and the two developed a high level of mutual trust. Schubert was a master at landing on knife-edge ridges that might be only two feet wide. He'd toe in first and let the skiers off on the ridge, then jockey forward two feet at a time, allowing them to take their skis and gear out of the basket, before he peeled away and left them there. At times, the slopes Schubert dropped Coombs and his clients off on were so steep that the pilot would guide them down over the radio, warning them about cliffs and other hazards that they couldn't see.

Equipped with Schubert's Eurocopter Astar, and fueled by the money coming in through Coombs's clients, Valdez Heli-Ski Guides flew deeper and deeper into the mountains. "Every day was like, 'Where should we take the client's money today? Ah, let's go up to the northwest and figure that area out,'" Coombs said. "Every run was a first descent for a while with the clients. The feeling of skiing runs where no one ever had been before was kind of an addiction. That's what got me hooked on the place."

But there was more than just Schubert's Astar keeping VHSG up and running. As the saying goes, behind every strong man is a strong woman, and that was especially the case with Coombs and the success of Valdez Heli-Ski Guides. Coombs was notoriously bad with money. "The first time I met him, he was living off his credit card," remembered Emily. "He didn't care about money; he just wanted to ski." The day-to-day logistics of running a company were completely lost on him. "I had no idea how to do the business," Coombs admitted. "I needed someone with the brains, and Emily's got the brains. She figured out the business end of it, and I figured out the mountain end of it."

Coombs's lack of business sense put the full responsibility of operating Valdez Heli-Ski Guides squarely on Emily's shoulders and often made her out to look like the bad cop. Coombs never wanted to disappoint people, so if clients called and asked to change the dates of their trip, he'd tell them it was fine without checking with her. Emily would then have to call up the clients and break the news that it wasn't fine. To which they inevitably responded, "But Doug said . . ."

"Running a business like this in partnership with your husband is stressful," Emily said, "but we were committed to each other and running it together." In the mountains, where Emily regularly served as Coombs's tail guide, the two shared an almost telepathic connection. "For three or four years, Emily skied every run with me," Coombs said. "There was sort of this magic stuff going on where she knew how I thought, and we wouldn't even have to talk out there."

With Coombs as the draw and Emily running the business, Valdez Heli-Ski Guides grew rapidly, from one helicopter to three, five employees to fifteen. Soon they dragged trailers up to Thompson Pass and operated out of the Tsaina Lodge. It became a polished business catering to three different types of clients. A "public ship" was a helicopter that carried an assortment of clients who booked the guiding operation for a week or so and would be split into groups with other like clients. A "private ship" was a helicopter rented out by a single group for the week.

Finally a "film ship" was a helicopter rented with a guide for up to seven weeks at a time, allowing the filmmakers and pros to wait for the perfect conditions and ideal light to fly, ski, and film. It all began when a couple of brothers from Cape Cod named Todd and Steve Jones followed Coombs from Jackson Hole to Valdez in the early nineties with little more than a couple of nickels to rub together. They lived in snow caves and army tents on Thompson Pass, working as guides for Coombs during the spring and as fishermen on the herring fleet during the summer. After saving up their money, the Jones brothers bought a film camera and began shooting footage of their friends skiing in the Chugach. "Our first films, *Continuum* and *Harvest*, were basically filmed on Dougie's dime," Steve Jones said. "Of course, he would go out skiing with us half the time." After a day of guiding, Coombs turned the Jones brothers loose to fly around with a pilot and film in the evening's magic light. The Jones's production company, Teton Gravity Research, eventually became one of the biggest names in the actions sports industry and brought clips of skiing in Alaska to VCRs around the country. Coombs had helped turn Alaska into a ski moviemaker's mecca.

12

THE LAST FRONTIER

Valdez, Alaska, 2015

I read the email on my phone while sitting on the floor at Denver International Airport, waiting to embark on my flight to Anchorage. It was from Tim Petrick, the former president and CEO of K2 Sports who signed Coombs to his first major sponsorship deal in the mid-nineties. Petrick had skied with Coombs all over the world, including in Alaska, where he blew out his knee falling down a couloir. "Never let your guard down," Petrick wrote to me. "You are not safe up there until you have your boots off in the Tsaina."

I'd been dreaming about Alaska since the third grade, when I first read Gary Paulsen's *Winterdance* about the Iditarod. My uncle and cousins spent a few summers fishing in Alaska, and when they returned, they regaled me with wild stories of grizzly bears, bush planes, and mountains so massive that looking up at them made your neck hurt. Then I watched my first ski movie and my fascination with Alaska exploded. Indeed, the first time I ever laid eyes on Doug Coombs was a scene filmed in Valdez, Alaska—exactly where I was now headed. I was going to ski at Coombs's original operation, Valdez Heli-Ski

Guides, which was still being run out of the legendary Tsaina Lodge on Thompson Pass.

I landed at Ted Stevens Anchorage International Airport a few hours before dusk, which, as it was late March, was around eight. After collecting my backpack at the baggage carousel, I made my way to the oversize luggage claim to pick up my skis. Standing there was a man who cut the unmistakable figure of a mountaineer. He was compact as a spring and had a leatherlike tan and a squirrelly air about him. I had spotted him sitting in first class on my flight, and I could just tell he was somebody.

"Fingers crossed for your skis, huh?" he said, looking up at me from his phone. "Where you headed?"

"Valdez."

"Oh man, I haven't been there in years," he said. "Probably since the nineties, skiing there with Doug Coombs."

Here I was, not fifteen minutes after arriving in Alaska, and the first person I met knew Coombs. The guy's web of contacts just seemed to be never ending. John Griber was from Jackson Hole and had gone on many wild adventures with Coombs over the years.

"Yeah, I was with Doug and Emily in Kyrgyzstan in '97 for the Outdoor Life channel," he told me. Tian Shan, Kyrgyzstan, was another one of those far-flung adventures that boggled my mind when I pondered the chronology of the Coombses' lives. *Where did Coombs find the time to do all that stuff?* I thought.

John Griber had since gone on to become an accomplished videographer for National Geographic, thus his first-class ticket to Alaska: he was here on assignment. "I also filmed Doug skiing the Otter Body," Griber told me. "He left an ice ax up there. Someone should go up and get it for his son, David." The Otter Body was one of Coombs's crowning descents in Jackson Hole. A fifty-degree patch of snow off the east face of the Grand Teton, the Otter Body might have been skiable only one day each season. It could also go years without ever being in condition. "If you fall on the east face of the Grand," Coombs had said about the elusive run, "that's a closed-casket funeral. One fall does it all."

The garage door to the oversize luggage claim rattled open, and our bags came sliding down. Griber shouldered three massive packs and bid me farewell. "Good luck up there," he said. "I'm jealous." Then off he went onto adventures unknown, yet another faint echo of Coombs's life reverberating around the world.

I schlepped my bags through the quiet yet sizeable airport to a rinky-dink wing where I'd be catching a puddle jumper to take me 115 miles east to Valdez. A clearly agitated man in the line ahead of me was having it out at the ticket clerk. From what I gathered, he too was headed to Valdez to ski—his buddies were there waiting for him, in fact—but his flight had been canceled that morning due to an isolated storm that was now pummeling the small port town.

"My friends said it's clearing over there," the man huffed, as if the poor guy behind the desk had anything to do with whether or not we would fly. The clerk informed us that there had been no break in the weather and no flights were headed to Valdez until morning. I'd be spending the night in Anchorage.

As luck would have it, my arrival in Alaska coincided with the start of the Iditarod, and almost every bed in town was booked. The only vacancy I could find was at a motel that might as well have had "SKEEVY" glowing in red neon lights out front. Cooties and bedbugs be damned, my jet-lagged bones needed a bed, so I booked a nonsmoking room and hoped for the best. Sure enough, the first thing I spotted when entering the room was a dirty Band-Aid sticking up from the center of the carpet like a middle finger. I stripped the bed and slept curled up in my down jacket. I guess it was better than a snow cave.

The next morning broke gin clear. The cab ride back to the airport took me through the outskirts of Anchorage, which looked like one never-ending strip mall. And yet there was beauty in the stark contrast between tire repair shops, Taco Bells, and the hulking mountains plowing the sky into the distance. Even the strip malls in Anchorage, it seemed, had million-dollar views.

"You here for the Iditarod?" the cabbie asked.

"No, headed to Valdez," I responded. "Going skiing."

"Not the best time for that," she said. "This has been a terrible year for snow."

Indeed, Anchorage itself was bone dry, having received only one-third of its typical annual snowfall, a measly twenty inches. I'd read in the paper that morning that crews had hauled in 350 truckloads of snow for the Iditarod's ceremonial start in downtown Anchorage. As the seventy-eight mushers and over 1,200 dogs made their way through nineteen city blocks before a crowd of thousands, the temperature was a balmy forty degrees. Even the race's official start had to be moved 225 miles north from Willow to Fairbanks due to the lack of snow.

The minimal snowfall also had serious implications for the skiing. "Right now, they're having a hell of a time up there," Jim Conway had told me over the phone right before I left Massachusetts. "It's gnar up there this year. Valdez has a bad layer, and it's just not a good time to be out." The lack of snow precipitation had created instability within the snowpack, which would flare up whenever new snow fell. Conditions were hardly ideal for me to be taking on the extreme skiing capital of the United States.

Back at the airport, I was reunited with the skier from the night before who was also headed to Valdez. A heart surgeon from Taos, New Mexico, he had been skiing with Dean Cummings's H20 Guides heli-skiing tours for a week every season for the better part of a decade.

"The scale is just so massive," the surgeon told me. "It's the hardest thing to wrap your mind around." He said the guide would take off skiing, and then the next thing you knew, he was this speck on the apron below. Without trees or exposed rocks to give you any measure of distance or size, the Chugach made you slow down, he told me. You couldn't charge everything like you would at your home mountain. He had learned this the hard way, he said, when he unexpectedly launched off a thirty-foot cliff one year. The terrain was so steep that he never saw it coming. Thankfully, the deep powder softened his fall, but he found the experience completely unnerving. "That might as well have been a hundred-foot cliff," he said.

In the back of my mind I was thinking about how this surgeon was the archetype of the heli-ski clients booking trips to Alaska. For someone with a high-intensity, high-powered job, heli-skiing in Alaska—where your every move needs to be calculated and precise—seemed a fitting hobby. Indeed, just as when you cut open a man's chest and slice into his aorta, heli-skiing ultimately distills into terms of life and death. More practically speaking, only the likes of a heart surgeon could afford the $10,000-a-week price tag. Long gone were the days of thirty-five-dollar heli-flights that Coombs and his cronies relished during the early nineties. As for me, I was just lucky enough to be getting a press discount, but even that was still costing my credit card around $1,000 a day.

When it was time to board, the surgeon and I walked onto the tarmac and climbed into a twenty-seat plane operated by Ravn Alaska. I hastened to a window seat. After taking off, we climbed over Cook Inlet and then eventually leveled out over the Chugach Mountains. My nose pressed up against the glass, excitement filled my chest and made my scalp tingle. This was the Alaskan vastness everyone told me about. The mountains just went on and on in every direction, and it was entirely feasible that none of them had ever seen a footprint, let alone a ski track. The glaring morning light struck their eastern faces, casting long shadows behind them that only amplified their grandeur. Each mountain looked like a kingdom whose civilizations had long since vanished, leaving behind an Atlantis buried in snow.

When we landed in Valdez forty minutes later, mountains towered over the tarmac. The flight attendant needed to shoo me off the blacktop and into the terminal because all I could do was stand there, completely dumbfounded by the peaks blotting out the sky.

"Don't worry, there's plenty more where that came from," she said.

In the miniature airport terminal, I collected my skis and met two Frenchmen who were also headed to the Tsaina Lodge. They had heli-skied extensively in Europe and Canada, but this was their first time in Alaska. We were met by a shuttle driver who was going to transport us up the thirty-five miles of Richardson Highway to the Tsaina. Immediately after we turned the corner from the airport, mountains exploded around us. I couldn't help but be totally giddy, repeatedly rolling down my window to snap photos.

I hounded the driver for names of the peaks, but again and again he informed me that many of them didn't have names. The road straightened out, and smack in the middle of the windshield appeared another gigantic massif. People driving down this road had been staring at this behemoth for generations. Surely this mountain had a name.

"What's that one called?" I asked.

The driver thought about it for a second. "Yeah, I don't think that one has a name either."

I was baffled. In any other ski town, this mountain would have been venerated and worshipped. It would have been printed on thousands of T-shirts and had beers named after it. But here in Valdez, it was just another mound of rock and snow.

At the sixteen-mile mark of Richardson Highway, the driver gestured to the left side of the road, where a wall of snow loomed three stories high. "That's where the avalanche happened last year," he calmly informed us. He went on to describe how a furious avalanche ripped down the side of Keystone Canyon, burying Richardson Highway in debris that reached one hundred feet high and stretched 1,500 feet wide in some places. There was so much snow that it dammed the nearby Lowe River, creating a lake that rose by an inch or more per hour at its peak. The highway was completely impassable from mile twelve to forty-two for weeks while cleanup crews carefully cut through the frozen debris, keeping a watchful eye on the snow dam plugging up the Lowe River. If the dam had broken, the workers would have been washed away into oblivion. The story reminded me that in Alaska, the mountains were judge, jury, and executioner. We were all just awaiting trial.

"That's Odyssey," the driver told me as we came around the bend, snaking our way up Thompson Pass. "That's where they had the competition. Cars were lined up all along the road here to watch." I could clearly see why Mike Cozad had picked this location for the second day of his World Extreme Skiing Championship. The long apron made for an ideal seating area, and it was directly off the road. I tried to imagine the scene: families climbing out of their cars after the long ride from Anchorage, schlepping hibachis and coolers onto the snow to watch the spectacle. Then I pictured a thirty-four-year-old Doug Coombs dropping into Odyssey for the second day of the competition. I traced the face with my eyes, imagining his crisp turns and iconic pole plants navigating this sprawling sheet of white.

Not long after, we pulled into the parking lot of the Tsaina Lodge. Although the sign out front looked exactly how I remembered from old photos circa Mike Cozad's era, the lodge itself was completely unrecognizable. In 2011, a clearly well-off couple from Jackson Hole bought the ramshackle Tsaina, which had fallen into various states of neglect. After painstakingly documenting all its historic elements, especially the bar, they bulldozed the structure and then erected this modern, 18,400-square-foot, twenty-four-room compound that stretched the term "ski lodge" to the absolute extreme. Frank Lloyd Wright would have no problem staying here.

The driver pulled around back, where an employee was shoveling away the two feet of snow dumped overnight. We dragged our bags across a big porch and into the lodge. The inside was more striking than its cubic-inspired exterior. Every detail, from the meticulous two-sided stone fireplace to the rich leather sofas, screamed luxury and rustic elegance. The water pitcher at the front desk even had cucumber slices floating in it.

"Hi guys, welcome," a beautiful blond said sweetly. "How was the ride up?" I'm not sure what I was expecting, but I never imagined the lodge staff to be beautiful. *Had my plane crashed?* I thought. *Was this heaven?* "I think Scott wants to get you guys skiing today. Let's get you suited up." One of these lovely angels showed me to my room and told me to get my ski clothes on when I was ready. The door clicked behind her. I flopped onto the mattress and then slowly sank into it.

"You gotta be kidding me," I said out loud. "A memory foam bed."

Today's five-star Tsaina Lodge was a far, *far* cry from what I imagined of Coombs's heyday living up here on Thompson Pass. Back then, if you slipped in the shower and cut yourself, you were destined for a staph infection. The shower in my room now had two heads with five settings apiece, one of which I believe was labeled "Champagne." Back in the nineties, the Tsaina's only luxury was a cold beer at the end of the day. Today, there were three staff members for every one client staying at the lodge, which also staffed two gourmet chefs and an in-house massage therapist. What hadn't changed, of course, were the savage mountains directly outside my bedroom window.

After pulling on my gear, I eagerly returned to the lounge area, where I was met by an old man wearing ski pants and holding a clipboard. He had shaggy gray hair, and his ruddy face broke into a road map of wrinkles when he introduced himself.

"I'm Jeff," he said in a gravely voice reminiscent of Jack Nicholson.

"Zell?" I asked.

"Yup, that's me," he said. "I'm your guide."

Jeff Zell was one of Doug Coombs's closest friends going back to the early Jackson Hole Air Force era. He was part of the original Air Force crew who followed Coombs to Valdez during the renegade days and then became one of his top guides. According to Emily Coombs, Zell has since amassed more vertical feet of skiing in Valdez than any other human being. I waited exactly one minute before bombarding him with questions about the early days of Alaska.

"It was wild," Zell said, pouring himself a cup of coffee and chuckling to himself. He walked me over to one of the tables. "There were two ski planes, and then a couple helis. And there was no guiding, so you'd find four people, put your money together, and then jump in the helicopter."

Even before he came to Valdez, Zell had logged hundreds of hours of heli-skiing time with Coombs in Canada. As winners of the 1993 World Powder 8 Championship, Zell and Coombs were awarded a free week of heli-skiing in British Colombia at Mike Wiegeles, one of the top heli-skiing outfits in the world. After their free week was up, Zell and Coombs just kept sneaking back into the helicopter. This lasted for weeks. "We wouldn't listen to the guides," Zell said with a grin. "Eventually they just said, 'Okay, you guys go last and go wherever you want. And then I would go down the run and point Doug to all the extreme terrain. The guides were like, 'Oh my God, what is wrong with these guys?'"

Zell belonged to the upper echelon of the Air Force fraternity that included Jon Hunt, Tom Bartlett, Dave Miller, and his younger brother Jimmy Zell, who passed away tragically from Lou Gehrig's disease in 2010. "We were like special forces," Zell said. Sitting there in the palatial, new-age Tsaina Lodge, sipping his coffee, Zell seemed like an artifact from a much realer, rawer time. All the frills of this place served only to enhance how truly authentic Zell was. He was crusty. He was a cowboy. He was exactly who I wanted to be my guide in Alaska—a living link to the old days, a living link to Coombs.

"From Bozeman to Jackson to here—they were stepping-stones to going bigger and bigger," Zell said when I asked him about the progression of Coombs's career. "I'll bet he had ambitions to ski Everest. Why wouldn't he? He probably wanted to ski K2."

"What do you think drove him?" I asked.

"The life of Patrick Vallençant had a big, big influence on him." Zell said, before retelling the story of Coombs's encounter with the ski legend in Chamonix, when Coombs was told "you ski the walls well." Zell said Coombs was "super proud of that. He wanted to be as good as him. He admired that he was an accomplished, polished skier."

The two Frenchmen soon joined us. After we signed our lives away in enough liability paperwork to buy a house, Zell gave us a mandatory safety briefing. He clicked through a PowerPoint quickly, all four of us knowing full well that this presentation was standing between us and a flight into the mountains.

We then went out into the parking lot to do an avalanche transceiver test. "It's pretty simple," Zell said. "If you can't find it, you can't go." What he meant was that if I couldn't manage to find and recover the test transceiver that was buried somewhere in snowbanks in the parking lot within five to ten minutes—the time a person had to live if they were buried in an avalanche—I wasn't getting on the helicopter.

Inexplicably, I decided to use a transceiver provided to me by the lodge, as opposed to using my own, which I'd been training confidently with since my first AVY course in Jackson Hole. I guess I figured the technology would be newer and more effective. I was mistaken. When Zell said go and I set the transceiver to search, I was instantly befuddled by this unfamiliar device, as if I were handed a PC after working on a Mac my whole life. I followed the arrow on the transceiver around the parking lot, up and over snowbanks, in aimless circles. The seconds were ticking away loudly in my mind. Sweat began dripping down my brow as frustration, embarrassment, and anxiety clouded my effectiveness. All the while I could hear Zell cackling in the background.

With my beacon test sufficiently botched, Zell stepped in to help. He pulled out his transceiver and began searching. To my surprise and relief, Zell himself started having trouble locating the bag, even though he knew exactly where it was buried. We hovered our transceivers inches away from the snow and probed the area, waiting to feel the soft strike of the buried backpack. Eventually we just started digging. Finally we found it and dragged it to the surface. I looked over to Zell, who was just grinning.

"Let's hope we don't have to do that for real today," I muttered, mostly to myself.

THE HELICOPTER LANDED WITH THE fury of a dragon, its blades whipping snow around the helipad. The intense roar of the machine hit my brain with a heaping shot of adrenaline.

Here. We. Go.

Zell opened the door and waved us forward. I scurried below the blades, dragging my skis behind me and thinking of what Chet Simmons had told me about heli-skiing in Valdez: "It's like going on an ambush at night . . . it's absolutely fucking real." He was absolutely fucking right.

I buckled up between the two Frenchmen on the bench seat behind the pilot and Zell. The pilot pulled back on the stick, and we lifted off and then pushed forward over the lodge. Compared to the chaos outside the chopper, the cabin was relatively peaceful. The Frenchmen and I exchanged shit-eating grins as peaks jutted out of the blanket of snow ferociously, black fangs tearing through white flesh. As we banked around mountain after mountain, Zell and the pilot pointed and exchanged inaudible banter over their headsets. Craning my neck, I stared down the steep faces and wondered which one we'd be skiing.

Before long, the pilot zeroed in on a summit. He buzzed around it a couple of times, and then made his approach. He touched down deftly in the snow. Zell said something to him, smiled, laughed, and then pulled off his headset, which was the sign for us to unbuckle. He climbed out of the cabin and held the door open for us. We poured out and collected behind him in the snow as he tossed out our skis and backpacks. Kneeling in the snow, we held down our gear as Zell moved to the front of the copter and raised a thumbs-up to the pilot, prompting him to take off. Snow ripped across my face as the chopper hovered up. In a matter of seconds, deafening silence replaced the din of the machine.

Standing up on trembling legs, I met my surroundings. In the helicopter I had felt powerful, but here I was miniscule, just an insignificant pebble on the mountainside.

"This is Stairway to Heaven," Zell said, pulling his skis apart. Across the way, I could see the fabled Dimond Peak. Even in the day's mellow light, Dimond looked like a killer.

Just above where we were standing was a memorial to Coombs made up of black slate stacked six feet high. After his death, guides and clients began stacking rocks here in his memory. The stone tribute seemed fitting for Coombs, a geologist who loved pointing out and naming various rock formations. Nearly a decade after his death, the memorial had grown so tall that guides now had to ask clients to add their stone to the sides. Any higher, and the memorial would prevent the helicopter from landing. The rock beacon reminded everyone who stepped foot in these wild mountains that it was Coombs who put this place on the map. We were all here because of him.

I dropped my skis to the ground, smacked the snow from my boots with my poles, and clicked into my bindings. The landing zone looked as wide as a tennis court, off the edges of which there was no telling what was to come. Buckling my backpack, I pulled out the handle to my avalanche air bag. If an avalanche ripped while I was skiing, which was highly plausible given the two feet of new snow on an already treacherous snowpack, I'd yank this handle and deploy an air bag from my backpack. In theory, the air bag would help me float to the surface in the rushing river of snow and protect my head from blunt trauma.

Ski technology had evolved dramatically since Coombs's early days in Alaska. Improved avalanche safety technology like my air bag was still years from being commonplace, while the proliferation of fat skis, which made skiing powder so much easier, was just beginning in the late nineties. After Shane McConkey ripped down an Alaskan slope on a pair of old water skis in the early 2000s, ski companies began producing wider planks that allowed skiers to float on top of the snow. While it would be hard to back up this claim, chances were good that if you threw today's young-gun pro skiers on the old, longer, narrower skis Coombs was dominating the slopes on, they would flail down the mountain.

Zell led us to the edge of the landing zone, which instantly confirmed everything I'd ever heard about skiing in Alaska. Below us, the slope plunged into oblivion. It was steep, rocky, and completely unwelcoming. There would be no warm-up run. No time to get my legs under me. This was full on right from the drop. Zell looked over to us and grinned.

"This is why you guys came, right?"

I began climbing into that headspace you need to be in when skiing high-consequence terrain. It required summoning a level of confidence beyond what I was naturally equipped with. I'm talking run-through-brick-walls, nobody-is-going-to-fuck-with-me, Clark Kent confidence, the mojo that Coombs was somehow able to instill in his clients.

Zell gave us some brief instructions and then set off down the couloir. In a matter of a single turn, this wizened old man suddenly became boyish, moving through the deep snow with the grace that came from billions of turns and millions of vertical feet. Watching him carve perfectly symmetrical turns in this steep couloir was like witnessing a man in a transcendental state of flow. Even after more than twenty-five years skiing in the Chugach, Zell's body, which was held together with steel rods and screws in some places, moved like a feather floating down from the heavens.

Reaching an island of safety, a relatively safe spot in the event of a slide, Zell gave us the sign to start skiing one at a time. I nodded to

LEFT: Doug Coombs, in the halo brace he wore after breaking his neck, with his sister Nancy *(Photo courtesy of the Coombs family)* RIGHT: Coombs skiing with his older brother Steve *(Photo courtesy of the Coombs family)*

ABOVE: A helicopter approaching Dimond Peak in the Chugach *(Photo courtesy of Emily Coombs)*
PREVIOUS: Coombs making a descent in the Chugach *(Photo by Ace Kvale)*

Coombs in La Grave, France *(Photo by Ace Kvale)*

LEFT: Coombs avoiding a freight train of sluff in the Chugach *(Photo by Wade McKoy–Focus Productions)* RIGHT: Coombs instructing students how to rappel into Corbet's Couloir in Jackson Hole Mountain Resort *(Photo courtesy of Emily Coombs)*

Coombs and Chad VanderHam in the téléphérique in La Grave, France
(Photo by Joe Vallone)

Coombs airing into Corbet's Couloir *(Photo by Bob Woodall—Focus Productions)*

Doug Coombs and Emily Gladstone in Bozeman, Montana *(Photo courtesy of Emily Coombs)*

Emily Coombs holding her son, David, in La Grave, France *(Photo by Josefine Ås)*

The view of Tuckerman Ravine from the Caretaker's Cabin *(Photo by Robert Cocuzzo)*

BELOW: The village of Les Terrasses before La Meije *(Photo by Joshua Simpson)*
NEXT PAGE: Coombs in the Chugach *(Photo by Ace Kvale)*

the two Frenchmen to go first. They, too, possessed surprising ability, nothing near Zell's level, but a classic, Old-World form that maximized the number of turns and looked quite beautiful.

As the second of the two men set off, I was left alone on the side of the slope with this sprawling mountain landscape stretching out before me to the edge of the earth. There was an aura to this place that I'd never felt before. It was neither ominous nor welcoming. Valdez felt truly magical. I'd dreamed a lifetime of dreams about Alaska, and the reality was now exceeding every one of them. I couldn't help but think of the man that brought me here and thank him.

With Zell waving me on, I broke from my perch and pointed my skis down the couloir, giving myself just enough speed to initiate my first turn. Sliding against my shins and up my thighs, the snow hummed and purred. It felt like I was moving through a sea of cats rubbing up against my legs. As I gained momentum and found my rhythm, I began rising up and floating through the snow. Therein lies the beauty of powder: you're momentarily freed from the laws of gravity, moving over the world like a satellite.

Each turn broke off a small amount of sluff that trickled down the slope alongside me. I thought about the Coombs form: keep my hands out in front of me, square my shoulders, plant the pole, turn, and collapse it. Pain began to ring out in my thighs and lungs, but it didn't register. My brain had become an ice cube melting away in a cocktail of adrenaline, endorphins, and the unmatched euphoria of skiing perfect powder in a place as profound as this.

Reaching Zell and the Frenchmen at the apron, I just grinned and grinned. I tried to say something, but the words got caught in my throat as if I was about to cry. So instead, I just kept smiling, hanging my huffing carcass over my poles like a wet towel. Before I could even take my goggles off and gather myself, Zell was already calling in the helicopter on the radio. Moments later, the aircraft appeared on the horizon, soaring toward us like a gunship.

I'd just skied the best run of my life, and now this machine was flying toward me for the sole purpose of allowing me do it again. As I climbed back into the helicopter, I was overcome by the realization that from this point forward, I would do anything to have this experience in my life again and again. Just like that, I was a full-blown addict.

What felt like thirty seconds later, the pilot zeroed in on another landing zone, except this one appeared to be only a fraction of the size of Stairway to Heaven's. Exposed rock walls corralled this patch of snow, and the pilot needed to be perfectly positioned so that his blades didn't strike them. When the helicopter touched down, Zell plucked off his headset and we unbuckled, then exited the machine and climbed down. The copter pulled up, showing us its belly, before disappearing behind the rock wall to our right.

We were again alone and surrounded by the Chugach. The sun lit up snow crystals and magic was in the air. "Looks like I'm going to need to pull out my handle for this one," Zell said, jolting me back into reality. He slung on his backpack and unzipped the handle to his avalanche air bag. For an old schooler like Zell, who had spent the better part of his early years skiing avalanche terrain with little more than a shovel, pulling out his handle indicated imminent danger to me. Then I looked down and fully grasped the gravity of what we were about to ski. Three couloirs broke steeply below our feet. The snow looked deep and precarious. Clearly our first run had been, in fact, a warm-up. Now we were getting to the real deal.

"Alright, I'm going to have one of you guys ski out here on the shoulder and watch me," Zell said. "If an avalanche breaks above me, I want you to blow your whistle." Zell asked one of the Frenchmen to test the whistle that was attached to his backpack. It sounded like it wouldn't even get a dog's attention. Zell made a face. There was no chance that he'd hear the meek whistle if hell broke loose behind him. "Well, if this thing slides, just scream."

As Zell finished buckling his straps and the rest of his gear, I thought of what I would do if this slope did avalanche and bury him. Keep eyes on him. Break out my beacon. Set it to search. Tell the Frenchmen to do the same. Make my way down to the debris and scan. Get my probe ready. Shovel like hell when I found him. I tried to forget about how miserably I had failed my beacon test earlier in the day, and how the real-life test would be infinitely more difficult.

Zell started by doing a series of ski cuts, driving hard across the slope to try to make it fracture, but it didn't. Apparently satisfied, he set off, once again assuming a beautiful form that I knew I would never possess. Like Coombs, Zell didn't ski just to get down the mountain. Rather, his skiing was an extension of his soul—doing it with style and grace was the fulfillment of why he was put on this planet.

As I stood there perched in the snow, waiting for my turn to ski, the truth of what drew Coombs to this place—indeed, what kept him here for over a decade—washed over me. Even among imminent dangers like crevasses, cliffs, and avalanche risk, Alaska was utterly empowering. The mountains, the helicopters, the deep powder, the air of lawlessness seeped into the marrow of my bones and made me feel painted into this epic landscape. The moment charged every shred of me. The combination of fear and adrenaline had turned my concentration into a superpower. I didn't feel invincible; no, quite the opposite: I was fully aware that my next turn could be my last. People would then ask, was it worth it? You're damn right it was.

Zell signaled for me to start skiing, and I didn't think twice about doing so.

13

THE PROTÉGÉ

Jackson Hole, Wyoming, 1994

"Who is this kid?" Coombs yelled out in amazement. He lifted his goggles onto his forehead to get a better look at the skier bombing down the mountain behind him. He was compact as a spark plug, his technique smacking of years running gates as a slalom racer, exploding through the snow with confidence and flair. He dumped speed with each turn, but still the kid was flying down the mountain like his hair was on fire. Duct tape was the only thing keeping his jacket from tearing at the seams. Coombs couldn't help but smile. He was genuinely impressed.

"What's his name again?" Coombs asked Emily.

"Chad," she said. "Chad VanderHam."

When it wasn't spring heli-skiing season in Alaska, Doug and Emily Coombs continued to spend their winters in Jackson Hole, where, in 1993, they started an extreme skiing camp. Much like Patrick Vallençant had done at the height of his career in France when opening Stages Vallençant, Coombs capitalized on his international fame by starting Doug Coombs Steep Skiing Camps in Jackson Hole. And just as

Coombs had when he went to Chamonix to ski with Vallençant, young skiers began flocking to Jackson Hole for the chance to ski with their hero. One such skier was Chad VanderHam.

Nineteen-year-old Chad VanderHam grew up over a thousand miles away from the big mountains of Jackson Hole in an upper-middle-class neighborhood outside of Minneapolis. Despite his suburban surroundings, VanderHam shared the same innate appetite for adventure that had drawn Coombs into the mountains as a kid. "He was feisty and spunky and full of piss and vinegar," remembered VanderHam's childhood best friend, Nate Kaegebein. "He loved to push himself. He genuinely enjoyed taking risks. Absolutely. One hundred percent. He liked to push any type of circumstance, whether that was snowmobiling, if that was water-skiing, if that was jumping off a bridge into a lake. Any type of thing. He was an adrenaline-junkie kind of guy."

VanderHam ski-raced for both his high school team, of which he was the captain, as well as a team on Buck Hill, a three-hundred-vertical-foot ski resort south of Minneapolis. Despite its modest stature, Buck Hill gained a reputation for turning out exceptional World Cup racers, including Kristina Koznick and Olympic gold medalist Lindsey Vonn, who is considered one of the greatest female racers of all time. VanderHam was no slouch himself. Although in his senior year of high school he didn't stand much taller than five foot six and tipped the scales around 120 pounds soaking wet, VanderHam was one of the most dominant slalom racers for his age in Minnesota when he left to attend college in Colorado.

Studying economics at Colorado State University (CSU), VanderHam excelled as a student but really got his education as a skier. "Chad was not just leaps and bounds beyond us; he was light-years ahead of us in terms of his skiing ability," said Simon Fryer, who met VanderHam during his freshman year at CSU and became a longtime ski partner. VanderHam moved down the terrain with the distinct stance, technique, and aggressiveness of a racer. No matter the conditions, VanderHam wanted to go fast and hard all the time.

VanderHam was an only child, and his parents owned and ran a successful paper company. His father was his best friend, instilling in him a strong work ethic, honesty, and humility. Although his parents were well off, VanderHam insisted on living a rather modest existence. "He could have had all the freaking gear he wanted," said Simon Fryer. But "he got the mileage out of everything he owned. He wanted to live a simple life." The family business would be waiting for VanderHam when he graduated from CSU. It was turnkey. But then VanderHam met Doug Coombs in Jackson Hole.

THE GOLD STANDARD FOR SKI instruction during the nineties in North America was the Professional Ski Instructors of America's Demonstration Team, known simply as the D-Team. The D-Team taught a rigid technique in an effort to create uniformity along the ski discipline. Before the D-Team, many skiers lamented that every time they took a ski-school lesson, they were taught a different method and were forced to relearn the sport from the ground up. The D-Team standardized ski instruction, teaching people what they considered to be the perfect turn, the perfect pole plant, and the perfect hip position.

"They were phenomenal skiers, but their benchmark was kind of a robotic, repeatable, cookie-cutter technique," described *Powder* magazine's Steve Casimiro. Although the D-Team's technique gave skiers the form to rip up the groomed runs and low-angle powder fields, when it came to steep, technical terrain, skiers needed a unique set of skills, a set that Coombs had been perfecting in the Chugach each spring and teaching all his Valdez Heli-Ski Guides clients. The Coombs's Steep Skiing Camp at Jackson Hole Mountain Resort aimed to spread these skills, as well as provide them another revenue stream. Not to mention that the camps allowed them to recruit future clients for their heli-skiing operation in Valdez.

The Steep Skiing Camp was a bold proposition for the ski industry. Two landmark liability cases had put American ski resorts on high alert, spurring a countrywide policy of minimizing inherent dangers as much as possible. In 1979 a skier was paralyzed when he struck a snow-covered bush at Stratton Mountain and then sued the resort for $1.5 million. Four years later, another skier broke his neck when he launched off a cat track in Aspen. He was awarded $5 million. "The effects of those suits, and the others that followed, rippled through every ski area in the United States," wrote John Steinbreder in *Snow Country* magazine in 1995. "Liability insurance premiums, which on average equaled 1 percent of ski-area revenues in 1978, climbed to as much as 15 percent in the 1990s."

Not surprisingly, the idea of guiding people into the most dangerous areas of the mountain didn't exactly fit the safety objectives of Jackson Hole Mountain Resort and its ski school director, Pepi Stiegler. "I don't know why Pepi said yes," Emily said. "But he did." With the backing of K2, Coombs's biggest sponsor, he and Emily took out a $500 ad in *Powder* magazine and invited the publication's editor to attend the first camp.

"The wonderful thing about camp was it was kind of like how to be Doug Coombs," Casimiro remarked later. "Frankly, for my money, I can't imagine a better lesson than to be able to chase Coombs around for a week. I learned as much as I ever did skiing in that one week, spending that kind of intensive time with him." The Coombses developed a daily curriculum described as "terrain progression." After a ski-off to determine each camper's abilities, the school was broken into three groups. "We'd start them off on something easy, and then we'd build them up to something more challenging, skiing something tight with a lot of turns," explained Emily. "Then we would always slow it down and end the day with confidence."

As the week progressed, the midday crux became more and more demanding until the last day, when skiers graduated by jumping into Corbet's Couloir. Rather than teaching skiers how to perform flawless turns like the D-Team, Coombs and Emily taught their students how to read terrain and how to react to it. They raised their awareness to avalanche risk, taught them backcountry etiquette, and trained them to be respectful of the environment while skiing. Most of all, however, Coombs's clients enjoyed being in his presence in the mountains. "He was sort of like this electrical wire," said Steve Casimiro. "He was always buzzing about skiing. You could feel the volts radiating off of him. His charisma around skiing was also very much like the way he skied: controlled, precise."

When Steve Casimiro's article came out in *Powder*, the Doug Coombs Steep Skiing Camps went gangbusters. "Pepi called me up and was like, 'What have you done? The phone is ringing off the hook,'" Emily remembered. The Coombses offered three weeklong camps per season, and each was booked up months in advance, bringing tens of thousands of dollars to the resort, of which the Coombses were entitled to 20 percent. The Steep Skiing Camps served as a huge marketing draw for Jackson Hole Mountain Resort, and Coombs was made an official resort ambassador. Prior to that, the world extreme skiing champion wasn't being compensated for the use of his image and reputation in the resort's marketing materials, beyond just promoting the Coombses' steep camp. He and Emily were living in a hotel. After much insistence by Emily, Jackson Hole Mountain Resort agreed to pay Coombs $20,000 to serve as an ambassador, which allowed him and Emily to put a down payment on a one-room condo in Teton Village.

Clients came from all over the world to learn from Coombs, but none showed more promise than Chad VanderHam. "We were amazed with him as a client," Emily said. "He could just rip." VanderHam was equally awestruck by Coombs and his entirely unique approach to the big mountains. "Afterward you could tell that this light went off," said Simon Fryer. When VanderHam returned to Colorado, he looked at the mountains completely differently and began venturing outside his comfort zone. "My experiences with Doug and Emily have shown me another side of skiing," VanderHam wrote in a testimonial for the Coombses' Steep Skiing Camps. "My eyes have opened from making turns within the restrictions of riding lifts, to the excitement of route-finding among the vastness of the living mountains."

14

CHAMOFIED

Chamonix, France, 2014

The rattle of the charming red trolley kept me from being completely consumed by travel fatigue. But I was too zonked to even look out the window and try to make out the mountainous landscape passing in the night. Instead, I stared blankly at the train's simple route map and awaited the next stop: Chamonix.

This trip was prompted by an invitation from Miles and Liz Smart, who took over Coombs's steep camps after his death, which by then had expanded globally to become Steep Skiing Camps Worldwide. We had been going back and forth over email as I was trying to glean the details of how Doug and Emily Coombs once ran their steep camps. Liz Smart finally suggested that I just come to Chamonix and experience the camp for myself. So here I was, stepping out into the epicenter of extreme skiing history much like Coombs had done some thirty years earlier when he came knocking at the doors of Stages Vallençant in search of his hero.

Snow was falling from the heavens in big, wet chunks when the train pulled into Chamonix. I dragged my skis out of the train and plucked a tourist map from a nearby kiosk. Miles and Liz had invited me to join them and the rest of the campers for a meet-and-greet dinner, which I was now very late for. When I couldn't make heads or tails of the map, I just started walking into the heart of Chamonix, hoping to stumble across the restaurant where they were dining. I mean, how many restaurants could there possibly be in this little village?

The reality was that Chamonix was far from the quiet French hamlet I'd imagined. Hundreds of people swarmed its snow-caked streets. The village was a bustling mini metropolis, complete with après bars booming techno music, garish storefronts, and the ultimate sign of cultural collapse: the golden arches of McDonald's. There were pieces of historic Chamonix sprinkled throughout, but the overall aura struck me as commercial, and I felt it quickly sucking me in like a vortex that led me in aimless circles.

After walking past the same sculpture a third time, I pulled out my map again, which was now soggy and breaking up into pieces. "Where the fuck am I?" I huffed, now wet and cold. I huddled alongside the window of a closed cell phone store in hopes of stealing their Wi-Fi to get an email out to Liz and Miles on my cell phone for directions. Mercifully, they responded quickly, and before complete despair set in, I burst awkwardly into the quiet, small Italian restaurant like a wet stray sneaking in to beg for scraps.

The group sat at a long table, the candlelight flickering in their faces. It was a motley crew to say the least, fifteen middle-aged men and a tall blond who could easily pass as a runway model. She quickly rose to greet me.

"You made it!" Liz Smart said. "We're just settling up the tab, but Miles is going to go over what we're doing tomorrow, so just grab a seat."

I pulled a chair to the corner of the table and introduced myself to the first of my fellow campers. William Wallace was a strapping young American naval officer who was stationed in Germany. He was the image of a man in uniform, with a chopping block for a jaw that had grown thick, black stubble from his days on leave. Jo Spehr was a big, bald German, maybe in his early fifties, who looked like he could play the villain in an *X-Men* movie. When I shook his hand, I realized Spehr was missing all his fingers, which I later learned he lost to frostbite in a climbing accident in Italy when he was just a teen. Bald and bespectacled, Filip Pagowski was originally from Poland but now lived in New York City and worked as a freelance illustrator for companies all over the world. Jeff Wilson was from Jackson Hole and actually used to be one of the tram operators at Teton Village. He had a shock of salt-and-pepper curls that he wore in Jerry Garcia style. Juan Torruella, of Puerto Rican descent, was a banker from New York City. Torruella told me that he had attended at least eight of Coombs's Steep Skiing Camps and I mentally noted that he was someone I wanted to talk to later in the week. Each of the fifteen campers came from very different walks of life. The only thing that we all shared in common—in my mind, anyway—was that none of us fit the description of an elite skier. They, like me, appeared to be amateurs, probably the best skier among their friends but not exactly ready for the race circuit.

Miles Smart stood up at the head of the table. He was short and compact, but what I had read about him during the trip to Chamonix made him seem like a giant in my mind. Originally from Washington State, Miles learned to ski on a small hill before graduating to Stevens Pass, in the Cascade Mountains. More than a skier, however, Miles had earned a reputation as a fearless speed climber. He had set numerous speed ascent records in Yosemite, at least two of which he did without the safety of ropes. And these weren't small routes. Miles attacked faces that took other elite climbers days, sometimes weeks, to ascend, and he did them in a matter of hours. The notion of speed climbing without the safety of a rope struck me as completely ludicrous, but nothing about Miles, as he stood before me now, appeared prone to recklessness.

He met Coombs in the early 2000s while working for Exum Mountain Guides in Jackson Hole. Even though Miles was half his age, Coombs was in awe of him as a climber. Despite all the time he'd spent in the mountains, Coombs didn't start getting serious about climbing until later in his career, and Miles became one of his favorite partners and a source for improving his own climbing. When he and Emily brought their Steep Skiing Camps to Europe, Miles followed shortly thereafter. In 2006 he was named American Mountain Guide of the Year.

"This is going to be a great week," Miles began. "We have snow in the forecast for the next few days, and from the look of it, tomorrow should be optimal conditions."

He briefly scanned the group with a guarded smile, his eyes not focusing on anyone in particular. I detected an air of seriousness in his voice that made me think Miles wasn't much for small talk.

"We'll be meeting at the hotel lobby tomorrow at eight thirty," he continued. "Anyone not have a harness?"

I raised my hand, along with most of the others. *A harness?* I thought. *Why the hell do I need a harness?*

"Okay, come grab one from Liz before you leave. And we'll see you bright and early tomorrow."

DAY ONE BEGAN WITH a ski off. Miles and Liz hiked us from the lift to an off-piste run called The Hotel Face, which had been one of the competition runs in the recent Freeride World Tour. There was no instruction at this point, but rather a dog-eat-dog test to separate the men from the boys. This would enable Miles and Liz to break us up into groups of similar ability. Before we got started, Miles asked each of us, "What percent power does your avalanche beacon have?" The question was like asking someone how much gas he had in his car while it was sitting in the garage, and it prompted each of us to unzip our jackets and pull out the device that could ultimately save our lives.

Grabbing mine, I had a momentary rush of dread that I might have taken out one of the batteries to use for my electric razor like a complete idiot. Thankfully, when I turned it on, the screen read 99 percent.

Accompanying Miles and Liz in guiding us this week was Thor Husted. At first glance, Husted looked like he had no right to be named after the Viking god of thunder. He was a small man with elfin features and a slight gap tooth. But my impression of him quickly changed when Husted began ferociously hammering out a boot pack through thigh-deep snow for us to follow, all while carrying two pairs of skis on his back. When we reached him at the top, Husted didn't seem to be breathing hard at all. Behind his loosely fitting ski suit, I imagined his body must be a sinewy mass of lean muscle encasing a giant set of lungs.

On the car ride earlier in the day, I had asked Husted about the process of becoming an internationally certified mountain guide. He told me it had taken him six years to attain his American Mountain Guides Association certification, although it takes most applicants around four. He explained that the process had been dragged out because he shattered his femur halfway through his mountain education. After I prodded for more information, Husted explained that he'd triggered an avalanche on the west side of the Grands Montets Glacier while skiing with three friends in Chamonix. The avalanche rushed him nearly a thousand vertical feet down the mountain before burying him under nine feet of snow for more than twenty minutes. "My leg was wrapped around my head," he said. When Husted was finally dug out, his ribs were broken, his lung was punctured, his femur was broken in two places, and he had been stripped of most of his clothes. His body temperature had dropped to 86 degrees Fahrenheit. A rescue doctor and crew were dropped on the scene by a helicopter, but when it came time to fly Husted out, a bank of low clouds prevented the helicopter from returning for nearly an hour.

He spent six days in the hospital, where his leg was pieced back together with metal rods and screws. The scars I was more curious about, however, were the mental ones. How was it that he was able to return to skiing after one of the most traumatic experiences in the mountains? Husted didn't offer a direct explanation. Perhaps it was too personal, or perhaps he simply didn't know any other way to live.

"Alright, guys, you really can't go wrong here," Miles said, surveying the slope below. "There are some obvious rocks to the right you should avoid, but otherwise it's all good."

An untracked powder field stretched below us like a canvas. About a foot had fallen since I had arrived yesterday, and Miles had raced us up here to get fresh tracks before other skiers arrived. "Thor, I'm going to go halfway down," Miles said. "Then you can send them one by one."

We watched Miles bound down the slope, making beautifully symmetrical turns through the powder, his blue-and-green ski suit glaring in the crisp morning light. He came to a stop above a rocky outcropping and gave Husted a wave.

"Have at it," Husted said.

One by one, my fellow clients descended the slope with varying degrees of success. Some started out strong, making their first handful of turns confidently until fatigue set in and they were forced to stop and catch their breath. The youngest, a nineteen-year-old Scotsman, hit the slope more aggressively, if not slightly out of control, jumping off every rock he could spot and sacrificing form for speed.

Determined to earn my way into the elite group, I set out to ski the whole face in control and without stopping. The snow was thick and heavy as I pounced from turn to turn and did my best not to think about the fact that Miles was probably eyeballing my every move and picking apart my form. He'd likely grimace when seeing my habit of holding my right turn a second or two longer than my left. Or my upper body lurching too far forward over my skis. And then there were my overzealous pole plants, which undoubtedly made me look like the leader of a marching band stumbling down the mountain.

But when I reached Miles at the bottom, he didn't utter a word to me. Not even a nod. He just kept staring up the mountain to watch the remaining skiers, so I turned and did the same. Our guides had their work cut out for them, as our abilities ran the spectrum. Since I made it down without stopping or falling, I mentally ranked myself somewhere near the top of the heap—flamboyant pole plants be damned.

"That was the steepest thing I ever skied," gasped a fisherman from Michigan. "Is the rest of the week going to be like that?" This would turn out to be the first and last run the man would make as part of the camp. He was simply too rattled to continue.

The last person down the face was in a purple one-piece ski suit. The figure absolutely dominated the slope.

"Whoa, is that Liz?" I asked Miles in disbelief.

"Yup," he said with an uncharacteristic glimmer of pride in his voice. Liz was the picture of control and grace. She reminded me of the first time I saw Emily Coombs skiing in Jackson Hole.

"Jeez."

Miles smirked as if to say, "Yeah, that's my wife." Miles met Liz around the same time he met Coombs. She was working at the Exum office while Miles guided clients around the Tetons with Coombs. Liz grew up in Aspen, where her father served as the ski school director. In fact, Liz's father was the person on whom filmmakers based the main character of *Aspen Extreme*, the cult classic ski film that Coombs starred in as a stunt double. But Liz didn't lead the charmed life one might imagine in the posh ski town of Aspen. She and her family lived in a trailer, with the mountains acting as her backyard. Liz ski-raced during high school, mostly to get out of class, but her father forbade her from ever becoming a ski instructor. After she and Miles started dating and Miles moved to Chamonix, Miles gave her a birthday present that would change both of their lives. He invited her to Chamonix for a ski trip. Liz's three-week trip to France turned into three months, and five years later she and Miles were married. Now, at the age of thirty-two, she was an internationally certified mountain guide and what looked to be one of the most dominant female skiers in Chamonix.

The Hotel Face was the only run Miles wanted us to make. He'd seen enough to split us up into three groups. We hopped back into the car and drove a short ways to the base of the tram to Chamonix's most iconic peak, Aiguille du Midi. The cable car was an engineering marvel that I couldn't wrap my mind around. I stood on the tram dock alongside Jeff Wilson, the former tram operator from Jackson Hole, who educated me on just how amazing this machine was. The cables stretched up to the castle-like tram dock at the top with no towers between them. We entered the tram, which swept us up over nine thousand vertical feet in twenty minutes.

At the top, I followed Miles and the rest of the campers through a tunnel cut into the mountain and then out into daylight. Emerging from the tunnel, I was filled with the wonder I remember feeling the first time I entered Fenway Park as a little kid—except instead of the Green Monster, I was now staring out at staggering peaks rising up from France, Switzerland, and Italy. Miles had us each clip into a rope as we walked down a precarious ridge in the snow and then onto a clearing, where he broke us up into our groups. I was put in Liz's group with four others. She guided us down steep couloirs that funneled all the way to the valley floor below. The run induced sensory overload. The jagged peaks. The deep snow. The glaciers. The helicopters and single-prop planes flying by. Chamonix was a playground of extremes.

At the end of the day, Miles and Liz brought us to the Moö Bar in Chamonix, a favorite skier watering hole where I got a chance to pick their brains about what it was like being a husband-and-wife team in the mountains, much like the Coombses had been. After Coombs's death, Miles and Liz moved in with Emily in Jackson Hole to support her. It was during that time that Emily asked the Smarts to continue running the steep camps. The passing of the torch seemed fitting, one mountain couple taking over for the other.

"What impact did Doug and Emily's relationship have on you and Liz?" I asked Miles.

"They were definitely role models for us," he said. "Showing us how you can make a living in the mountains, and how you can have a relationship together living in the mountains. I think in so many ways we really looked up to them."

"What are the challenges of working with your spouse and sharing a life together in the mountains?"

"We're very aware of the mountains and the risks they pose," Miles explained. "It's always hard when one of us happens to be at home and the other person is out there on some big climb. We're always more concerned or more worried when we're apart. But when we're both out there working together in tense situations, or watching the other person do something really serious, we're both very relaxed. We both have full faith in the other person's abilities and judgment."

"For some people who aren't familiar with the lifestyle of a guide, they might look at some of the risks that Doug took, especially at the end of his life, and not understand them. What's it like being a husband while also taking risks on a day-to-day basis in the mountains?"

"First and foremost, our job as guides is to manage risk," Miles answered. "What we do out there is inherently risky, but it's not more risky than a lot of other things people do in their lives. The big thing for us is that we're constantly aware of what the risk is. We're constantly making a very educated calculation. That's what we do for work. For us, it's not risk taking; it's managing risk. Just like a doctor would manage risk in an operation."

"How much of the steep camp is still driven by the idea of continuing Doug's legacy?"

"I think everyone that comes to the camp still has some kind of interest in Doug Coombs. He's such a big presence in the ski industry," Miles said. "For some clients, Doug was their idol for their whole youth, while others just knew of him loosely. But his legacy still lives on in the camps."

As the Moö Bar began to fill up with more skiers, the din quickly consumed our conversation. Miles and Liz went off to say hello to some friends, while I stayed back with the rest of the clients. Then I spotted a face I instantly recognized.

"Holy shit, do you know who that is?" I whispered to one of the others.

"Who?"

"The guy at the bar."

"No, who's that?"

"That's Seth Morrison."

"Oh yeah?" he said.

"Do you know who Seth Morrison is?" I asked breathlessly. I didn't give him a chance to answer. "I grew up watching that guy ski with Coombs. He's an absolute legend."

Many in the ski industry thought that if there was any American skier better than Doug Coombs in the big mountains, it was Seth Morrison. He was at the forefront of the next generation of skiers that came up behind Coombs. They skied together on many occasions, and Emily told me that her husband had tremendous respect for him. Despite their mutual admiration, Coombs and Morrison couldn't have been more different, both on the mountain and off. Beyond his rock-solid technique, Morrison made a name for himself by jumping off giant cliffs and landing impossible backflips and barrel rolls that made him look like he was skiing on a trampoline. His jaw-dropping ski style matched his punk-rock appearance. Morrison's hair was dyed wild colors; he wore black nail polish; and his tongue, eyebrow, and ears were pierced. Morrison's bad-boy reputation became the stuff of legend when he was arrested in his twenties for getting drunk and stealing a car for a joyride, but since then he had cleaned up his act, battling through injuries and surviving a helicopter crash that killed the pilot and a fellow skier. Today, Morrison was a venerable icon who still did backflips off eighty-foot cliffs and dyed his hair. Right now, it was long and dyed pitch black.

I sat there quietly nursing my beer, pretending to listen to the others while an internal debate raged loudly in my mind. *Do I go up and talk to him?* Morrison starred in all my favorite ski movies, often alongside Coombs. In fact, the movie clip that now came to mind was of Morrison skiing with Coombs as a celebrity instructor in one of his steep camps. In some cosmic way, Morrison was partially responsible for my being here right now. *Maybe he could tell me some of his stories with Coombs,* I thought. "I'm going to grab a beer," I told the others.

Meandering up to the bar, I decided that if Morrison happened to come over to get another drink, I'd offer to buy it for him. *Play it cool,* I thought to myself. *Don't come off as some starstruck fan.* Sure enough, Morrison wandered over. It was all too serendipitous not to just go for it. I tapped him on the shoulder and introduced myself with an outstretched hand.

"Hi, I'm Seth," he responded.

"Sorry to bother you," I said, not knowing where I was going with this, "but I just wanted to . . . wanted to tell you that I—I grew up watching you ski." *So much for playing it cool.* "I'm actually here skiing in one of Doug Coombs's Steep Skiing Camps, and one of my favorite Warren Miller scenes was of you skiing with him at one of the steep camps. When I saw you come in, I just thought I had to say hi."

"Oh nice," he said. "You skiing with Miles and Liz?"

"Yeah, we had an amazing day today."

Despite his fame, Morrison struck me as supremely modest, almost to the point of being shy. There was no ego about him at all. Even though I was a complete nobody in the professional ski scene, he seemed genuinely tuned in to our conversation, as the bar became more and more boisterous around us.

"What was it like skiing with Coombs?" I asked.

"He lived to ski," Morrison said. "He always made it the best time. He had a powerful effect on people. Everyone will tell you they skied the best runs of their lives with him. That's what Doug did—blew people's minds and kept them alive."

"And what impressed you about his skiing?"

"He was so fluid and could make turn after turn without ever stopping. Legs of steel. He had such control on the hardest snow and just made everything look easy—like he was always skiing powder even when he was on ice."

"Where does he stand in your mind compared to others you've skied with?"

"One of the best," Morrison said in a flash. "He skied gnarly lines that others wouldn't even think of. He had a different look at terrain and how to ski it. Sometimes I wonder how he would ski some of these lines I see today."

Morrison shuffled slightly in place. He had to be around forty years old by now, but he didn't look a day past twenty-one. There was obvious wisdom in the contemplative way he spoke.

"We worked together a few weeks before his passing," Morrison continued. "The last time I saw him, he was sitting in the Vancouver airport reading the paper, having a coffee and a muffin. He was alone, and people were passing him not even realizing who this guy was. I didn't bother him. It was a different light that I hadn't seen him in before: a superstar skier in the normal world. I watched a bit from a distance to see him in a moment of peace."

WE HIKED THROUGH THE WAIST-DEEP snow as methodically as a chain gang. Miles was breaking trail while my group and I did what we could to keep up with him. The three of us had no choice but to hike hard, as we were all attached to the same length of rope, with Miles at the front end. Any of our steps could break through the snow and pull us all into a crevasse, so it was all for one and one for all.

The day's objective didn't need much explaining to sound completely audacious. Miles had told us we were going to hike from Italy and ski back into France. That was how Miles conveyed most bits of information, in short bursts that came off like "well, of course." Earlier, at lunch over spaghetti and espresso, I had asked Miles what he thought extreme skiing was.

"The definition of extreme skiing is if you fall, you die," he shot back.

"Well, yes, but do you think it's changed with marketing and all?" I asked, hoping to broach a bigger conversation about how extreme skiing had gone through a few different iterations since Patrick Vallençant's day. Everything seemed to be marketed as extreme in the nineties, from tacos to razor blades, and I was curious to know whether Miles thought extreme skiing had been bastardized in the process? Was it something different today?

"The definition of extreme skiing is if you fall, you die," he repeated, his eyes fixed on me as if to say, "You came all the way to Chamonix and you don't know what extreme skiing is?" He said again, "That's the definition."

I decided to leave it at that and bury my face back in my spaghetti. Clearly Miles thought there were such things as stupid questions, and I planned on choosing what to ask more wisely next time.

Now, a couple of hours into our hike, Miles motioned for us to stop. "Hold it up here, guys. This is where it gets tricky," he said, nodding to the vast open expanse before us. "This is the top of the Géant Glacier. Just wait here for the others, and I'll wave you over when I'm ready for you."

Miles detached us all from the rope, then deftly wrapped it up and put on his skis. He then pushed himself out on the glacier. He went on and on, until he was just a tiny figurine sticking out from the snow. I imagined his loneliness out there, listening to the snow, waiting to hear the groan of a crevasse. Liz's group caught up with us, their faces red and glistening with exhaustion.

"Where's Miles?" Torruella huffed between breaths.

I nodded out to the snowfield.

"Shit," he said.

Miles finally came to a stop in the distance, looked around, and then gave us the signal to come by waving his arms.

"Don't stack up," instructed Liz. "Keep a bus length between yourselves and keep moving."

I waited for my turn and then pushed out onto the snow, gliding over Miles's track. I tried not to think about what was under my feet—or rather what *wasn't* under my feet. Miles had explained earlier in the day how layers of snow formed over the cracks in the glaciers, creating snow bridges. With our skis distributing our weight over the snow, we could pass over these bridges with relative safety. A skier got into trouble if he fell while descending a glacier and lost both his skis. Walking over snow bridges was a death wish.

When I reached Miles, he seemed uncharacteristically giddy. "This is Vallée Blanche Noire," he said in a voice like he had just pulled the sheathing off a brand-new Bugatti and handed us the keys. Dead ahead was a low-angle powder field that ski bums dream about. Beyond the slope and to our immediate right, massive icefalls clung to the sides of the mountains. These tractor-trailer-size slabs of ice could fall at any moment, and death would pretty much be guaranteed. Being stuck squarely between something so heavenly and something so hellish was exciting, like I had just stolen a handful of Christmas cookies off the pan and I could hear my mom about to enter the kitchen.

"Have at it," Miles said with a grin, and then he took off.

My fellow clients and I took one look at each other and then hustled into action. "No friends on powder days," as Coombs used to say. Gaining momentum, I floated through the snow and felt like a god. There were no obstacles in my way, and I let my eyes wander and feast upon the surroundings. The ferocious icefall. The towering peaks. The sublime snow. Suddenly a single-prop plane tore through the sky directly in front of us. I laughed out loud, hooting and hollering. *How the hell did I get here?*

THE MOOD AT DINNER THAT night was off the charts. Everyone was buzzing from the day, and suddenly we were blood brothers, throwing arms over one another and ribbing each other. The wine list landed in my lap.

"What should I order?" I asked.

"Get a bottle of Saint-Émilion Bordeaux," Miles said. "That was Chad's favorite. Right, Liz?"

"Right."

"What would Chad say about today?" Miles asked her, wearing an inside-joke smile.

"It was *niiiiiice.*" Liz laughed.

"Did you spend a lot of time with Chad?" I asked Miles.

"Oh yeah, we were close friends. We lived together in La Grave for at least two winters in the same apartment. Three winters, maybe. Skied a bit together on our days off."

"What was he like?" I asked.

"He was very relaxed, very even keeled, calculated. He had a good head for being in the mountains. He had the patience you need to be a good skier and be able to wait for the right conditions. Had the accident not happened, he definitely would have been working for Doug down the road."

"Do you think that having a good head is something you develop, or is it something that you're born with?"

"I think it's a combination of both," Miles said after giving it a moment of thought. "You know certain people are never going to be that good under pressure. Never going to be able to make sound decisions in stressful situations. But it's also something that you learn and develop over time, especially in the context of the mountains."

"I actually skied with Chad when he was a client," Torruella chimed in. "I remember the moment I first saw him. It was at the airport. He had this huge smile and his boots around his neck. He was a very nice guy. I can't overstate that."

"Where was that?" I asked. "In Jackson?"

"No, La Grave," Torruella said. "I was there with my dad for one of Doug's steep camps. It was our first time. My dad ended up leaving after the first day."

"Why did he leave?"

"The skiing was over his head, but Doug was so cool about it. I remember that night we stayed up late with him, and he told us the story about breaking his neck as a kid."

I was surprised to hear this. I had thought Coombs never talked about his neck, especially not to clients.

"We were talking about taking risks," Torruella explained, "and Doug put the story of his neck out there as an example. He was conveying that as a younger person, he had taken bigger risks, but now that he was getting older, he had a safer risk-taking mentality."

"What was it like in those camps?" I asked.

"Doug had more confidence in my skiing than I did." Torruella laughed. "Somehow he had this ability to convey that he had no doubts in my skill. I remember the first day, we got caught in this whiteout, and I was pretty rattled, and he just pulled me out of it with this big smile on his face. He had this way about him that said, 'If I'm relaxed, you should be relaxed.'"

"How many times did you attend the camps?"

"I went back eight consecutive years," Torruella said. "Those trips were so special to me. I could have spent the last twenty-one years working on Wall Street, being a working stiff, getting old, but Doug amped out the nineties for me." Torruella looked down at the table and then back up at me again. "He made my life infinitely more interesting. I can't tell you how much I miss him."

15

SWIFT. SILENT. DEEP.

Jackson Hole, Wyoming, 1997

The two skiers tried to quiet their heavy breathing, but their lungs were screaming for air. They huddled behind a grove of trees, waiting and watching. They were being hunted. When their pursuer finally appeared, his red jacket glared out against the white-and-green backdrop of the Jackson Hole backcountry. He scanned the snow, looking for the two men's tracks as their hearts beat like jungle drums. The ski patroller looked deep into the trees where they were hiding, then reached for his radio.

"Looks like they're gone," he muttered.

Even after they were left alone, the two men waited anxiously in the trees. The ski patrol was known to set traps, and they wondered if this was just another ambush. Minutes before, they had been spotted ducking the ropes of Jackson Hole Mountain Resort, violating its boundaries to ski the deep, untracked powder of Teton National Forest. Skiing out of the bounds of the resort was a criminal offense in Jackson Hole that could cost the skiers their $1,550 season passes if they were caught. Or worse, they could be banned from the ski area indefinitely.

The skiers brushed the snow from their jackets and finally continued on down the mountain. As they gained momentum, they began to float in the waist-deep powder. The sensation of riding weightlessly through the snow was utterly addicting, justifying all the risks of getting caught and losing their skiing privileges at the resort. Here in the backcountry, they could find miles of this magical powder between trees, flowing over boulders, and blanketing steep slopes where they could launch off cliffs and land as softly as feathers. Powder snow made these ordinary men feel like superheroes, if only for a few moments.

Suddenly there was a flash of red followed by the dull thud of bodies colliding. They hadn't even seen him coming. The patroller tackled one of the skiers into the snow like a linebacker and wrestled him into submission. The jig was up.

"When are you Air Force punks going to learn?" the patroller spat, holding the skier by the scruff of his jacket. "Your pass. Hand it over."

In the late nineties, a war raged in Jackson Hole between the resort's ski patrol and the Jackson Hole Air Force. Since he had been pulled into their ranks when he first arrived in the mideighties, Coombs had ascended to become a revered member of the gang. His victories in the World Extreme Skiing Championship served to stake the Air Force's claim as the top skiers in the United States. Indeed, three of the top four places at the first WESC were all occupied by Air Force members. They went on to dominate the podium for the next three years, with Hunt taking first in 1992 and Coombs again in 1993. Some of his most trusted employees at Valdez Heli-Ski Guides were members of the Air Force.

Despite the Air Force's growing reputation in the ski world, certain members of the ski patrol looked upon Coombs and his fellow Air Force members as nothing more than a bunch of reckless punks, and they were on a mission to see to it that the Air Force was grounded permanently.

Ski patrol strictly forbade anyone from venturing outside the boundaries of the resort. Once skiers ducked the ropes, they entered the national forest, where the terrain was unpatrolled and potentially deadly, and the consequences of being caught were severe. But Coombs and his gang remained undeterred. "As soon as we got a taste of it, there was no way we were going to stay away from it," said one Air Force member. "Basically the attitude was that those little orange closed signs said, 'This way for good skiing.'"

To evade the ski patrol, the Air Force employed guerilla tactics of deception. They dressed in all white to slip under the ropes unseen. They carried radios tuned in to the patrol's frequency and learned their daily routines to stay a step ahead. They stashed jackets in the backcountry, so if the patrol spotted them leaving the resort in green coats, they swapped them and reentered wearing red ones.

The Jackson Hole Ski Patrol had good reason to forbid the Air Force from venturing into the backcountry. Jackson Hole Mountain Resort leased its land from the national forest through a special-use permit, and the mandate was handed down by the Forest Service to keep the boundaries staunchly intact. The ski patrol's concern was not for the safety of the Air Force, which had developed the backcountry savvy to survive, but rather for the unknowing skiers that might follow their so-called "sucker tracks" out of bounds. Corky Ward, the ski patrol director at the time, explained: "Our worry was that someone from Boston would jump on an airplane and be here in eight hours, skiing in ten; they'd see a nice set of figure eights in the backcountry, and they would find their way out there."

Ward and his fellow patrollers knew of the grave dangers that lurked on this mountain better than most. In 1985 they had watched as two members of the patrol were killed by avalanches that ripped inbounds. The first came on the ski patrol's inaugural day of duty that winter while they were setting up closed-area signs and roping off boundaries. At 4:15 p.m., forty-eight-year-old patroller Paul Driscoll joined seven others in their final responsibilities of the day, fixing signs and ropes to the skier's left of Rendezvous Bowl. Driscoll was skiing ahead of the others, shouldering a stack of closed-area signs, when a small avalanche ripped across the slope above him. The patrolman attempted to self-arrest by jamming the signposts into the ground, but when he did, the entire slope shattered around him. Driscoll struggled to swim through the rushing snow, making his way to a grove of trees and latching onto the smallest of the bunch.

When the snow finally slowed to a stop, he was nowhere to be seen. Patrollers frantically began to search with their avalanche beacons. Yet despite a full force of experienced patrollers, locating Driscoll's beacon signal took over ten minutes. Once he was located, it took another ten minutes of digging to reach Driscoll, and then another twenty to extricate him from the snow. Driscoll had been buried six feet deep. As darkness descended on the mountain and a storm began to rage, the ski patrol raced Driscoll to the base, where he was ultimately declared dead after several attempts to resuscitate him.

Paul Driscoll's was the first death in Jackson Hole Mountain Resort's history, but his would not be the last. Just two months later, a blizzard raged for twelve days, closing the resort. The storm came in off the Pacific, dropping eight-and-a-half feet of wet snow and gusting winds up to one hundred miles per hour at the top of the tram. Throughout the storm, the ski patrol battled the resort's building avalanche risk by throwing handheld explosives and ski-cutting the slopes. At 8:00 a.m. on the fifth day of the storm, patrollers Tom Raymer, John Bernadyn, and Paul Rice were given the green light to ski to Moran Face and throw handheld explosives. It was snowing at a rate of one inch per hour when the three men arrived at Moran Face. After throwing two charges from above the slope with no success, the patrollers skied out onto the upper section of the face and threw three more. Still nothing. As they stood there discussing what to do, Bernadyn spotted the slope fracture a hundred feet above Raymer. He screamed to warn him, but Raymer had no time. The giant avalanche engulfed him, rushing him through the trees below before erupting in a blinding cloud of snow.

When they found Raymer's beacon signal six hundred feet down the slope, furious probing and digging ensued. Raymer had been buried for forty-five minutes when they finally pulled him out from under twelve feet of snow. Both his legs were broken and he wasn't breathing. Rescuers attempted CPR, but despite their best efforts, Tom Raymer was pronounced dead at the medical clinic at the base.

If there had been any lingering doubt after Paul Driscoll's death, the avalanche that killed Tom Raymer served as a stark reminder that even the most elite skiers could be consumed by this mountain's perilous wrath. Some members of the ski patrol looked at the tracks left by the Air Force leading out of bounds as an affront to their authority, and perhaps even a sign of disrespect to their fallen patrol brothers. They took it personally and began cracking down hard on the boundaries. "It was a pain in the ass," recalled Corky Ward. "You had to go out there and stand on the boundaries and chase people around and be a law officer."

The ski area turned into the Wild West, with cowboy patrollers chasing cavalier Air Force members through the backcountry. "They treated people skiing out of bounds like vandals," recalled Porter Fox, who wrote for the *Jackson Hole News* at the time. "The patrol was out of control in how they were trying to bust people."

Certain members of the ski patrol's old guard, some of the same patrollers who watched Raymer and Driscoll die, made it their primary objective to bag the Air Force. It became a personal vendetta for them. Even Corky Ward admitted, "Some were just abusers [of power]." They threw sticks of dynamite into the Air Force's secret hut on the mountain, blowing it to smithereens. They hid in the backcountry, sometimes with police officers by their sides, waiting to bag unsuspecting skiers. When Air Forcer Rick Hunt got caught out of bounds by one of these headstrong patrollers, he was asked to turn over more than just his ski pass. "After he chewed my ass and took my pass, he had the gall to say, 'Okay, who's holding? Let's get stoned,'" Hunt remembered. "He wanted me to break out my weed and get him high."

Beyond revoking a skier's season pass, the ski patrol also had the power to banish someone off the mountain indefinitely. "We had repeat violators, year in and year out," explained Corky Ward. "If you were caught three times, the ski corporation had the option of denying you ski privileges, not only for that year, but for the proceeding three years." These repeat violators were blackballed and prevented from buying a ski pass for extended periods of time, which, for someone whose life revolved around skiing in Jackson Hole, felt like a death sentence.

The Air Force didn't take the fight lying down. The backcountry was national forest, they argued, and what authority did the ski patrol have to tell them they couldn't access public land? To make their point abundantly clear, Wilson and some Air Forcers plucked a number of closed area signs off the mountain. The following day, Wilson burst through the doors of the ski patrol's annual Swinehearts and Sweathogs fundraiser event dressed as the grim reaper and carrying a miniature coffin over his shoulder. "All the ski patrolmen were hanging around this pool table," Wilson remembered. "I walked over and yelled, 'Hey guys, here's a history lesson for you.'" He slammed the coffin down on the pool table, causing the lid to flip open. Mortified members of the ski patrol looked down into the casket to find their orange closed-area signs lying there like a corpse. This meant war.

Of all the members of the Jackson Hole Air Force, no one had a bigger target on his back than Coombs. "Doug was among the best at ducking the ropes," said one member of the Air Force. "If there was ever a prize for being able to ski under a rope at high speed, Coombs would definitely be the winner." Coombs violated the boundaries on a daily basis, and although he was caught several times, he always managed to ski away with just a slap on the wrist. His Steep Skiing Camps were generating tens of thousands of dollars for the resort each year, and Coombs himself had become a key component to the resort's marketing strategy—a Jackson Hole icon. Flocks of people followed him around the mountain looking for a chance to make turns with the extreme skiing champion who had honed his skills in the last of the old West.

"He was an ambassador," said Connie Kemmerer, one of the owners of Jackson Hole Mountain Resort. "He loved the resort. He talked it up. He was passionate. He was friendly. He was engaging. He was knowledgeable. He didn't judge people. He was just a perfect representative of Jackson Hole." Given Coombs's friendship with the ownership, most members of the ski patrol were content to look the other way when catching Coombs out of bounds. Moreover, Coombs counted the majority of them as personal friends.

But some of the older generation of the ski patrol was not so lenient on him. They looked at Coombs as a direct challenge to their authority. His carefree attitude came off as arrogance to them, and as long as he was on the mountain, violating the boundaries, they felt they would never receive the respect they thought they rightfully deserved. "The older guys had a chip on their shoulder," described Porter Fox. "If they could bust Doug Coombs, it would serve as a lesson to everybody else that they were in charge and you don't break their rules or you're getting booted." Coombs became public enemy number one in Jackson Hole, caught firmly in the crosshairs of the old guard. A handful of patrollers were gunning for him, but nobody more than Dr. No.

16

DR. NO

Jackson Hole, Wyoming, 1997

On January 22, 1997, Doug and Emily Coombs were celebrating their fourth wedding anniversary. It was a deep powder day in the middle of what was shaping up to be an epic ski season. Two hundred twenty-five inches of snow fell in the month of December alone—the most monthly snowfall ever recorded in Rendezvous Bowl—and skiers were calling it the winter of "1996/ninety-*heaven*." Adding to the year's mystique was the fact that Jackson Hole Mountain Resort was celebrating its own anniversary: it had been thirty years since Paul McCollister's tram carried its first paying passengers to the top of Rendezvous Mountain, and now his vision of Jackson Hole Mountain Resort as international ski destination was solidly confirmed. As an ambassador, Coombs was helping herald a new era for the resort.

Coombs spent that afternoon skiing with Emily and another pro skier they had met during the second World Extreme Skiing Championship in Valdez named Dean Conway. Coombs led them to the Cirque, a steep powder field inbounds that ran down to an intermediate cat track below. Emily skied the gut of the Cirque, while Coombs and Conway traversed high to the far skier's left to a run called Pair-a-Chutes and its far skier's left side, where exposed rocks would normally force them back in toward the Cirque. But the snow had filled in the rocks, allowing them to push farther across the rocky ridge toward a closed area. They skied down the ridge, ten feet from a closed-area sign. When they reached the cat track at the bottom, somebody was there waiting for them: Dr. No.

Dr. No was a member of the ski patrol's old guard. He was one of the first responders to the avalanche that killed Paul Driscoll in 1985 and took to enforcing the law of the land with unwavering sternness. Back in the seventies and early eighties, skiers needed permission from the ski patrol to access certain parts of the mountain. Dr. No became legendary for denying every request, thus earning himself the nickname. "He was one of those guys that had a Napoleon complex," said Wilson. "He was short and squat but was always trying to be the big man on campus." Dr. No had already caught Coombs out of bounds two times that season. Many believed he had it out for the famous skier and wanted to catch Coombs in a situation that the resort couldn't turn a blind eye to. Dr. No wanted Coombs gone.

When he spotted Coombs skiing down the ridge, the patroller claimed that Coombs had blatantly violated a closed-area sign and skied out of bounds. "The whole thing could have been resolved," Coombs told the *Jackson Hole News* later that week, if Dr. No had skied the run in question with him. "But all he could do was yell at me in four letter words and tell me I was going to jail." Dr. No demanded Coombs's ski pass. The situation escalated quickly from there.

"It was my day off," recalled Corky Ward. "I got called from Jim Gill, the mountain manager. He said, 'Hey, you have to come in, one of your patrolmen just caught Doug Coombs skiing in a closed area within the ski area.' And oh shit, here we go." Corky Ward drove in and met with Dr. No and Gill. An hour and a half after the incident, Ward went up to the run in question and looked for Coombs's ski tracks. He agreed with Dr. No that Coombs had violated the boundaries and his season pass should be revoked.

In meetings with the Jackson Hole Mountain Resort Corporation, Ward demanded that if other skiers were going to be kicked out of the ski area for violating the boundaries, then Coombs had to be held to the same standard. Coombs vehemently pleaded that he had never violated the boundaries or ignored any closed-area signs. He insisted that there was no sign where he skied and that the section in question was a "gray area," which was made all the grayer by the season's unusually deep snow. "I wasn't trying to be malicious or look for powder; the whole mountain was untracked that day," Coombs told the *Jackson Hole News*, adding that after the last time he'd been caught, "I made an oath that I would not cross any ski boundaries. And I haven't."

The proof should have been in the snow, where Coombs's tracks couldn't lie. Corky Ward, after he had surveyed the area, claimed that Coombs had skied within eighteen inches of a closed-area sign. "In my opinion, he intentionally skied out of bounds," Ward told the *Jackson Hole News*. "He knows our sign placement better than we do." Jim Gill also canvassed the area the following day, but sixteen inches of snow had fallen overnight, effectively covering any tracks. He had to go on his head patroller's word.

The situation became increasingly confusing and tense when news leaked that the patrol had actually moved the closed-area signs inward after the incident. "By moving the sign the next day, they admitted their guilt," Coombs insisted to the *Jackson Hole News*. "You are admitting that the sign wasn't in the right place." According to Porter Fox, who diligently reported the incident for the newspaper, Gill first denied that the signs had been moved, before recanting and saying that they had been moved, all in the same interview. "He gave me two totally different versions of what happened in the same phone call," Fox recalled decades later. "So there was confusion on their end." Fox went on to explain that "in those days it was a lot of times the Jackson Hole ski corp versus the ski bums of Jackson Hole. I won't say it was antilocal sentiment, but it was a very insecure place the Jackson Hole ski corp was coming from in regard to policy. Very reactionary. Very drastic."

Opinions within the Jackson Hole Ski Patrol and the Jackson Hole Ski Corp ran the spectrum. Many patrollers were good friends with Coombs and believed he should be given leniency. But Corky Ward held his ground. "We have extended more privileges to Doug than anybody on the mountain, but he continually gets into some kind of trouble," he told the *Jackson Hole News*. "He continues to ski into our hands. We are not looking for him. We are not waiting for him."

Despite Corky Ward's insistence that this was entirely business and not personal, many in the community believed that the situation was ego driven. Coombs was arguably the best skier on the mountain. For some self-righteous patrollers, Coombs's very existence stuck in their craws. "I think they got a little bit worked because he was so impossibly good," Air Force cofounder Howie Henderson said later in the TGR documentary *Swift. Silent. Deep.* "He had so much bravado and so much force of personality. He truly was like a rock star. He was like Ziggy Stardust. It just came off him in waves. And you'd be like, 'Who is that guy? Jesus!' Most of us said, 'Damn, I want to try and be like Dougie.' Some people said, 'You know, that Coombs guy kind of pisses me off.' And unfortunately some of the ski patrol fell into that category."

Whatever the motivation, the verdict was handed down from the corporation: Doug Coombs was to be banished from Jackson Hole Mountain Resort for the rest of the season, as well as all of the following year. He was allowed a special ski pass to conduct his last two Steep Camps that season, but thereafter he was forbidden to set foot on the mountain. "Doug had to be held to the same standards," insisted Corky Ward. "We had to be consistent. Otherwise I couldn't enforce it to anybody. He couldn't live outside the standards of everyone else, even though he was a close friend to the owners."

Ever since she had attended her first steep camp with Coombs, Connie Kemmerer had been good friends with the Coombses, both "on snow and off," as she put it. In fact, Kemmerer herself had once been scolded by the patrol for skiing a closed area with Coombs. Now she was thrown into a conflicting position. "I was devastated by the event," Kemmerer recalled. "For some reason I wasn't right on hand, and I wasn't there to stop it. I really feel that I would have wanted to express a voice that might have stopped it, but I couldn't. And as part of the leadership of the resort, it would have been really awkward at that time to take a stand against the mountain manager and the patrol that made the decision. It was a tough one. It divided the company and the resort." Kemmerer shared the view of most of the Jackson Hole community, which saw Coombs as the future of skiing and the future of their mountain community. In her eyes, Coombs epitomized everything it was to ski and live in Jackson Hole.

The news of Coombs's banishment hit the ski world like an atomic bomb. "Oh my God, it was one of the biggest scandals ever," remarked Casimiro. "It was huge. Doug was beloved. Outside of Jackson, the reaction was just outrage. Just outrage." Local skiers were furious too. Howie Henderson stormed into the corporation's office and pleaded with them: "This guy represents everything that's about to happen in skiing; don't you see that?" A chain reaction ensued. In a show of defiance and solidarity, the Jackson Hole Air Force began flagrantly breaking the boundaries with full force. "Once that happened, all bets were off," said Rick Hunt. "We did whatever the hell we wanted. We didn't give a rat's ass. We poached even more just to put it in front of their faces."

Meanwhile, Coombs and Emily were shocked and devastated. "Doug was like a trophy hunt for them," Emily said. "They finally got their trophy. They got the bad guy." Doug and Emily's world had been flipped completely upside down. "The thing that is sad for Emily and me is we have to move out of the community, leave our friends, cancel our livelihood, and stop using this place as a headquarters," Coombs told the *Jackson Hole News* after being banished. "We were planning to live the rest of our lives here."

Behind closed doors, the reprimand handed down by the Jackson Hole Mountain Resort Corporation was far worse. According to Emily, not only was the corporation banishing Coombs from the mountain and cutting off a critical source of his family's income, but they also demanded that he pay back the $20,000 they gave him for serving as a resort ambassador, the sum of which the Coombses had used as a down payment on their condo two years earlier. "I've never seen anything like it," said Porter Fox. "I really haven't seen an administration make a move like this against an entire family." A legal dispute ensued. Eventually Coombs's lawyer won the battle over the $20,000, and the resort conceded, allowing them keep the money and their condo. But Coombs's banishment from Jackson Hole would stand.

Coombs didn't know what to do. Even though Jackson Hole Mountain Resort was going to continue to run his Steep Skiing Camps in his absence, he and Emily wouldn't see a cent of the money brought in. While they were still spending their spring seasons in Valdez and Valdez Heli-Ski Guides was earning them a modest income, it was not enough to support them year round. More significantly for Coombs, who cared less about money than skiing, he had lost the mountain he loved so dearly. Since arriving in 1984, Coombs had given so much to Jackson Hole, and now it had completely turned its back on him. He felt betrayed.

Scrambling to figure out what to do next, Coombs received a call from the president of Marmot. John Cooley had just returned from a trip to Europe, where he had discovered an unknown skiing village hidden in the French Alps. When he heard about Coombs's banishment from Jackson Hole, he called up the star skier. "Doug," he said. "Forget about Jackson Hole. Have you ever heard of La Grave?"

17

STEPPING INTO LA GRAVE

La Grave, France, 2014

I woke up on the morning of my flight to France filled with an all-consuming sense of dread. I had spent months thinking about this trip to La Grave, and now with my flight finally here, the realities were sinking in. There was a laundry list of things for me to do to prepare for my departure later that day, but instead I sat in my kitchen, drinking cold coffee in my underwear, and reading about tragedy in La Grave.

"Skiing Beyond Safety's Edge Once Too Often" read the headline in the *New York Times* article that described Coombs's death in April 2006. "Mr. Coombs slipped off a cliff and fell 490 feet to his death," reported Nathaniel Vinton. "He was forty-eight. He was trying to rescue Chad VanderHam, his thirty-one-year-old protégé and skiing partner from the United States." I'd been putting off this part of my research for months—much like when you're rewatching a movie and you already know the ending, but somehow hope it's going to change. Of course, the facts remained the same: after decades of outrunning avalanches and dancing around crevasses, Coombs died the one way no one would have ever predicted. The man who never fell finally did in

La Grave's Polichinelle Couloir. I was now headed to that quiet French village to get to the bottom of what exactly happened on that fateful run.

As I poured through accident reports and news clippings, I came across another piece entitled "A Ski Mountaineer and a History of Tragedy," written by Nick Paumgarten for the *New Yorker*. One line jumped off the page and grabbed me by the back of my eyeballs. It was a quote from Bruce Tremper. "People get in trouble by trying to be their hero," Tremper said. "Because they don't have his talent or experience. Life gives us cheap lessons sometimes." I read the quote and paused.

At the root of my quest to understand Coombs's life was this idea of pursuing heroes. Coombs idolized Patrick Vallençant and went all the way to France to ski with him. Similarly, Chad VanderHam idolized Coombs and followed him to France. Now, as I prepared to follow Coombs's tracks to France and spend the winter in the mountains that claimed all three of the men's lives, I had to ask myself: Was I trying to be like my hero?

TWO PLANES, TWO BUSES, AND one night sleeping on the floor of Heathrow Airport delivered me to the sleepy streets of La Grave, France. The bus from Grenoble had taken me 169 kilometers west through the imposing Romanche Valley, where sheer cliffs plummeted off the roadside and tunnels were cut into the mountains like something out of a fairytale. Although my face was pressed up against the glass the whole ride, the bus very nearly passed through the tiny village of La Grave without my noticing. I had to shout for the driver to stop.

Stepping down from the bus, I had no choice but to just gawk at it: La Meije. The mountain monopolized the sky. Every point seemed to give way to another point; the whole massif looked like a tall wave of broken glass cresting over me. Snow clung to some aspects of the summit, but mostly the peak was ragged and exposed. Below it, glaciers beamed sapphire blue, and there were black crevasses between them. A long, grim cloud lingered across its face, and the rock looked foreboding even backlit by the sun. Some mountains on my journey had inspired awe. Others respect. La Meije instantly filled me with raw fear.

I forced my gaze back down to the miniature town, mainly to compose myself. One partially plowed street meandered between stone buildings out of another century. I watched as a slab of snow slid lazily down one of the tin roofs. Every storefront was dark and shuttered. There wasn't a person in sight. The only movement in the scene came from directly behind the town, where a small group of gondolas ascended painfully slowly up a ridiculous cliff. Following the cable higher and higher with my eyes, I got my first glimpse of the ski area, which looked entirely unskiable. Every stretch of snow appeared to end in a cliff, or a crevasse, or dense trees, or a ravine, or some other hazard that would surely result in injury or death.

Just as I was taking all this in, a tiny black helicopter pounded across the horizon in front of me. It banked around La Meije and then swooped down into the ski area and fell out of view behind one of the peaks. A few moments later, the chopper hovered straight up and then buzzed back from whence it came. *Heli-skiing is banned in France,* I thought. *So what was that?* Then it dawned on me: I'd just witnessed a rescue.

I balled up a handful of snow and squeezed it tightly in my fists, allowing the cold to sink in and letting the water run down into my shirtsleeves. I lobbed the snowball weakly to the sky, watching it arc before breaking against the pavement. I then asked myself the question that had risen again and again on almost every stop of this adventure: "What the hell am I doing here?"

THE STONE TOWN OF LA GRAVE was built on a foothill, a couple of kilometers above which were a series of even smaller villages wedged into the mountainside like tiny toeholds. With Emily's help, one of Coombs's old friends had arranged for me to stay in a small chalet in the village of Les Terrasses, the closest of the three villages above La Grave, where the

Coombses had lived. There was just one problem: I had no idea how I was going to get up there from where I was standing. With two big bags, two pairs of skis, boots, poles, and other miscellaneous luggage, there was no way I could hike up there by nightfall, and the chances of hailing a cab in this one-road town were even less likely—that's to say, impossible. So I stuck out my thumb and hoped someone would pick me up. As an American, hitchhiking in a foreign country felt as natural as walking down the street naked, but I was out of options.

Two hours passed but no one stopped. Each car sputtered by without giving me much more than a nod through the window. It wasn't that they didn't want to give me a ride, I decided, but rather my heap of luggage simply wouldn't fit in the trunks of these European compacts buzzing by with chains on their tires. As snow began to fall and darkness seeped into the sky like spilled ink, a young lady from the small tourist office, who was locking up for the day, took pity on me. We stuffed my bags into her coupe and motored our way up the steep switchbacks to Les Terrasses.

Her English was choppy but fluent compared to my French, which consisted mostly of butchered attempts at the requisite *oui*, *merci*, *bonjour*, and *voilà*. I asked her about the helicopter I had seen earlier in the day. "Was that a rescue?"

"Probably," she responded without taking her eyes off the road. "There are rescues here all the time. Helicopter is the only way to be taken off the mountain."

Oh, c'est la vie.

Ten minutes later, I stood on the side of a snow-caked road in the village of Les Terrasses. Big, fat snowflakes fell from the darkness, catching the rays of a lonely streetlight that turned them golden yellow before they hit the ground. The silence was heavy. If La Grave seemed old, Les Terrasses felt biblical. Even in the darkness, I could see that the buildings' ornate masonry harked back centuries. Built on the hillside, the stone structures leaned into one another, as if they had shifted over millennia along with the earth's tectonic plates. The woman at the tourist office let me out in front of the village's church, which had a small but magnificent bell tower and adjoining portico.

The only bit of directions Emily's friend had given me to find my apartment was "150 paces up from the church." No house number. No landmarks. I stowed my bags in what looked to be an old horse corral and set off in search of my lodgings. As I trudged up a snowy alleyway between the buildings, chickens and goats and cows called out from the shadows. The air smelled sweetly of burning wood and manure.

Despite searching for an apartment in the dark, in a foreign land, in a snowstorm growing more and more intense, I was completely at peace. There was a charming, old-world tranquility to Les Terrasses that made me feel like everything would eventually work itself out. There were only thirty or so houses in this tiny village—I'd eventually find mine. This was my first glimpse of Doug Coombs's private life in France. He and Emily had lived in one of these stone buildings. I remembered the picture she had shown me of her husband holding up their son on their apartment's terrace. The boy had his fist raised to the sky Superman style, and Coombs beamed his big, toothy grin. It was one of the last photos she ever took of him.

Through the curtain of falling snow, I spotted a small note stuck to one of the apartment doors. Sure enough, my name was scrawled on it in neat cursive. An old skeleton key hung out from the lock. Elated, I bounded back to my bags and schlepped them one by one up to the apartment. I pushed open the door to behold a perfectly quaint living quarters. The studio couldn't have been more than fifty square feet, combining bedroom, kitchen, and living room in one area, but the space possessed all the delightful details I could ever have hoped for in a French chalet. Three picture windows dressed in lace curtains looked directly out to La Meije, which now glowed blue in the moonlight. The church bell tolled dully outside. The snow continued to fall. I was here. Man, oh man, was I here.

18

BACK TO THE ROOTS

La Grave, France, 1997

When Pelle Lång first arrived in the village of La Grave in the winter of 1986, it was a ghost town. All the shop windows were shuttered and people were scarce. A former sniper in the Swedish military, Lång had spent the last six years whittling out a modest career as a ski model in Chamonix, France. He appeared in ski magazines and competed in contests, but besides earning some free skis and the local prestige of being a professional skier, Lång's sponsorships didn't earn him much of a living; he spent his summers and falls working as an electrician. During his first winter in Chamonix, he slept in a camper van in the parking lot.

Much like Coombs, Lång idolized the legendary extreme skier Patrick Vallençant, and also like Coombs, Lång had the serendipitous fortune of meeting his hero while in Chamonix. It was during this chance encounter that Lång learned of an obscure village 247 kilometers from Vallençant's birthplace of Lyon. "He told me about La Grave," Lång remembered. "He told me that there was this small village with a big lift. It was like Argentière, but nobody was skiing there."

La Grave was a farming village of fewer than five hundred people; its stone buildings had been built in the twelfth century. By the end of the nineteenth century, La Grave had emerged as an epicenter of alpinism that rivaled Chamonix. The road between France and Italy passed right through the town, making the village rich with travelers and alpinists looking to hike and climb the surrounding Alps in the summertime, most notably La Meije.

Tearing 13,068 feet into the sky, the north-facing massif of La Meije was as ferocious a mountain as Pelle Lång had ever set his eyes upon. Although it had been summited in 1877, La Meije looked completely unwelcoming to human life. Steep, exposed granite jutted violently from the snow, and glaciers and icefall were strewn all over the face. Nothing about La Meije indicated that La Grave was a ski area. Even on the sunniest of days, the mountain cast a long, foreboding shadow over the village that was palpable. The only part of the mountain that betrayed its wild mystique was a cable car running precariously up the side of it.

The *téléphérique* was installed in 1976 to ferry hikers up to the glaciers in the summer months. The two-stage gondola was never intended for skiers, but when Lång arrived to town, the lift was being operated during the winter for two runs a day exclusively on the weekends. "The first season, there was never more than a handful of people skiing there," Lång remembered. "There were times you were skiing there and you'd be happy to see someone." Due to this infinitesimal amount of business, the téléphérique went bankrupt by the end of the ski season in 1986. It was then leased back to the engineer who originally designed it, but he shut it down for two years.

Despite its early reputation among many serious alpinists, La Grave was a far cry from Chamonix when it came to being a skiing attraction. By the late eighties, Chamonix was a full-fledged international ski destination, complete with glitzy après bars, posh accommodations, and thousands of skiers visiting each winter from around the world. Meanwhile, La Grave had ski terrain similar to Chamonix but not a fraction of the crowds. Lång recognized a business opportunity, and that's when fate swept in.

In 1988, after competing in a mogul competition on a mountain near La Grave, he heard rumors that the engineer was going to reopen the téléphérique. Back in Chamonix, Lång bumped into a fellow ski bum, a Brit named Les Harlow, who just so happened to be considering buying an old hotel in La Grave. He asked Lång if he was interested in becoming his business partner. The next day, they drove to La Grave and discussed the venture over a few bottles of wine. By that summer, the two had opened the hotel, La Chaumine.

In an effort to attract more winter business, Lång petitioned the operator of the téléphérique to run the lift starting a month earlier, but still La Grave remained largely a ghost town. "There was no gas station open. They were closing down the schools. You really couldn't get any bread. The supermarkets were closed. It was only Hotel Edelweiss and us that were open," Lång recalled. "I knew that the business would take off sooner or later. I thought it would take off after five years, but I spent ten years there, and I didn't make any money at all. But at that time it was not about the money. It was an alternative life. Not having to go back to industrial work was a dream."

While Lång's business barely made him enough money to pay for gas to get back to Sweden each summer, his life as a professional skier took off in La Grave. Much like Coombs in Alaska around the same time, the early nineties, Lång became legendary for pioneering first descents in La Grave's surrounding mountains. By 1996, he was an internationally certified mountain guide and began leading others to his secret stashes in the shadow of La Meije. From the top lift station, he accessed glaciers, couloirs, and over seven thousand vertical feet of completely unchartered, often terrifying terrain. La Grave had every imaginable danger—crevasses, avalanches, cliffs, icefall, exposed rocks, tight trees, unpredictable weather—immediately accessible from the lift.

Another defining feature of La Grave was the variability of the snow from season to season, month to month, and elevation to elevation. Some seasons the snow came in deep and stable, while other seasons, the snowpack could be thin or muddled by rain that left sheets of deadly, slide-for-life ice in its wake. If a skier lost an edge in those conditions, he wouldn't stop until he reached the bottom, fell off a cliff, or hit a rock or tree. Because the mountain was so massive, this variation in the snow quality could manifest itself at different elevations from top to bottom. The top might have deep powder while the lower elevations could have bulletproof ice. With all these factors working in unison on many runs, La Grave required flawless skiing.

By the midnineties, La Grave began creeping out of obscurity. Lång and a group of skiers produced a series of films that started grabbing the attention of other pro skiers who were looking for an alternative to Chamonix. Ski magazines soon followed, along with ski companies. "In the middle of November in 1996, the marketing from all over the world came here," Lång said. But the biggest game changer was yet to come. The following year, John Cooley of Marmot came to La Grave. He took one look at the terrain, the no-nonsense atmosphere, and turned to Lång and said that he knew the perfect guy to help him put La Grave on the map.

"I GRAVITATED TO LA GRAVE because everyone said it was the last frontier of wild skiing," Coombs said after he and Emily moved there in November of 1997. "It's *ski sauvage*, as they say. You can easily get off the lift here and get in the most amazing, dangerous situations of your life. You can go from sipping a nice café au lait to almost killing yourself in five minutes. It's like no other, no other. I love it." In La Grave, Coombs found another Valdez, an obscure village nestled in wild mountains that were just begging for him to explore.

Having been banished from Jackson Hole Mountain Resort for violating its boundaries earlier that year, Coombs now planned to spend his winters in La Grave, where there were no boundaries. In fact, there were no ropes or signs at all. There wasn't even a ski patrol. Coombs had complete and utter freedom. He found skiing in its purest form, stripped down to its alpinist roots, away from movie cameras, big business ski corporations, helicopters, contests, and fame. Off the mountain, the low-key, old-world attitude of La Grave suited the Coombses perfectly. Back in Jackson Hole, Coombs had been a superstar, trailed around by fans and admirers. His fame had also drawn the ire of others, like the members of the ski patrol who got him kicked out of Jackson Hole. "Over there in La Grave, nobody cared about that stuff. In fact, it was almost taboo. They would tease him, like 'Oh, *Doog* the legend . . .'" Emily said. "Nobody cares who's who. If you were a good skier, so what? Everybody from Sweden and France is a good skier. It was just refreshing to ski with people and then not talk about it afterward. There was a different conversation. More soulful."

Coombs could be just another skier in La Grave. He could go back to being that kid from Bedford who loved nothing more than exploring the mountains and playing in the snow. "People here, they slow down. They slow down for life," Coombs said. "Sometimes in the States, people don't slow down. Life goes by them too fast. I love France. I love the food. I love the mountains. I love the people. I love the attitude—the c'est la vie attitude." Coombs took to learning French and read the French newspaper every morning, even if he didn't know most of the words.

From a business standpoint, La Grave was perfectly suited for the Coombs's steep camps for one very obvious reason: it was extremely steep. "We're talking about 2,500 meters of vertical, starting at 3,600," explained Per Ås, a Swede who came to La Grave shortly after Lång and later served as one of Coombs's steep camps guides. "Everything is steep compared to most resorts. Basically from top to bottom it's a steep-ski mountain, technical with all the different rope work."

In La Grave, Coombs's clients could learn ski mountaineering techniques. They could strap on harnesses and rappel into couloirs. They could ski over glaciers where layers of deep snow bridged the gaps of yawning crevasses. They could navigate around sheer cliffs and tour through valleys miles away from civilization. Coombs developed an outing called "couloirs to bars," in which the clients would ski down from La Grave to another tiny French village for a beer.

Of course, all these wild and exciting experiences required assuming a tremendous amount of risk as a guide. In La Grave "the challenge of a guide is timing and bringing the right people to the right places," said Per Ås. "It can very fast become a disaster if you make mistakes. It's so easy to bring people on the wrong day to the wrong run."

Beyond La Grave's inherent dangers, there were some logistical hurdles in bringing their Steep Skiing Camps to Europe. Coombs wasn't legally allowed to guide in France at all. Just as during Patrick Vallençant's time, becoming a certified mountain guide in France required being a master of all things mountains, not just in skiing, but also climbing and alpinism. More specifically, Coombs needed to get his International Federation of Mountain Guides Associations (IFMGA) certification, an intense and costly licensing process that required weeks of class time, rigorous examinations, and years to complete. "When you're an international guide in Europe, you're like this god walking around," Coombs said. "They see your little badge and they know what you went through to get it. A million other people tried to do what you did, but so many people fail."

The IFMGA certification was the equivalent of getting a Ph.D. in mountaineering. Over his fifteen years of guiding in Jackson Hole and Alaska, Coombs had a 100 percent safety rating, had performed numerous rescues, and had actually developed some of the protocols that were now standards of American guiding, but it was all for naught when he came to La Grave. In the eyes of the IFMGA, Coombs was just another good skier.

Unlike the boundaries in Jackson Hole, Coombs respected the law of the land in La Grave. He vowed not to guide without his IFMGA certification. In the meantime, he and Emily would run their Steep Skiing Camps by hiring local certified guides like Pelle Lång, Xavier Cret, and Per Ås. "He was very clear from the start that he was not guiding; he was coaching," said Per Ås. "That was good for the local guide scene; we appreciated that."

As might be expected of a hardcore ski community in France, breaking into the tight-knit, sometimes-standoffish guiding circle in La Grave could have been harder than navigating some of its ski runs. "In France, sometimes we worry about when people arrive," said Xavier Cret, who grew up in La Grave and later became one of Coombs's most trusted ski partners. "But Doug was rapidly appreciated for his courage and his love of skiing. He became a legend in La Grave." Pelle Lång agreed: "Doug had all this charisma as a person. He was funny. He couldn't piss off people. He could make a fool of himself and laugh about it. It wasn't about prestige for him."

More importantly, Coombs wasn't stealing business from the local guiding community but was rather connecting these guides with new paying clients. He wasn't coming to town and using their mountains to make money; he was injecting money into La Grave. "In Europe he wasn't a big name; he was just a very keen skier," explained Per Ås. "For the local guides, he was just someone bringing clients to do his camps, and he was coaching." The respect Coombs exhibited for the local guiding community won him quick friends. Soon skiers who had followed him from Jackson Hole to Alaska over the years were now booking rooms in Lång's hotel and buying lift tickets at the téléphérique. Much like he had been doing in Valdez for nearly a decade, Coombs was putting La Grave on the map. A new door was opening in his life as a skier, just as another was about to slam shut.

19

BURIED ALIVE

Valdez, Alaska, 1999–2000

There was blood and hair stuck to the ice. *Well, this is where his head hit,* Mike Fischer thought to himself as he rappeled deeper into the crevasse. Surrounded by blue ice with nothing but darkness below him, Fischer thought this place felt haunted. Crevasses were not meant for human life. Doug Coombs, Dave Miller, Jeff Zell, and Jim Conway were looking down from the ceiling of the crevasse. Forty feet down, Fischer spotted the body of the snowboarder lying on a ledge and covered in snow. The victim's skull had been crushed by the fall, and there was a gaping hole in the back of his head. He was clearly dead.

An hour earlier, this snowboarder had been very much alive, riding down through the powder on a run called School Bus when he cranked a turn over an indentation in the snow, completely oblivious that the snow was covering a crevasse. He was not a client of Valdez Heli-Ski Guides but rather was riding without a guide; when he fell in, his head slammed against the ice wall, killing him instantly. Minutes later, when the snowboarder's friend ran frantically into VHSG's trailer on the airstrip, screaming for help, Coombs and his team shot into rescue mode.

Fischer began by clearing the snow off the body and then yelled for Coombs to lower down a rope so that they could pull him out. It took a half hour to get the body out from the crevasse, after which they wrapped him up in a tarp and skied down to Richardson Highway. An ambulance and a state trooper were waiting at the airstrip to meet them. The ambulance took the body away, and then the state trooper approached the five skiers.

"Who made the rescue?" he asked.

Fischer raised his hand.

The next thing the state trooper said would stick with Mike Fischer for the next twenty years. "Why did you do that?"

"Do what?" Fischer responded.

"Why did you rescue him?" he said. "We have lots of people fall in crevasses in the greater Anchorage area, but we never bother to go get them. There's probably dozens and dozens of snowmobilers that have spent eternity at the bottom of a crevasse, and nobody is ever going to go get them."

The fatality on School Bus illustrated not only the imperative need to ski with guides in the Chugach, but also the need for search and rescue. As more inexperienced people found their way up to Thompson Pass to ski without guides, more accidents happened. Coombs and his VHSG team soon found themselves responding to emergencies in the mountains like an ad hoc search-and-rescue outfit. They plucked a number of skiers out of crevasses and became a source of information for snow stability and avalanche cycles. During the off-season, Coombs and Emily trained their guides in crevasse rescue on Mount Hood in Oregon. "We were basically 911 up there," said Miller, "because we were the only ones that had the skills."

Keeping people alive was the central mission of VHSG, but this became increasingly difficult as the operation grew to three helicopters, fifteen guides, and well over a hundred clients per season. Being responsible for people's lives weighed heavily on them. With all this risk spread out over the treacherous Chugach Mountains, Coombs and Emily feared that the odds would eventually catch up with them. They saw a fatality on the horizon.

Since arriving in Valdez at the beginning of the decade, Coombs and his crew had been blessed with an incredibly stable snowpack. Unlike the Ridge of Bridger Bowl or the backcountry of Jackson Hole, which were riddled with the ever-looming threat of avalanches due to their finicky intermountain snowpacks, the snow in the Chugach initially appeared to possess the same degree of stability that skiers enjoyed in the Sierra—heavy, coastal snow that stuck to the slopes. But nothing could have been further from the truth.

"The first three years, it was so ridiculously stable," said Conway. "We'd talk about how stable the snowpack was, and some of the old-timers would just shake their heads and laugh at us. 'Yeah, guys, you just wait, you'll see.'" The reality was that the Chugach was the ultimate laboratory for studying avalanches. As the warm Gulf of Alaska and the frigid Alaskan interior pushed back and forth against each other, the Chugach, sandwiched between them, experienced a dynamic snowpack. Storms from the Gulf of Alaska buried the Chugach in heavy, wet snow that, generally speaking, created a more stable maritime snowpack. But storms from the Alaskan interior brought Arctic, high-pressure cold that resulted in a more continental snowpack, which is significantly less stable. Depending on how these two weather systems rolled in, and depending on how these two different types of snow stacked up, the stability in the Chugach could range from being either bombproof or violently avalanche prone. The winter of 2000 was a horrific case of the latter.

Coombs brought in Mark Newcomb from Jackson Hole to serve as his avalanche forecaster that year. Although Newcomb had only a few years of avalanche forecasting in the Tetons and brief stints in the Colorado Rockies and Utah's Wasatch Range under his belt, snow science was in his blood. Newcomb's father, Rod Newcomb, founded the American Avalanche Institute in the midseventies and once served as the avalanche forecaster for Jackson Hole Mountain Resort. While most kids talked sports around the dinner table, Newcomb and his father discussed slabs, surface hoar, and avalanche trigger points. During the spring of 2000 in Valdez, he had plenty of avalanche case studies to learn from.

"We had two layers of surface hoar that formed in late February and early March, and as the season went by, that got buried with more and more snow," Newcomb explained. Surface hoar is a highly unstable layer of snow, similar to frost, that forms on the surface during frigid Arctic nights. When heavy snow falls on top of surface hoar, it prevents the layers from bonding.

In the early weeks of the season, Coombs and his guides mitigated the avalanche risk by ski-cutting the slopes, essentially making a hard turn to intentionally trigger an avalanche, but as more snow fell on top of those two weak layers, controlling the avalanche risk became impossible. "The nature of those kinds of weak layers is that you might have two or three skiers ski the slope and not trigger an avalanche, but then the fourth or fifth skier will," Newcomb said. "Even if you thought you could trigger an avalanche on your own, you didn't know if it was going to release above you."

The best way to deal with these extreme avalanche conditions was to ski lower-angle slopes where the risk of sliding was less. Coombs and his team resorted to doing this, but soon they ran out of terrain for their many clients to ski. VHSG had grown so popular that they were guiding up to thirty clients a week. After about a half day of skiing lower-angle slopes with four or five groups, the powder runs were entirely chewed up. Clients were coming from around the world and paying thousands of dollars to ski Alaska's legendary steeps and deep powder, and of course, Coombs wanted to deliver. "We were working as hard as we could to find safer slopes where this combination of weak layers didn't exist," Newcomb explained. "We found one zone known as the Cauliflowers that had good skiing, but then weather prevented us from returning." With more clients on the way and the avalanche risk growing more extreme, things were shaping up for a perfect storm.

"We had guides trigger huge avalanches that fractured maybe almost a mile wide in some instances," described Newcomb. "We had instances of remote triggers where a helicopter would land and slopes a quarter mile away would avalanche." Avalanches were breaking naturally not just on the steeps, but also on low-angle slopes that were typically stable and safe. It was only a matter of time until skiers started getting caught in these furious monsters.

The first accident had come earlier in the season, when a guide named Greg Miles was caught in an avalanche that snapped his femur. Then Coombs was skiing with a film crew on a run known as Butterfly when the slope fractured a meter deep. Miraculously, he was able to ski out of it safely. One of Coombs's guides from Jackson Hole, Theo Meiners, was skiing with a private group when he triggered a massive slide that very nearly buried him. He was able to grab onto a bush before it dragged him under. "It got to the point that rather than have your avalanche shovel in your pack, you just started having it sitting on the floor of the helicopter," said Newcomb, "so you could jump out faster to get to your buddy and dig him out." Soon nearly every guide in the entire operation had experienced his own brush with death. "We had five employees get hurt to the point where we could no longer work," said Emily. "We then had to hire some new guides." It all came to a head on a fateful day in April.

Hans Saari was a Bozeman native and Yale graduate who started guiding with Coombs in Alaska in the midnineties. On this particular day in 2000, Saari was guiding two clients along with a tail guide on the last run of the day. One of the clients was in Valdez to compete at that season's World Extreme Skiing Championship, which was to be held the following week. Saari skied down and stopped on a raised point on the slope that he considered an island of safety. The second skier followed him down and met him there. When the third skier pushed off, he triggered a gigantic slab avalanche that rushed right over that island of safety and buried Saari and the client. The third skier was able to safely outrun the slide. When the snow settled, the tail guide went into rescue mode, but when he started skiing down, he ended up triggering a second avalanche. Amazingly, this second avalanche launched the buried client off a small cliff, bringing him to the surface, while Hans Saari remained deeply buried.

Word of the slide immediately shot over the radio frequency. Coombs and Emily were far away skiing in another zone with a group of clients. All they could do was listen helplessly as first responders frantically said they couldn't locate Hans Saari. They didn't know if he was dead or alive. Then another voice came on the radio—it was Hans Saari. He'd been buried with a big air pocket and was able to communicate that he was okay. The guides dug him out, and tragedy was avoided.

"That was a really nerve-racking day for me," remembered Emily. "Everything was sliding on all aspects, all elevations. We all decided to go home. I just had enough." News of the extreme avalanche danger in Valdez spread so wide that the manager of Era Aviation, who contracted the helicopters and pilots, flew in to see the carnage for himself. He took a flight around, saw all the avalanche debris, and then released Valdez Heli-Ski Guides from their contract. With the Coombses no longer needing to fulfill the remaining hours of their contract with Era, the writing was on the wall. They decided to shut down Valdez Heli-Ski Guides for the season. "We wanted to avoid a fatality," Emily said. "Maybe no one would have died, but there were just too many close calls. I was relieved we got out before a friend or a father was killed under my responsibility."

As all the helicopters took off immediately for Anchorage, Coombs broke the news to the crowd of guides and clients. He had tears in his eyes. He knew he'd exhausted all the options for guiding people safely in these mountains, but still, shutting down the operation deeply pained him. What the group gathered outside the Tsaina didn't know was that this was the beginning of the end of Valdez Heli-Ski Guides as they knew it. Later that year, Coombs and Emily would sell their operation, concluding a chapter of exploration in Alaska that redefined the skiing industry.

"I was setting off class-three avalanches, six-foot fractures, four-foot fractures, going one thousand meters, three thousand feet," Coombs said. "You're looking down at fifty, sixty feet of snow that you could be buried in, and I was getting numb to it. I felt like I could predict it. Something in the back of my mind said, 'Why don't you just step back and take a look at all this, because you have seven years getting away with literally murder and nothing's happened yet. Maybe it's time to step back.' And so I left Alaska."

20

FEAR

La Grave, France, 2014

Fear.

Unremitting fear plagued me during my first week in La Grave—to the point where I couldn't muster the courage to step foot on the mountain to ski. Even from the safety of my bed, La Meije haunted my dreams. Night after night, I tussled in my sheets through fitful sleep, tormented by a recurring nightmare of being caught in an avalanche that buried me at the bottom of a crevasse. Just as my head was being violently pinned between my legs under tons of snow and ice, I'd jolt awake, panting and soaked in sweat.

My waking hours were no less comforting. Over mugs of coffee that grew cold in my hand, I'd catch myself staring out the window at La Meije, wondering what was up there and why it was frightening. I couldn't shake the thought that if the best skier in the world had perished up there, my own demise was entirely feasible.

Each day during that first week, I skied down from my chalet in Les Terrasses to La Grave, to buy groceries and access the internet—and eventually to make my way to the lift to ski. The daily ritual began by putting on all my gear and then ambling down from my apartment through the village with my skis over my shoulder, passing by chickens pecking at the snow and a few of my very French neighbors, who avoided me as if I had the bubonic plague.

I walked to the edge of the road and put on my skis. Below was the run Coombs made every day. I stepped up and over a snowbank in my skis, then shoved off down the slope. I made lazy turns through the deep, low-angle powder. Skiing soothed the fear and anxiety that had flared up since I arrived, but I knew the only way for me to truly extinguish my terror was to get up on the mountain and ski La Grave for real.

This was easier said than done. La Grave was not a ski area in any traditional sense, where I could take the lift to the top and piece my way down. The téléphérique, which I learned locals just called "the bin," was essentially a gondola to the backcountry, and up there, following someone else's ski tracks could lead me to places where only a rope and a harness could get me out. Because I didn't have either of those, my only option at that point would be to call the rescue helicopter. There was no avalanche control. There was no ski patrol. There were no ropes marking cliffs. No signs marking runs. To ski in La Grave, I either needed to hire a guide or make a friend.

The Hotel des Alpes Skiers Lodge was the most conspicuous building on La Grave's sleepy main drag. Pelle Lång opened the lodge after leaving La Chaumine in 2003, and now I learned he ran a guide service out of it. Below the lodge itself, which could accommodate up to forty-five guests at a time, was an underground pub. K2 became the pub's title sponsor after Coombs introduced Lång to the president of K2 at the time, Tim Petrick. Now the company's insignia beamed out front in bright neon lights that stood in stark contrast to its subdued, twelfth-century surroundings. I could only imagine the bewilderment of the cheesemonger across the street when he had seen the sign being fastened in place: "There goes the neighborhood."

When I descended into the K2 Pub at the end of my first week in La Grave, the first thing I saw, after my eyes adjusted to the darkness, was a ski fastened to the barroom wall with "DOUG COOMBS" stenciled across it. Except for the bartender, who was polishing pint glasses behind the till, the joint was empty, so I pulled up a stool and ordered a cold one.

Unruly black curls flowed down around the bartender's face, which could best be described as Roman. He introduced himself in French—his name was Kristof Orlans—but when I stuttered to reply in French, he quickly switched to English.

"Where you from?" he asked in an accent I couldn't quite pinpoint.

"The States. Originally from Boston, but I mostly ski in Jackson Hole," I said, figuring that playing the Jackson Hole card might earn me some credibility around these parts. Hearing my own voice out loud made me realize that this was probably the first conversation I'd had with anyone since I arrived a week earlier, save for the woman at the grocery store who seemed to genuinely hate my guts.

"Oh man, I was just in Jackson last year," Orlans said, his eyes lighting up. "Place is amazing. I worked as a liftie for the winter."

Skiing in Jackson Hole for a winter was the equivalent of graduating from the same college, and Orlans and I got along famously from that point forward. He told me that he was from Belgium and that he had spent the last handful of years romping around the globe—India, Sri Lanka, Nepal, far-off villages in Africa. He spoke a number of languages, and although he looked barely in his twenties, I could clearly see that Orlans had a lot of worldly miles on his tires.

"Yeah, I just got here a month ago," he said. "Pelle gave me a job over Skype."

I drained pint after pint, peppering Orlans with questions about the mountain. "How does it compare to Jackson?" "Is it as dangerous as everyone says?" "Is it really that scary?" Behind every question was my burning hope that Orlans would invite me to come skiing with him and show me around, but the invitation never came. When I realized drinking another beer would make my hike back up to Les Terrasses an adventure all its own, I splayed out some Euros on the bar and thanked him.

Just as I zipped up my jacket to leave, he stopped me. "Hey, man, if I see you on the mountain, I'll show you around. I'll be up there tomorrow."

Bingo.

OPERATION ORLANS STARTED EARLY THE next morning. I skied down to La Grave and then walked to the base of the téléphérique, where I planned to stake out the area and "bump into" my new and only friend. Orlans was my ticket to learning this mountain, and in turn, the only way I was going to overcome my growing terror of it. I clunked around at the base of the téléphérique, kicking snow and staring up at La Meije, which was poised over me like the jaws of a shark waiting to chomp me to bits.

The base area looked nothing like the polished resorts of the American West—more a truck stop than a ski lodge. A nondescript building served as both ticket counter and base of the lift operations. Nearby, a small wooden shed housed the Bureau des Guides, a commission of guides hired by La Grave's mayor, who decided whether the mountain opened each day. It was the guides' job to make the first run down from the top after a storm and assess the snow stability and other object hazards that might have formed overnight. If nothing tragic happened by the time they got to the bottom, the lift was given a green light to load skiers.

I walked up to the shed and studied the trail map pinned to the outside, which appeared not to have any trails on it at all. Instead, a red line indicated the direction of the lift, and yellow triangles with exclamation points inside indicated glaciers, bergschrunds, cliffs, and other potentially deadly hazards. Next to the map was a whiteboard with today's avalanche rating, which showed three out of five, or moderate.

After thirty minutes, no one showed up at the base. No Orlans. No anybody. The woman behind the glass of the ticket desk sat paging through a magazine, and every twenty minutes or so a pack of gondolas descended from the heavens and entered the lift station. Finally I just decided to get on the lift. If Orlans was in fact skiing today, I'd catch him at the top. And if he wasn't, I'd take the lift back down at the end of the day with my tail between my legs.

Boarding the cable car was like entering a time warp. The bin was an absolute relic, painted in retro colors with doors that groaned when they opened. I jammed my skis into the slots in the door and then grabbed a seat. There was plenty of room to spread out. As the car left the dock, the doors malfunctioned and refused to close. I tried to shut them manually, but then the bin took off and I was suddenly staring down at a gorge gaping hundreds of feet below. I shot to the back of the bin in fright as it ascended excruciatingly slowly up the side of a ragged cliff, swaying precariously side to side and up and down in the breeze.

Finally the bin came over the cusp of the cliff and continued creeping to the first lift station, which looked like a giant steel jungle gym. Five or six people stood around with their skis in hand. One by one, the doors to the bins opened again—of course, mine was already open because it had never closed—and the skiers entered the other bins. That's why I hadn't seen Orlans at the base. People weren't skiing all the way to the bottom; they were doing laps to this midmountain lift station. Just as my bin was about to leave the lift station, an operator came over and squeezed the doors shut.

The trip to the top took the better part of an hour, during which time I wrestled through anxiety and claustrophobia. The long, slow ride up the mountain did nothing to alleviate my concerns of this place. Staring at the terrain passing slowly below, I still couldn't piece together how the hell people got back to the base. In fact, I hadn't even seen one skier skiing down. I needed to find Orlans.

Exiting the bin, I grabbed my skis and made my way out of the top lift station. La Meije was there to greet me. The peak looked fierce but also quite beautiful, with the sun illuminating its eastern dimensions and leaving its northern face shrouded in shadows. Skiers sauntered around wearing harnesses with ice screws dangling from them like pistols; some were smoking hand-rolled cigarettes. To my right was a tiny restaurant with "Chalet 3200" painted on its exterior wall. Inside the restaurant, I found Orlans.

"Hey man!" he called over. I played it cool like I was surprised to see him.

"Kristof?" I said, pulling off my helmet. "How you doing, brother?"

"Good, man, just taking a break," he said, swirling the last of what looked to be a hot chocolate. "Want to join us?"

Orlans was skiing with his roommate, a Kiwi named Ryan.

"This guy's from Jackson Hole," Orlans told him. I decided not to correct him.

"Nice," Ryan said. "Never been but want to get there."

Ryan's Kiwi accent gave him the distinguished air of a classic mountaineer, although I learned that he had just picked up skiing less than a decade earlier. Before that, Ryan got his kicks through competitive paragliding. "We're thinking about skiing Trifide 1," he said, gathering his gloves and goggles off the table. "You should be fine on it, being from Jackson and all."

Having no idea what Trifide 1 was, I just smiled like an idiot and nodded. "Sounds good."

After clicking into our skis outside the restaurant, we passed under a rope attached to a yellow sign reading "DANGER. DANGER. PELIGRO." I followed Orlans and Ryan down into a sprawling valley, which they informed me was called the Vallons and was one of two main routes leading to the base. But that's not where we were headed. Instead, we traversed hard right until Orlans and Ryan disappeared around a bend. I had no choice but to follow them. What else was I going to do? I slid uneasily along the small traverse and came around to find my two impromptu guides perched over a steep maze of rocks. My stomach soured. What had I gotten myself into?

Unbeknownst to me, Trifide 1 was the deadliest run on the mountain. It wasn't the deadliest from a danger standpoint, necessarily; there were way more technical, high-consequence runs in La Grave. Rather, Trifide 1 was the deadliest quite simply because it had killed the most number of people—thirty, I heard later. Given their easy proximity to the lift, the Trifides, a series of five steep couloirs, saw a lot of traffic, thus increasing the likelihood of accidents. I learned later that one particularly gruesome fatality resulted in the mountain being closed for a week after the victim left a frozen streak of blood in the snow. The scene was simply too grim to let people on the mountain.

Sizing up the situation, I immediately regretted every decision that delivered me to this perch in the snow: taking the lift to the top, meeting Orlans, entering the K2 Pub, coming to La Grave, watching my first Doug Coombs movie.

"Alright, don't fall here," Ryan said.

No shit, Sherlock.

"Once you get through the choke, the couloir opens up."

Directly below us, a tiny sliver of snow snuck through the band of jagged rocks.

"I'll go first," Orlans volunteered.

As I watched him navigate the choke, the sum of my existence began pooling up in my mind. Everything could end right here. This mountain didn't give a damn about me. It didn't care where I went to school, or who my parents were, or what I'd done in my life to tip the karmic scales in my favor. I was out of options. *I could hike out of here, I guess, but then what?* I thought. I had no idea where I was. I had to follow these guys, and yet every fiber of my being wanted absolutely nothing to do with any of this. Vertigo swirled around my body, rising up in my throat and pressing against my chest. If I stood here any longer, I was going to hyperventilate.

"Cool for me to go?" I nodded to Ryan.

He smiled. "All you."

I began slide-slipping down to the entrance of the choke, where rocks pinched together and gave me little more than a ski length to get through. The snow between the rocks had been scraped raw by the skiers before me, and I scratched my way through with as much confidence as I could muster. After I passed through the choke, the slope opened up and I came to a stop.

After thirty feet or so, the stretch of snow rolled over an edge that I couldn't see beyond. Rock walls lined either side of the couloir, gradually doglegging the slope to the right. The snow had been buffed by the wind and it looked fast. If I caught an edge here, gravity would careen me down until I hit one of the rock walls.

I turned my tips down the couloir and began driving my edges hard into the snow like I was hammering railroad ties into the mountainside. My mind and body functioned moment to moment. The whole world distilled down to the patch of white directly in front of me. *Inhale. Plant your pole. Exhale. Turn. Inhale. Hold your edge. Exhale. Plant your pole. Inhale. Turn. Exhale. Hold the edge. Inhale . . .* There was no room for fear, no time to think. With my quads screaming out in agony, I finally reached the bottom of the couloir and met up with Orlans.

"Shit, that was steep," I yelped.

"Yeah, steeper than I remembered it," Orlans laughed.

We looked back up at Ryan navigating down the couloir, but although I was staring directly at him, I wasn't really seeing him. Instead, my mind was occupied by a new thought—a revelation, really. I'd just looked into the eyes of a killer, and the killer had blinked. I was alive; my God, was I alive. The air tasted cool and delicious. My body felt strong and light. The world was beautiful. Colors were vivid.

Temperature comfortable. I could feel everything and nothing all in the same breath.

This was why people risked their lives, I thought. Why some soldiers yearned to be back on the battlefield. Why Doug Coombs continued to walk this lethal line, even though he had so much to lose. This was life fully lived, and getting just a taste of it made everything else taste that much better. Facing my own mortality, when each moment could have been my last, made me realize how many other moments in my life I'd let pass by without stamping an exclamation point on them. Each of my heartbeats screamed out, *I'm alive! I'm alive! I'm alive! I'm alive!*

After Ryan rejoined us and we continued skiing down to the lift station, my euphoria was gradually replaced with a very different emotion: guilt. *I'd just risked my life so needlessly,* I thought. There was no reason for me to be up there. I wasn't a professional skier. I wasn't rescuing someone or doing anything brave or heroic. Yes, I got down without incident, but just. I then imagined my parents' gut-wrenching sorrow if I were killed in these mountains. The news probably wouldn't reach them for days. No one knew who I was here. I was just some American being too bold in a foreign land. It would take them weeks to get my body back to the States; that is, if I wasn't buried in a crevasse somewhere on this mountain. In which case, I'd never return.

This rollercoaster of emotions came to define my existence in La Grave. Over and over, day after day, the experience pulled at the roots of my sanity. I rolled around in bed each night, wondering where the mountain would bring me the next day. I didn't need to ski, I'd tell myself in the morning. I could just sit here in my chalet, eating bread and cheese, drinking wine, feeding the chickens. And yet, at the same time, something primal within me wanted to be back on the mountain risking my life. My boots were on and I was out the door before my coffee got cold.

21

THE PIN

La Grave, France, 2000

It looked no bigger than a nickel and yet it held the power to propel Coombs's career to the highest level. The International Federation of Mountain Guides Association (IFMGA) pin hung on the backpacks and jackets of the most elite mountaineers in the world like a medal of honor. Earning it would allow Coombs to legally guide clients throughout Europe, thus creating another income stream for him and Emily. But more fundamentally, the IFMGA pin would confirm Coombs into a distinguished class of mountaineers the likes of Patrick Vallençant. Coombs never wanted to be labeled as an extreme skier. He despised the very word "extreme." The pin would rightfully establish him not only as a world-class skier, but also as an expert climber and alpinist—a full-fledged mountain guide. "That's really important to me," he said. "Having that little badge, that certification, is the highest respect you can get." So as Coombs fell deeper and deeper in love with living in La Grave, he set out in pursuit of his pin.

At the time he embarked on his first course at the age of forty-two, only a handful of Americans had been admitted into the IFMGA.

Founded in October of 1965 by nine sitting and former presidents of the French, Chamonix, Swiss, Valais, and Austrian guide associations, the IFMGA established an international standard for mountain guiding. In the years that followed, other national guiding associations came under the umbrella of the IFMGA, like members of the United Nations. Once these associations were vetted by the IFMGA, any guide certified by that association was also legally recognized on the international level.

In 1997, the same year Coombs was kicked out of Jackson Hole, the American Mountain Guides Association (AMGA) earned its accreditation from the IFMGA. As a result, Coombs could now pursue his pin in America, where all the courses and exams would be administered in English. Despite the advantage of being able to understand his instructors in English, however, pursuing his pin through the AMGA proved to be a nightmare for Coombs.

When the AMGA received its IFMGA accreditation, the then-small organization saw a huge influx of new applicants. The original members of the AMGA, who had worked intensely to get the accreditation, might have feared that passing too many applicants would threaten their international status. As a consequence, they made a concerted effort in the early years to be extremely stringent; this was especially the case when it came to Doug Coombs. The examiners weren't about to pass the great Doug Coombs just on account of his name and his fame. Quite the opposite: they were going to intensely scrutinize every step of his certification.

"I always felt kind of bad for Doug because he was a little bit older generation, and he had a name in the ski industry and the guide industry. Then he stepped into the certification process and got run through the wringer by the old guard," explained Simon Fryer, who served as the AMGA's program director during the time Coombs was pursuing his certification. "They were like, 'Alright, hotshot, you're not going to step in here and get a pin. You're going to earn this.' And man, they made him earn it by really testing him left and right."

The AMGA certification process was divided into three disciplines: skiing, alpine, and climbing. Within each of those disciplines, there were two training courses and two exams—all told, twelve steps to becoming an AMGA-certified guide. An aspirant guide needed to be an expert in all things mountains: self-rescue, mountain medicine, snow science, meteorology, risk management, environmental protection, high-altitude mountaineering, climbing, skiing, orientation, and on and on.

The courses were grueling, spanning between two and twenty days each, during which time the AMGA examiners did everything they could to make an applicant crack under the pressure. Even if an applicant was really motivated, the most steps he or she could usually accomplish in the course of a year was three, according to Simon Fryer. Some aspiring guides were known to spend the better part of a decade struggling to pass all their courses and exams to get their pin.

Despite having been a guide in some of the most dangerous mountains in the world for nearly twenty years, and despite having a 100 percent safety rating during those years, Coombs was criticized and critiqued on his every move by the AMGA examiners. Even his skiing came under harsh scrutiny. As Emily remembered, "He came back from one of the courses and said, 'Those guys need to take a Steep Camp. They can't even ski. They were getting on me for my pole plant.'"

During one of his alpine exams in Washington State's North Cascades, Coombs got into an argument with one of the examiners over the safest location to pitch their tents. In the end he pitched his tent in the location he thought was best, while the examiners stuck with their location. That night, Coombs and his partner slept soundly, while the rest of the participants and examiners suffered through howling wind that blew down their tents and hurtled ice chunks upon them.

After returning from that particularly grueling course in Washington, Coombs was invited by a friend to take a trip into the mountains. "'I don't even want to see a mountain,'" Emily remembered him responding. "AMGA tries to make you snap. They want to see how you handle stress, and they kept pushing him and pushing him." Moreover, getting the pin was financially taxing. Each course and exam cost thousands of dollars, and Coombs eventually needed to borrow money from his mother-in-law to pay for the last of his exams.

Above all, the real crux of Coombs's certification process was the climbing component. He had been climbing recreationally since he was a kid, scaling the church steeples in Bedford, but he didn't take it seriously until later in his life, in Jackson Hole. Mark Newcomb remembered first meeting Coombs at the Teton Rock Gym in the late eighties, and one of the gym's owners asked him to give Coombs some pointers. "He wasn't that smooth yet. He hadn't developed that coordination for climbing that he had for skiing," remembered Newcomb. "He had a couple fused cervical vertebrae, and so there were certain kinds of moves as a climber that you could tell he didn't have the flexibility to do."

Nevertheless, Coombs took to climbing with gusto for his certification. Many times, Emily found herself on the other end of the rope, belaying him and wanting to hide her eyes as Coombs hacked his way up precarious rock faces. "He basically had to learn to climb so that he could pass," she said. Pursuing his climbing certification late in life was like taking up golf at the age of forty and then trying to play on the pro tour. "It was massive, especially at his age," said Miles Smart, who also became one of Coombs's climbing partners. "It's one thing to go through and get your international certification in your twenties, but to do it in your midforties, to have not grown up as a climber, and to try to reach that level in climbing and climbing guiding—at the age he did it, it was a huge deal."

Coombs's final climbing exam was held at Red Rock Canyon, outside of Las Vegas. He had taken everything the AMGA had thrown at him in stride, and now he was in the homestretch. This was his final hurdle, but the AMGA was going to make this hurdle as hard as possible. If Coombs wanted his pin, he was going to have to pry it out of their hands. Over the course of two long days, Coombs was assigned not one, but two examiners who grilled his every move and did everything they could to break him. "He called me so angry," Emily remembered. "I said, 'Doug, you just have to hang in there. Bite the bullet and get out of there with your pin. Don't snap.'"

"They were just having a full epic," said Simon Fryer, who arrived on Coombs's last day. Coombs's exam went into the night. Fryer waited around the campsite, quietly rooting for Coombs, who was off somewhere in the rocks guiding the two examiners on a long, technical climb. Eventually Fryer couldn't wait any longer and went to bed.

"I woke up the next morning; it was super early. Coombs's van door was open and he was passed out inside the van," remembered Fryer. He walked over and asked Coombs how it went. "He didn't even open his eyes; this huge smile came across his face and he pulled down his sleeping bag, and on his T-shirt was his pin."

The pin opened a world of possibility for Coombs and Emily's steep camps and guiding operations. In the years that followed, their steep camps expanded throughout Europe in Chamonix and Verbier, and to far-flung places like Greenland. In 2004, back in Jackson Hole, Coombs and Mark Newcomb successfully guided a client down the Grand Teton on skis. It was the first guided descent of the Grand, and the story landed on the cover of the *Jackson Hole News & Guide*. In his own personal quests, Coombs would take ski mountaineering to wild places like Antarctica and Kyrgyzstan, but no matter how far they explored, he and Emily always found their way back to La Grave for the winter, where their hearts were.

22

THE EXPAT

La Grave, France, 2014

Throughout my journey, I'd found that living in any mountain town requires a level of personal sacrifice, but La Grave took that to a whole new extreme. Nothing was particularly convenient here. There were only a handful of restaurants, and the two small grocery stores were closed for most of the day and stocked only with the bare essentials. Of the après scene, the most luxurious amenity I came across was a bootleg hot tub built in the trailer of an old dump truck parked at the base of the lift. The girl-to-guy ratio was such that if you came to La Grave as a bachelor, you would leave as a bachelor. I found that the sheep started looking pretty good come mid-January.

And yet beyond the mountains, it was this stripped-down existence that was La Grave's appeal to the people I observed here. Living simply wasn't so much the ethos as the only option. People moved slower. They drank wine at lunch. There was a palpable air of old-world Europe wherever I went.

And thus it was no surprise that this mountain town of extremes also yielded a hardcore ski culture that made the Jackson Hole Air

Force seem like a youth soccer team in my mind. The guides walked around town stoic as lions, smoking hand-rolled cigarettes that left tobacco stuck in their teeth. The ski bums were just as crusty, some living in RVs in the parking lot and going what looked to be weeks without a shower. No one really boasted about their daily conquests in the mountains. Claiming to be the best skier in La Grave was treated as taboo. La Grave was about coexisting with the mountains, not conquering them.

While there was an obvious sense of community, I knew entering into its fold wouldn't be easy. The hundreds of skiers who sacrificed so much to live here were fiercely protective of their home. Making things all the more challenging for me were that I didn't speak French, I was alone, and, worst of all, I was a writer. When Coombs and VanderHam were killed, some of the mainstream media pointed to La Grave itself, with its flagrant lack of safety and regulation, as largely responsible for the accident. The stories painted this mountain community with a broad, grim brush that alluded to the need to regulate this type of skiing. What the media didn't understand, at least from the community's perspective, was that this lack of regulation was exactly why they were here. Only in La Grave could a skier take a lift and experience the mountains in their raw, pristine state. It was a mountaineer's mountain. La Grave offered a portal to the skiing of yesteryear, free of commercialism and full of soul. All the negative press attention threatened to take that portal away from the community.

The negative press also served as a deterrent to potential clients, many of them American. Coombs put La Grave on the map, but after his death, it was for a very different reason than when he first arrived. "The place just felt haunted after Coombs died," Juan Torruella had told me. "I didn't want to go back." That was one of the reasons why Miles and Liz Smart moved Steep Skiing Camps Worldwide to Chamonix. Coombs's death cast too dark a shadow on La Grave to attract enough clients to run the camp there.

Nearly a decade after the accident, La Grave was still wary of journalists. When Coombs's friend, who arranged my apartment in Les Terrasses, discovered that I was a writer, he said, "Don't tell anybody that . . . at least not for the first few weeks." And that was the last time he spoke to me beyond nodding hello. So it was that breaking into La Grave's tight-knit skiing community felt not unlike infiltrating the Mob. I couldn't force my way in; I needed to be invited. I played my hand slow, letting locals get used to seeing my face as I bellied up to the K2 bar each evening to chat with Orlans and sip beers with Ryan. Meanwhile, in the back of my mind, I was sizing up the room as it filled with guides and ski bums, keeping a mental checklist of people I needed to talk to. Top of the list, I decided, was Joe Vallone.

BEFORE I LEFT THE STATES, an editor from *Powder* magazine had advised that I seek out an American guide named Joe Vallone when I arrived in La Grave. Vallone had become best friends with Chad VanderHam after the two met in college, and they later became study partners through the AMGA certification process. When VanderHam moved to La Grave, Vallone soon followed. They spent almost every day skiing together, and both idolized Coombs. The day after the accident, Vallone was among the first group to investigate what had happened. If Doug Coombs left a legacy in La Grave, Joe Vallone was part of it.

I'd spotted Vallone during my first couple weeks in town, but it wasn't until a month into my stay that I finally introduced myself. He burst through the door of the K2 Pub, his eyes wide and intense, his cropped hair drenched in sweat and exploding from a bandana. He made for the bar, ice screws clinking off his harness, a rope slung over his shoulder.

"May I have a beer, Kristof?" Vallone asked politely before grabbing the stool next to mine. "And some popcorn?" Orlans poured popcorn into a container from an old-fashioned popper located behind the bar and slid it in front of Vallone, who began devouring it by the handful. After stowing his gear, Vallone pulled off his jacket, revealing two balaclavas around his neck and an avalanche beacon across his chest, which he unstrapped and stuffed into his pocket. Even while sitting quietly, Vallone's energy radiated off of him like a force field.

In a mountain town with no shortage of lions, Joe Vallone had become a pride all his own. When big-budget ski-film crews and magazine photographers wanted to get the epic couloir shot, they hired Vallone as their guide. Born in New York City and raised in suburbs outside of Chicago, Vallone learned to ski on an old landfill that installed a rope tow. In high school, he joined a free-style ski team and competed in park and mogul events. By the time he enrolled at Colorado State University in Fort Collins to study music and be closer to the big mountains, Vallone was a sponsored skier. Yet when he began to stray from the half-pipe and mogul events to pursue his AMGA certification, his sponsors dropped him. Vallone spent his years after college trying to establish himself as a guide in the United States before moving to La Grave full time in the mid-2000s.

Now a fully certified guide, Vallone left lines on the mountain that were unmistakably his own, mainly because he was one of the few with the skill, knowledge, and downright moxie to carve them. More often than not, I watched someone enter the chalet at the top of the mountain after spotting some death-defying ski track and simply walk over to Vallone and pat him on the shoulder: "Nice one, Joe." Stories of his conquests were told with such frequency around the K2 Pub that although there were a couple of Americans named Joe in La Grave, everyone knew who you meant when you said, "Did you see what Joe did today?" He once skied Pan de Rideau—one of the most exposed lines in La Grave that required traversing over a nine-hundred-foot cliff onto a steep, crevasse-riddled glacier—completely naked. All he had on besides his skis was a harness and backpack. Suffice it to say that some in town thought

Vallone was too much of a cowboy, always pushing for more exposed lines that he wasn't exactly shy to tell you about at the bar later.

When I finally mustered the nerve to tell Vallone why I was in La Grave, he was surprisingly thrilled.

"Chad and I were Jedi," he said, a light clearly flipping on in his mind. "Coombs was the master." He swiveled on his barstool to face me. "I first met Doug in Jackson Hole during one of our AMGA ski guide courses. He was a bit dumbfounded that I was a park skier pursuing IFMGA certification. To this day, I am a jibber gone guide."

"Did you ski with Doug here in La Grave?" I asked.

"Yeah, a bunch. In fact, he technically gave me my first guiding job in La Grave," Vallone said. "I was an aspirant guide, and I spent a few days tail guiding for him. Ironically, the first day I tailed for Doug in La Grave, he took me down the Polichinelle with one of his top clients."

I was surprised to hear this. The Polichinelle was the couloir Coombs and VanderHam had been skiing when they were killed. Having no real knowledge of the run, I had just assumed the Polichinelle was too dangerous to take a client.

"I was at the top having a coffee," Vallone continued. "Doug stormed in and said 'Joe, come with me; I need you.' I had no idea where we were even headed. I remember rolling over the entrance of the Poli and looking into the line, then looking at Doug before the client caught up with us, and asking him, 'You guide this shit?' He chuckled, but when the client got there, it was all business."

"How did he guide it?" I asked.

"As we skied the first couloir, Doug pulled out about fifteen meters down. He backed up into the couloir under a tiny nook of protection, but still close enough to monitor and coach the client down. Doug guarded the exposure as he coached him. It was mind-blowing to watch how he orchestrated the descent like a puppeteer. The client was practically on strings."

I pictured Coombs pressed against the rock walls of the couloir, calling up instructions to the client while also guarding the cliff below. If the client had begun to fall, Coombs would have had to tackle him and stop him from falling off the cliff.

"I watched the client reach Doug," Vallone continued. "He stopped right in the middle of the couloir in front of Doug to catch his breath. He was in awe of the turns he had just made. I figured the client was done and was going to pull to the side, so I started to ski. When I made my first turn, a piece of snow sluffed through the couloir. I yelled 'Sluff!' from above and stopped skiing immediately. The client was too busy celebrating his small accomplishment and just stood there taking the sluff through his skis, doing nothing about it. The mood changed quickly. 'Don't you ever stand in the middle of a couloir,' Doug yelled at him. 'Look at me. Look at where I am. Look at where my skis are facing. Get over here.'"

Vallone said that when he reached Coombs, he apologized profusely for sending sluff down on his client. But Coombs wasn't mad. "Doug looks back up at me with that classic Doug grin and says, 'No, you keep doing that. Next time he stands in the middle of the couloir, you sluff him again. We're going to teach him a lesson in couloir etiquette.'" Vallone took a sip of his beer. "I have been teaching what I learned that day ever since."

"What did you learn?"

"I learned a magic lesson about guiding. Most guides just move you through terrain and get you to the bottom or whatever, but Doug wanted to make you a better skier—not just guide you. A day in the mountains with him was not a hold-your-hand experience. He made it part of his day to make you better at what you do."

"Do you still ski the Polichinelle?" I asked.

"I used to ski that run a lot, but I have not been down it again since the day after the accident."

"Do others still ski it?"

"Yes, it gets skied all the time. Mostly by a handful of locals," Vallone said. "Folks have asked me to guide them down it, and I ask them how they even know about it. They say they want to see where Doug died. I have been asked by journalists, too." Vallone polished off the rest of his beer. "I tell them to fuck themselves. Go find it yourself. I don't guide it."

I slid back into my barstool. The question of whether I should ski Polichinelle had been plaguing me since I boarded my flight a month earlier. *Wasn't that the whole point of coming to La Grave?* I thought to myself. *To ski Coombs's final track?* But Bruce Tremper's words kept ringing out in my mind: "People get in trouble trying to be their hero." I wasn't a pro skier. I wasn't a guide. I was just a writer, and I had not earned the right to ski that line. Vallone had just confirmed that without my needing to ask.

"I didn't care for how the media ran the story," Vallone continued. "A few days after the accident, I wrote something online about who Chad was. I poured my heart into it because it was killing me that no one was ever going to know about this amazing person. All eyes were on Doug. Understandably so, but in my eyes Chad's potential was unimaginable."

23

THE PROTÉGÉ RETURNS

Verbier, Switzerland, 1999

Chad VanderHam drove his probe as deep as it would go into the snow. "*En bas*! *En haut*! *Un pas en avant*!" a voice commanded. Following orders, VanderHam pulled out the twelve-foot probe, took one step forward, and then drove it back into the snow.

"Down! Up! One step forward!" the command rang out once again in French. VanderHam was standing shoulder to shoulder with a line of other skiers. They were probing for bodies.

Avalanche dogs sniffed the snow frantically as recue helicopters buzzed overhead. Word was that three skiers were buried under at least twelve feet of snow beneath their feet. The avalanche had ripped big, running five hundred feet down the slope. Two people had already been killed that week. Suddenly VanderHam heard a commotion down the line: one of the probers thought he had struck a body. Furious digging ensued. Fifteen shovels dug all the way to the frozen ground only to discover that it was a false alarm. There was no body. And so the probing continued. "*En bas*! *En haut*! *Un pas en avant*!" This was the beginning of Chad VanderHam's third Steep Skiing Camp with Coombs, and he was getting a long, hard look at the dark underbelly of life in the big mountains.

Using La Grave as their European base of operations, the Coombses were running the camp in Verbier for a second year. For Emily, it was something of a homecoming, reminding her of her ski-bumming years after college, before she moved to Jackson Hole to be with Coombs. But the mood on this day was somber. All told, avalanches had already claimed six lives that week. "Every time I've been through a European storm, someone has died," Emily had told VanderHam and his fellow campers. And this was just their second day of camp.

Joining VanderHam on this Steep Skiing Camp in Verbier were at least seven others, including François von Hurter, who since his life-changing experience heli-skiing in Valdez had continued to follow Coombs around the world and ski with him at every opportunity. There was also a thirty-eight-year-old retired investment banker from New York, a thirty-eight-year-old Scottish geologist, a twenty-four-year-old student from Stanford, a retired commercial airline pilot, and a writer and a photographer from *Powder* magazine named Keith Carlsen and Dave Reddick. Coombs's camps cast a wide net, pulling together unlikely ski partners to learn from the master.

Despite their varying abilities and Verbier's level five avalanche risk, VanderHam and his fellow campers were given a full-on clinic on ski mountaineering by Coombs, Emily, and their fellow guides. They rappeled into couloirs using nothing but a broomstick jammed in the snow to hold their weight. They slinked around avalanche-prone faces. And they skied every minute of every day, for six straight days. "Before there's time to reflect on one day's adventure, we go to bed, wake up sore, and have another," wrote Keith Carlsen. "It's starting to feel like boot camp."

But twenty-four-year-old Chad VanderHam lapped it up. He fed off the adventure and was tickled to be skiing in Coombs's group for the week. VanderHam skied with the same aggressiveness that had impressed Coombs back in Jackson Hole, but here in the Alps that kind of hotshot style could easily get him killed. "He hadn't skied any real exposure before," said one of Coombs's Steep Skiing Camp guides. "He skied too fast. We had to slow him down every single run." Gradually, VanderHam adjusted his run-and-gun American style to the slow, methodical European approach. "I feel the camps offer an aggressive, educational approach to the freedom and vitality of the mountains, within some of the most amazing settings in the world," VanderHam reflected. "The skills, memories, and friends that are born under these circumstances are truly powerful."

At the end of the week, when his fellow clients returned to their normal lives, VanderHam didn't want to leave Europe. He was looking for direction in his life. He had a degree in economics and a family business waiting for him to run. "But he knew in his heart that's not what he wanted to do," said VanderHam's college buddy Simon Fryer. "He didn't want to go back to Minnesota and run a paper company. That's not where his heart was."

VanderHam respected his parents and the sacrifice they made to put him through school. He knew that whatever career he picked, it needed to have value—not monetary, necessarily, but in the seriousness with which he approached it. Spending time with Coombs in the mountains exposed VanderHam to a life that showed intrinsic value to him. "When he went to those first steep camps and then immersed himself in that La Grave culture, you could see that it was coming together for him," Fryer explained. "He said, 'This has meaning for me, my passion is here, and this is really a path for me.'"

FOLLOWING HIS HEART, VANDERHAM OFFERED himself up to Coombs as an apprentice, willing to do anything he asked. Coombs took him as a protégé. First he put VanderHam in charge of schlepping gear around and picking steep camp clients up at the airport. Then he enlisted him to film the clients during the steep camps. Every job, no matter how menial, VanderHam did with the utmost seriousness and professionalism. "I remember Chad would hang precariously from ridges and rocks to get the perfect angle to shoot his videos of us," remembered one of the steep camp clients. "His narration was priceless and an excellent reflection of his character—his words were sparse but incredibly funny in an understated sort of way, and reflected his deep love and awe of the mountains."

While filming the steep camps, VanderHam liked to pan over to La Meije and mutter with wonder, "La Meije, there she is!" His love and enthusiasm for being in the mountains, especially with Coombs, wafted off of him. At the end of each day, VanderHam took the video footage home with him and watched it over and over, obsessing over every nuance of Coombs's ski technique. He did everything he could to mimic it: Coombs's square shoulders, his snappy turns, his collapsing pole plant. "Chad was always aspiring to be like Doug," said Miles Smart, who came to La Grave to help guide Coombs's steep camps. "You could tell that he spent a lot of time skiing with Doug and had an ability to make smooth, controlled turns in the fall line." Eventually VanderHam got it into his mind that not only was he going to ski like his hero, he was going to become a mountain guide like his hero.

The longer VanderHam lived and skied in La Grave, the more he adapted to the mountain and the mountaineering ethos of the guides. "He started to understand very quickly exposure and all of the challenges involved with skiing this kind of terrain," said Per Ås. Pelle Lång agreed: "When he came, he was a kid in my eyes—a wild late teenager, but he grew up and got his mileage in." Under Coombs's direction, VanderHam began focusing less on speed and more on safety. At guide dinners each night, he soaked up the wealth of knowledge being discussed around the table by Coombs and the local guides. When it came time to pursue his pin, VanderHam approached his studies for the IFMGA certification with dogged dedication. "He trained really hard," remembered Miles Smart. "The year leading up to his exam, he was living up in Ventelon, and every morning he would ski down to La Grave, and then skin home every single day." He skied with a full guide's pack all the time, hauling around sixty pounds of ropes, crampons, ice axes, ice screws, and a myriad of other tools.

As he began applying these mountaineering skills, VanderHam also became painfully aware of the moods of the mountain and the high cost that can come when one provokes her wrath. One night, he and another aspirant American guide named Keith Garvey set out on Le Tour de la Meije, a signature ski tour in La Grave that required skinning from town, up through the Vallons, around the 13,068-foot summit of La Meije, and then down the other side. They navigated through the cold under the light of a full moon, but when they reached the summit, a storm rolled in. VanderHam and Garvey were forced to spend the night on the mountain. Coombs and his fellow guides waited anxiously down in town. When they finally got off the mountain the next morning, VanderHam's foot had been badly frostbitten. Happy to be alive, VanderHam threw his blue foot up on the dinner table, and the guides took a photo of Lång pretending to cut off his toes. "We were laughing at the time, but it was quite serious," remembered Lång. "I think it could have gone the other way." It took a full year for him to regain sensation in his foot.

The longer VanderHam lived in La Grave, the more he evolved from client to protégé to peer in Coombs's eyes. "Chad came into Doug's life as a client that evolved into a friend," said Emily. "In Chad's eyes Doug was a mentor." Still, when they skied around together, Coombs watched over VanderHam like a father might a son. He might have even looked at Chad VanderHam as his son if he wasn't about to have a child of his own.

24

THE OUTLIER

La Grave, France, 2014

Ptor Spricenieks told me to come over sometime after ten in the evening so he would have time to put his two little boys to bed. He drew me a map on a bar napkin showing me how to find his home, which was located at the top of the village of Ventelon, less than a mile walk down the road from my chalet in Les Terrasses. Although I'd heard his name uttered in reverential tones around town by the likes of Joe Vallone and Orlans, I knew next to nothing about this mythic ski mountaineer. The only thing I knew was that he had been one of Coombs's frequent ski partners here in La Grave. I bumped into him one evening at the K2 Pub, and after I got around to telling him why I was in town, he invited me over to his house for a beer.

I spent the hours leading up to nightfall reading whatever I could find about Spricenieks, the contents of which made me realize why I'd never heard of him: Spricenieks didn't necessarily want to be known. "Is it the case that the ski world at large knows the myth of Ptor better than it knows the man? Only most skiers know neither man nor myth," wrote Leslie Anthony in a *SKI* magazine article I dredged up online. "Despite a stunning catalog of first descents that places him among the elite of the elite, he isn't sought out to pronounce upon the state of the sport, is not awash in gear and expedition invitations, and has yet to earn a decent living from his feats." Anthony's article went on to describe Spricenieks's habitual fallouts with sponsors, his wild ski adventures, and his periods of going mad, like when he quit skiing entirely and roamed the jungles of Costa Rica. It was ultimately Coombs's death that brought Spricenieks back to La Grave, where he met his wife and started a family.

So it was that I set out into the darkness with a headlamp and a crinkled napkin showing me the way. Spricenieks answered the door still wearing his long johns from a day of skiing and welcomed me in warmly. After I pulled off my boots in a small mudroom lined with skis, we padded up wooden steps to a candlelit living area. "I built this place," Spricenieks said in a whisper, so as not to wake his two children. Handing me a beer, he led me to a handsome wooden table, where we sat facing one another. His Roman features were carved by the candle-light, a long ponytail falling behind him out of sight.

"Life . . . life sure isn't the same without Doug," he said, opening up my beer and then raising his to toast. "Here's to your project." The clink of our bottles rang out, and we sat there in comfortable silence after taking a swig.

"He was just this immaculate, precision-skiing machine in any conditions," Spricenieks said. "He was so technically razor on his skis. And that was part of his billy-goat nature. He'd stand on the edge all the time."

"What do you think enabled him to stand on the edge like that, and just be comfortable?" I asked. "Was it something about his demeanor?"

"I mean, it's not even personality. It's just his soul. His being was that way. He had a comfort being there. Maybe it was just miles of being there and knowing yourself. Feeling it. That you're dialed. That's kind of what you need. You need to be confident. Reasonably confident."

He took another draw from his beer. "At the same time, Doug always said, 'Overconfidence eventually weeds itself out.'"

"Did he ever express to you what this place was for him, and how it resonated with him?"

"Well, he didn't really—I can't remember him saying it, but I know he loved the culture. He loved the access. He loved the lifestyle here." He leaned back and looked around. "We're living *on* the mountain here—it's not in the valley. It's different than North America. You don't really live on a mountain in North America. Very, very few places do."

This sentiment resonated with me fully. Living at eye level with the surrounding Alps felt so much more intimate than being in their shadows. I could feel their moods, the joy of clear skies, the gloom of impending storms—and the moods had a way of seeping into you and becoming your own. Living on the mountain allowed for a rare kinship between man and nature, and I fully appreciated how perfect it was that Coombs had ended up here.

"And it's the scene here," Spricenieks continued. "You've seen it. What you experienced is what he loved here. Going up the lift. Hanging out at the top. Nobody's kicking you off the mountain. Skiing down in twilight with a good buzz and ending up at the road hitchhiking back. All that stuff."

"You said, when I first met you, that he really enjoyed being a dad, a family man—"

"Yeah," Spricenieks said with a smile.

"How did you see that impact the way that he was in the mountains? Was he any different? Was he—I mean, what changed in him, if anything?"

"You never know until you have a kid how that love transforms you and prioritizes things for you," Spricenieks said. "You have to do things for them. Then again, his life as a skier—my life as a skier—it's kind of your job. You have to go and do your job. It's like papa going out to a nine-to-five; it's totally normal. Somebody's gotta work. Doug had confidence in what he was doing, so he wasn't going to stop. And he was enlightened enough to realize that you can die doing anything. That you have to do what you love and do it well. And . . . yeah, he didn't really change."

"Should he have changed?"

"That's the lesson that was missed and somewhat misinterpreted at Doug's death. It was just his time to go. He didn't screw up. It wasn't like this weight of percentages that crushed him. He didn't make an error or ski a slope that was bad. He was so dialed that he was never jeopardizing his family. It might as well have been a car accident. It was great that he died in the mountains doing what he loved, but it's also irrelevant. It could have been anything. It was just his time."

Spricenieks studied the contents of his bottle for a moment, then looked back up at me. He didn't strike me at all as the uncompromising recluse that some of the articles I had read made him out to be. Rather, he sat there like a sage, and I felt as though I could ask him anything.

"How would you, um, rate Polichinelle?" I asked Spricenieks. "What would you compare it to, as far as its being a technical run?"

"It's kind of technical, but for here, it's no big deal. There are no gnarly cruxes—well, there can be. You have to get it in the right condition. But it's not exceptionally steep. It's a bit exposed. If it's powder, you can fall over and stop. If you're skiing it when it's boilerplate, that can be extreme, of course. 'Intricate and exposed' would be the realistic way to describe it, but not extreme. Like the woman that was skiing with him that day, Christina. Have you met her?"

"No, I haven't."

"She lives down here," Spricenieks said nodding out the window.

"She lives here?" I asked incredulously.

"Yeah, yeah. Christina Blomkvist."

"I didn't know that."

"She might not be here right now, but I'll totally introduce you. I don't know if she's skied Polichinelle since. She's a very good skier, but she's not the kind of skier that you'd expect to be skiing around with Doug. She's into the mellow stuff. So that says it all about the day, that she was along. It was great conditions for her. It wasn't a big deal—until that third part of the couloir."

"What do you think happened?"

"I talked to Farmer, who was there, and I talked to Christina, and Christina told me exactly what happened," Spricenieks said, pulling out a piece of paper and a pencil. "And I talked to Colin, too, who climbed up there the next day." Colin was the friend of Coombs's who helped me get my apartment and since hadn't uttered a word to me. "He climbed up there with ice gear to look at the tracks and see what happened. And the one thing he noticed was a twig sticking out near the bottom of the couloir; he thinks that screwed Chad's cadence and made him make a turn to the skier's right, where there is usually a bit of ice. So that was the theory, that he made his last turn too low. His tails slid out, and he just lost it and bailed over the cliff. And then Doug went down."

Spricenieks started drawing out the couloir on the piece of paper, narrating as he went. He showed me how the run consisted of a series of three couloirs that passed over a series of cliffs. He drew out how they skied down, and where they stopped above the third and final section. Spricenieks then offered a theory I'd never heard before.

"Chad went down and fell, and then Doug came down and realized what had happened. He went to the edge and called up for the rope. So then Farmer comes down this pitch. It's impossible to come down without kicking any amount of snow down—and Doug's perched right on the edge." There was a long silence. "Doug easily could have been knocked off by the sluff."

I'd read everything that had ever been written about the accident. I'd practically memorized Matt Farmer's account of what he said happened that day. When the first news of the accident came out, it was falsely reported that an avalanche took Coombs over the cliff, but then the story was corrected, indicating that he had slipped. What Spricenieks was saying, however, was that Coombs hadn't slipped off the edge. He was pushed off by sluff.

25

THE RISING SON

La Grave, France, 2004

When Coombs and Emily first got married, they had absolutely no intention of having children. "We liked our life the way it was," Emily explained. It was a life full of adventure, of world travel, of endless powder days, and of dangerous skiing. It was a life that didn't offer a lot of room for raising a child, especially given that Emily already had her hands full with Coombs, who was like a big forty-year-old kid himself. But in April of 1999, when she turned thirty-nine and sensed her maternal clock ticking, Emily raised the topic to her husband. "It's now or never," she remembered saying to him. "You have to decide if you want to have a kid or not. Don't tell me in five years that you want one." They eventually decided to try.

"When I got pregnant, it was like, 'Oh my goodness, what have we done?'" Emily remembered. "When I told Doug I was pregnant, he sort of got all fidgety and left. Then he came home that night with a pair of baby socks. I guess that meant he was sort of digesting [the news]." But the couple wasn't given much more time to let the idea of having a child really sink in. Two weeks later, Emily had a miscarriage.

The failed pregnancy gave the Coombses an out to return to their former lives, but after talking about it, they decided to keep trying. Once again Emily got pregnant, and once again she miscarried. "Every time we miscarried, we had our out, but we kept trying again, so we must have both wanted a baby," Emily explained. "But we never knew for sure. You never really know what you're getting into, unless you're the kind of person that knew your whole life that you wanted a family. We just weren't like that."

After three years and three failed pregnancies, doctors told Coombs and Emily that they weren't able to have children. "We had kind of given up," Emily said. "And then, all of a sudden, I just conceived him." Given their track record and the doctor's prognosis, she and Coombs didn't hold out much hope for the pregnancy. When she sensed her body heading toward another miscarriage, Emily called the doctor, who told her to come right in. The ultrasound showed that the baby still had a heartbeat. The doctor told Emily to quit everything and rest, not a small request for the wife of Doug Coombs.

For two weeks, she remained bedbound, while Coombs was off on one of his many adventures. "I didn't really see him at all during that time," she said. Going stir crazy in the house, Emily eventually started taking little walks. She kept her life very mellow, maintaining a low heart rate, eating good food, and resting. "Then I started getting bigger and bigger," she remembered. At the seven-month mark, Coombs and Emily flew to La Grave. She spent the last months of her pregnancy staring out the window at La Meije, where Coombs was out skiing every day. With no hospital in La Grave, the baby was going to be born an hour and a half away in Grenoble.

Around five o'clock in the morning on January 22, 2004, Emily's water broke. Coombs called up the hospital. The doctor told him that the delivery wasn't going to happen for several more hours. Coombs then asked a question that for anyone else would have been ridiculous:

"Can I go skiing?" The doctor, who apparently had no idea that this soon-to-be father was calling from La Grave, an hour and a half drive away, told Coombs he could go skiing. So while Emily went deeper and deeper into the throes of labor, Coombs was making turns with a client in the shadow of La Meije.

Finally Emily couldn't wait any longer. "When I called him, he was at the midway lift station," she remembered. "He thankfully answered the phone, and I said, 'Doug you have to come down here now. We got to go.'"

"Should I ski fast?" Coombs asked.

"No, just get here, and don't stop and talk to anybody," Emily said.

By the time Coombs reached Emily, she was wildly in labor. He loaded her into their van and embarked on the voyage through the Romanche Valley to the hospital in Grenoble. "I kept screaming 'Go faster, go faster!'" Emily remembered. "Every time we got behind a car, I'd yell out 'Pass him!'" Like a naïve little kid, Coombs kept asking Emily what was wrong whenever she had a contraction. "Just drive!" she yelled.

Within two hours of Emily's admission at the hospital, complications arose. From the heart monitor, Coombs noticed that the baby was going into distress. He ran and got the doctor, who came sprinting down the hallway, pulling on his scrubs midstride. The baby wasn't getting any oxygen and had to come out immediately. The doctor performed an emergency C-section.

So it was that at ten minutes before midnight on the twenty-second of January 2004—the anniversary of the day Dr. No caught Coombs out of bounds—the miracle baby, the baby doctors said was impossible, came into the world at a healthy seven pounds four ounces. Deep down, Coombs and Emily had been hoping for a son, so when the doctor told them they'd had a healthy baby boy, they were overjoyed. "They asked me, 'What's his name?'" Emily remembered. "We hadn't really done our homework." Although he had named hundreds of ski runs over the course of his career, Coombs was at a loss when it came to naming his new son. In the last conversation he and Emily had had about it, she had suggested the name David, which she thought went well with what they had picked for his middle name, Douglas. As the nurses swaddled the boy, Coombs told them that his son's name was David.

"We were just totally blown away by how much we adored him," Emily remembered. "We had no idea that we were going to love him so much and that he was going to be so perfect." Coombs and Emily lay in the hospital bed through the early morning hours, beaming down at their new son. "We're your parents," they gushed again and again, still unable to believe it themselves.

EVEN THOUGH HE WAS AN INFANT, Emily and Coombs both agreed that David had inherited his father's legs. They were long and skinny, with pronounced kneecaps. Throughout his infancy, the parents loaded their son into a backpack and skied him around the mountain.

When Coombs wasn't working, he loved to spend every second of every day with his son. He loved being a dad. Whenever he and Emily went out on a date, they brought David with them like their mascot. If Coombs was stuck in the house, he put the toddler in a little harness, attached him to a rope, and belayed him as he climbed up and down the stairs. By the time David was two years old, he was already pizza-cutting down the slope with his father holding him up by his armpits.

"My philosophy with our son is that I'm going to turn him on to all this skiing and climbing, and I'm going to give him the opportunity to like it," Coombs said. "If he doesn't like it, well, I'm not going to be one of those pushy dads. I don't want to be that. If he wants to play the piano, that's fine. He'll probably be really good at it."

David's addition to the Coombses' lives impacted each parent differently. Emily knew her former days as a risk-taking skier were now over. She was still going to ski, of course, but she had absolutely zero interest in skiing the extreme terrain that had defined much of her career. Emily was a mom now, and that's all she wanted to be. "There was just no way I could keep doing what I was doing," she explained. "My brain changed. I was taking care of an infant around the clock, so I couldn't do that stuff, and I really didn't want to—that confused Doug a little bit."

Coombs still wanted to go off on the same adventures that he shared with his wife over their seventeen years together. Even after she insisted that she didn't want to ski dangerous runs, Coombs occasionally led her on them anyway. "Doug, I don't want to do that right now," she would say. "I don't want to feel like I'm going to die today." He would respond by saying that he knew she could do it. "That's not the point," Emily would say.

One day Coombs led Emily down Polichinelle. "I was like, 'I don't want to do this kind of run today,' and he took me on it anyway. I was so mad at him," Emily remembered. "I said, 'What was it that you didn't understand about the fact that I didn't want to ski something that if I fell, I died?'"

For Coombs, having a son didn't change the way he lived his life or the way he skied. Eventually he accepted that the days of wild adventures with Emily were no more, at least for the time being. "Now that we have a child, that's all stopped, because I think she knows that she's gotta be a mom for a long time," Coombs conceded. "She still knows that I love them, [but] to make me stop doing something that I love, for that long, she knows it is not possible."

This was not to say that Coombs didn't acknowledge the inherent dangers of the life he'd chosen. Over the course of his skiing career, he'd seen a number of his friends and colleagues be taken by the mountains. Even his hero, Patrick Vallençant, had fallen to his death in a freak climbing accident in France. In La Grave these stark realities were especially conspicuous. The year before David was born, an avalanche in La Grave claimed the life of one of Coombs's friends, a beloved local guide named Philip Jaerschky. He was thirty-three years old and left behind a young wife.

"You know what they say in the mountains around here—all the birds, all the blackbirds, that's a dead person," Coombs said during an interview in La Grave on March 6, 2006. "And there's a lot of birds in the mountains here. And they're all blackbirds. That's their spirits flying around. That's the rumor."

He continued, "The sad fact of mountains, and any extreme sport, like car racing or whatever, [is that] there's going be bad accidents and deaths. I remember being really shocked when a friend died skiing. And then the next friend died skiing. And then the next friend died skiing. And you're like—I don't know what it is, it's weird—you just become numb to it. It's still terrible, and you don't like it, but it doesn't make you stop. It makes me think more. I try to learn from everybody's mistakes. But I hate seeing people that I know die; but I know it's going to happen. I think that's just part of it, you know? Just like saying you know someone who's died in a car accident. What's worse, the car accident or falling off the mountain? I don't know; I think a car accident's worse. At least when they're falling off the mountain, they loved what they were doing."

26

MAN MADE LEGEND

La Grave, France, 2006

Coombs held his two-year-old son on their apartment's terrace in Les Terrasses. Still wearing his pajamas, David felt like a warm loaf of bread in his father's arms. His cheeks were rosy, and the sun glared off his wispy blond hair. Immediately behind them, appearing so close it almost looked fake, La Meije was awash in the same warm spring light that turned the sky a regal shade of blue. It was one of those magical mornings in La Grave when the mountains felt so welcoming and friendly. With Emily at his side and David in his arms, forty-eight-year-old Doug Coombs gazed off into the distance. He was content.

Earlier that winter, the same week they left for La Grave, the Coombses had made an offer on a home in Jackson Hole, where they were now planning on spending their summers. Jackson Hole Mountain Resort had long since lifted Coombs's ban from the mountain, and the ski patrol had actually instated an open gates policy to the backcountry, allowing skiers to freely access the national forest. Many believed that the uproar caused by Coombs's banishment in 1997 was a catalyst for this dramatic change in resort policy.

Meanwhile, Emily was enjoying her life as a mother. Three days earlier, after much pleading with her husband, Emily had bought three horses for their new property in Jackson. "I wanted a sport that I could do while being a mother of a young child," Emily said, "because I could no longer join Doug in the mountains in the same way that we had done before we had David." Emily was glad to be settling down and happy to be in La Grave with her family.

When Coombs woke up that morning, April 3, he told Emily that his neck was really bugging him. The old childhood injury still flared up every now and again, but he rarely, if ever, talked about it. Despite his soreness, Coombs and his wife and son spent the morning meandering around the pastoral French village that had become their neighborhood. David rode his bike, while his parents switched off taking pictures as they discussed how they were going to spend such a beautiful day. Emily suggested they head down into town, but Coombs had his mind set on skiing. He and Emily hadn't been able to ski together much that season, and Coombs wanted to enjoy this day with his wife in the mountains like the good old times.

The Coombses decided to try to put their son in day care again. When they had attempted to do so a week earlier, the boy flat-out refused to leave his parents, especially his father. "He was having full-on tantrums," Emily remembered. "It was on an unusual level. He just didn't want to let Doug go." David had convinced his parents not to leave him that time, but this time, Coombs held strong and said good-bye to his son.

The conditions on the mountain were spectacular. It had snowed in recent days, and there were still boot-top powder runs for them to ski. Emily told Coombs she didn't want to ski anything high risk, and he honored her request. There was no telling how many runs Doug and Emily Coombs had skied together over the years. Since Coombs had landed at her feet in Bozeman, he and Emily had been through a lot together. They pioneered an industry. Ran two successful companies.

Faced controversy. Reinvented their lives in Europe. Had a child. And were still just as committed to one another as they were when they exchanged vows on the banks of the Kelly Warm Spring in Wyoming ten years earlier. "I don't know how my wife puts up with me," Coombs had said a month earlier when he was interviewed for a documentary. "She's the most tolerant person I know." As for Emily, she was still madly in love with her husband.

By the late afternoon, Doug and Emily Coombs caught one of the last bins to the top of the mountain. As fate would have it, Chad VanderHam, Matt Farmer, and Christina Blomkvist joined them in their cable car. Just a week earlier, VanderHam had passed his ski exam for his AMGA certification, this after failing the exam once before. Thirty-year-old Matt Farmer, a newly minted aspirant guide from the United States, was in La Grave for his AMGA ski guide course and had spent the last few weeks skiing around the mountain with VanderHam. The third in their group, Christina Blomkvist, was a longtime local skier from Sweden who had become dear friends with VanderHam, as they both lived in Ventelon.

Much like Coombs and Emily, VanderHam's party had enjoyed a fantastic day of skiing. There was more than a foot of fresh snow in some areas of the mountain, but the avalanche rating was low, only two out of a possible five. Conditions were perfect for most every run, allowing them to make descents down the glacier, the couloirs to the road, and even the Pan de Rideau. Although spirits within the cable car started off high, the tone took a somber turn at some point. "Chad kept saying, 'I don't want to die,'" recalled Emily. "I can't remember the details, but I remember Chad talking about how he didn't want to die, and it had to do with the Pan de Rideau and glacier holes and seracs, crevasses and stuff. He was really talking about that pretty profoundly."

When they reached the top of the mountain, the five continued on to the restaurant. Emily stopped to talk with some of her friends, while Coombs followed VanderHam and his party to another table. A carafe of *vin chaud* was brought over and a festive buzz broke out within the restaurant. Coombs sat with his neighbor and close friend Colin Samuels. Just as he had done as a boy around his family's kitchen table in Bedford, Coombs told Samuels about a dream he had the night before. "I had this wild dream," Samuels remembered Coombs saying. "I did this big ski descent—I think it was a first descent. But the dream was about the whole thing: the conceiving of it, the planning of it, the scouting, then the actual climb up and the ski down, and the celebration afterward. It was a wild first descent, but I don't remember where it was. I think it was a place I have never seen before, a place I have never skied."

As they sat around the table, Coombs and VanderHam began hatching a plan for their last run of the day. Their energy fed off each other exponentially. With Coombs's time typically consumed with guiding clients and VanderHam busy studying for his AMGA exams, they were thrilled to have the opportunity to ski together: the master and the protégé reunited on a picture-perfect day. The two decided that they would end the day by skiing Polichinelle. Coombs broached the idea of skiing the couloir with his wife, but she refused. "I'm a mother now," she pleaded with her husband. "I don't want to ski something that if I fall, I die." Instead, Emily decided to ski down the Chancel with a friend, and they would meet at the bottom. With that, she set off skiing.

Coombs, VanderHam, Farmer, and Blomkvist skied down to the road runs, a series of couloirs that ran down the face of the mountain and all the way to the highway below, a few short miles from the center of La Grave. Each of the road runs posed its own degree of risk, but Polichinelle could be especially treacherous.

The route consisted of three couloirs, each about forty feet wide and pitched between forty and forty-five degrees. The element of danger wasn't necessarily in the runs themselves, steep as they were, but rather the traverses connecting them. Each of the traverses passed over cliffs. If you were to fall in the couloir and could not self-arrest, you could tumble off the side. In certain conditions, Polichinelle was the definition of a no-fall zone.

"Doug and Chad were definitely in the driver's seat," remembered Matt Farmer. "I was less familiar with the area, so Doug and Chad were in charge. They were kind of our guides. They were just psyched to be skiing together." Less familiar with the terrain, Farmer took it slow, followed by Blomkvist, who also took her time. The snow was untracked and gripping nicely to the steep slope. It wasn't sluffing.

After reaching the entrance of Polichinelle, VanderHam took the lead down the first couloir, which descended in a straight line to the traverse at the bottom. Each couloir was longer than the last, stretching from a hundred feet to three hundred feet, and this was the shortest of the three. Coombs watched him from above, admiring VanderHam's confident turns. His protégé had come a long way since attending his first Steep Skiing Camp in Jackson Hole. All the years of obsessing over Coombs's technique had turned VanderHam's form into an almost carbon copy of his hero's. He'd matured in these mountains. He was no longer a reckless hotshot. He was a ski mountaineer. When the thirty-one-year-old reached the end of that first section, he pulled to the side, and then Coombs took off, followed by Blomkvist and Farmer.

They all collected at the top of the second section, where Coombs then took over the lead. The three others watched him descend from above. Even now, two years shy of his fiftieth birthday, Coombs was at the top of his game. He'd evolved from a ripping renegade in his youth to a sage-like ski mountaineer revered around the world for his knowledge and impeccable safety record. His legend was cemented in hundreds of first descents, on the covers of magazines, on the reels of ski films, in contests and certifications. Throughout it all, Coombs's own love for skiing remained unchanged from the days of sliding down his backyard in Bedford in the glow of porch lights. Now, as he snapped his turns down the second section of Polichinelle, he looked to be having as much fun as ever.

At the top of the third section, the group gathered on a spine. From where they were standing, they could see all the way to the valley floor below. The sun lit up everything. There was not a cloud in the sky, not a breath of wind in the air. Farmer pulled out his camera and snapped a photo just as VanderHam took the lead once again down the final section, which was the longest and curved immediately out of view. From where they were standing on the spine, the group couldn't see VanderHam skiing. Only when you entered the couloir could you see down the final section, which was shaped like a funnel that ended in a rocky constriction, and below that, a giant cliff.

After VanderHam set off skiing and disappeared from view, Coombs waited and then entered the final couloir. As she had on the previous two sections, Blomkvist followed shortly after Coombs, but when she pulled into the couloir, she heard him yelling up to her. At first Blomkvist couldn't understand what he was saying, but then it became clear.

"Chad fell!" Coombs screamed. "Come down with a rope!"

Meanwhile, Farmer was still on the spine above her and couldn't see what was happening. "I couldn't hear very well," Farmer said. "Christina relayed across to me that Doug was basically calling for a rope." Farmer then traversed into the couloir and rejoined Blomkvist.

They got a visual on Coombs at the end of the funnel. He was down past the exit of the couloir screaming VanderHam's name. The snow was peppered with rocks. Coombs was sidestepping down, trying to get a visual on VanderHam.

"Chad!" Coombs screamed. "Chad!"

With his skis clinging to the snow, rock, and ice, Doug Coombs descended deeper and deeper into the abyss.

27

BLACKBIRDS

La Grave, France, 2014

I was almost there. A few more steps, and I'd be through the turnstile and into the bin and gone, but just as my ski pass turned the light green for "Go," I heard my name yelled from across the parking lot. *Damn. Almost.* Stepping back, I spotted a small figure standing in the snow waving something over his head.

"I got you a harness!" he yelled. "I'll meet you at the top." Joe Vallone had finally caught me.

I wasn't avoiding Joe Vallone himself—he'd become a friend and an invaluable source for understanding the nuanced inner workings of La Grave—but rather what Vallone had in mind. Two days earlier, Vallone had offered to take me out skiing. His schedule was clear for the next few days, he said, and it was now or never. La Grave was scary enough when I wasn't following the tracks of one of the most fearless skiers in town, and I shuddered to think of where Vallone might take me.

"Bring a harness," he had messaged me over Facebook. Not having a harness, I thought that was a good enough excuse to wiggle out of skiing with him. "Joe—thanks so much for your invitation, but I don't have a harness," I wrote back. "I don't want to muddle your plans for the day, so don't worry about me. We'll ski together eventually." Now as Vallone waved the harness over his head, I realized he had called my bluff and I was out of excuses.

The lifts had been closed yesterday due to extreme winds that gusted one hundred miles per hour on the summit that night. As the bin crept up, a strikingly different mountain passed outside the window. The high winds had scoured the snow, revealing sharp black rocks that had been deeply buried just days earlier. The light was flat and ominous. At the midway station, hazard lights blinked around the avalanche safety sign. Today's rating was four out of a possible five—hazardous. As instructed, I waited for Vallone at the restaurant at the top of the mountain.

Vallone busted through the doors of the restaurant like I'd seen him do so many times before at the K2 Pub. There was a possessed look in his eyes. He slung his backpack on the table and began unloading gear. Out came a rope, an ice ax, crampons, ice screws, avalanche beacons, a belay device, and finally a handful of nylon webbing that he balled up and tossed over to me.

"Here's your harness. It's a bit of a diaper, but it will hold you."

I began threading my ski boots awkwardly through the loops of the harness, wondering for the millionth time what I had gotten myself into.

"I'm taking you to the *classic* classic," Vallone said, fastening his ice ax on the back of his pack for swift access. "La Voute."

I'd heard about La Voute, which was indeed a classic at the top of La Grave's prerequisite runs, but it wasn't exactly a cakewalk. It was one of the road runs and required skiing over the glacier to the edge of a cliff, where we would rappel about a hundred feet into a couloir and ski seven thousand vertical feet to the road. All the guiding operations took their clients down La Voute, and it was regarded as an entrée to true ski mountaineering. And yet La Voute was not without inherent danger. Just two years earlier, a thirty-year-old guide, one of Vallone's friends, and a fifty-year-old client had been killed when they fell after the rappel point. I looked at Vallone and then followed him out of the restaurant.

As we clicked into our skis on the fringe of the glacier, Vallone gave me the rundown of the first sequence of turns. "Count to ten and then follow me," he said. "When I stop, always stop above me, never below, and then I'll tell you about the next section." Vallone's demeanor had changed. He was serenely calm. His words were clear and measured. He was in guide mode, and despite not knowing what was to come, I suddenly felt supremely safe in his care.

Watching him take off down the glacier's packed powder, I marveled at his technique. With a few beers in him at the K2 Pub, he was a live wire, but here in his element, Vallone was a swan. His body moved down the glacier with each turn committed to the form. He looked efficient and in control. He looked like he was having fun. After counting to ten, I shoved off after him. The snow pushed back against my skis, springing me through each turn. The snow had a zip to it, but also a grip. Locals had mused to me about the dynamic variability of snow in La Grave, but I only now understood what that meant.

"You're standing on air right now," Vallone said to me after I came to stop above him.

"Yeah, man, that was amazing."

"No, we're literally standing on air right now."

Then I understood what he meant: we were standing on the glacier. Only layers of snow stood between us and the ice, and maybe a bottomless crevasse.

"Interesting, huh?" he asked with a grin.

Gradually leaving the open expanse of the glacier, we started heading down avenues lined with rock walls. After twenty or so turns, Vallone would pull to the side and wait for me to rejoin him, and then he'd give me a briefing on the next section. Before long, we reached the point of rappel.

"Take your skis off and strap them to your pack," he instructed. Vallone pulled the rope from his pack and then fished from the snow a chain-link anchor mounted to a rock. He swiftly set up the rappel, threading the rope through the anchor and then on through a belay device attached to his harness. "Here, clip this to your harness," he said, handing me a carabiner tied to the other end of the rope. "I'm going to lower you in. It will be faster this way."

I clipped the carabiner to my harness.

"Okay, now walk to me," he said, "and then lean over the edge."

I walked over on wobbly legs and got caught in an awkward little dance with him on the small platform of snow.

"Lean over the edge," he said again.

I leaned back and felt the harness squeeze my crotch, reminding me that I did indeed have the balls to do this.

"You know, I've always wanted to ski this," Vallone said to me, straight faced.

"What do you mean?" I snapped back, hanging over the edge. "You've never skied this?"

He smirked. "No, I mean really *ski* this. Ski it without a rope. No rappeling."

Suspended over the cliff, I looked around. The cliff showed no signs of being even remotely skiable. "Is it possible?" I asked.

"I know of only five people to have ever done it," he said, his face serious again. "Doug Coombs was one of them."

SEVEN THOUSAND VERTICAL FEET LATER, Vallone and I stared back up at La Voute and the rest of the Alps peeling across the horizon. "It goes on and on," he said, dragging a nubby finger across the peaks. "There is a lifetime of lines to ski here. That's why I haven't left. La Meije cast her spell on me and I was doomed." There was no question how much Vallone loved these mountains. His face beamed with wonder and respect, and yet at the same time, I knew these mountains were also a source of deep sorrow in his life. They had claimed the lives of his best friend and his hero.

"Chad was as close to family as I had here. He was my brother," Vallone said. "He was the most positive person I'd ever known. Chad just did things sometimes that blew you away. He'd always say things were 'niiiice.' We'd ski shitty breakable crust all day, and at the bar at the end of the day, Chad would tell people it was the best breakable crust he'd ever skied. 'It was niiiice breakable crust.'" Vallone laughed softly and then paused. "I have a hard time understanding the whole accident. Two of the best skiers who ever lived made fatal decisions inside of minutes of each other in terrain that they could ski with their eyes closed." The airiness that Vallone had exuded after our descent now left him. "I went into the couloir the next day with Miles. We got the rope out so we could go through the terrain they fell over to retrieve gear and try to understand what happened." Vallone explained that he and VanderHam had been scouting another possible exit in the couloir earlier that season. "I don't know if he went for it. I will never know," he said. "I think he could have just had an equipment failure. He was skiing on a pair of skis that were worked and some beat-up bindings."

"How do you think Doug fell?" I asked.

"I tried to stand up in his tracks where he slipped, and I was clutching at the rocks trying to hold on and stand on my skis. I was blown away that he was standing there. He was on an exposed slab of rock," Vallone said. "Doug saved lives and probably broke the number-one rule of rescue: scene survey. Don't become another victim."

Vallone looked back up at the mountains and continued. "I can speculate all day, but I can say that they were well within their limits, not pushing any envelopes or doing anything 'extreme' by their definition."

Vallone led me to the road, where we'd be hitchhiking back to town. He went on to describe the days after the accident. Vallone had been completely devastated. A couple of days after the accident, he went and skied Pan de Rideau by himself. He was so out of his mind with grief, he said, that he couldn't focus on the traverse and very nearly slipped off the edge. Returning home, shattered with fear and anguish, Vallone threw his skis in the corner. He didn't know if he'd ever be able to ski again. "But I knew that's not what Chad and Doug would have wanted," he said. So three days later he grabbed his skis and went to the top. The weather was stunning, much like the day of the accident. Vallone strapped on his skins and hiked the glacier. First he skied the Pic de la Grave. Then he skinned back up and skied the Col de la Girose through the ice. Then he skinned back up and skied Col de la Girose around the rocks. These were all of Coombs's movie lines, and now they were Vallone's tribute to his fallen friends. He dragged himself back to the restaurant and collapsed on the deck, sobbing. Friends looked up at the lines and knew what they meant. They patted him on the shoulder. "Nice, Joe."

Once we'd taken the bin back to the top of the mountain, there was enough daylight left for only one more run, so Vallone suggested we relax and hang out at the restaurant. He ordered us a carafe of *vin chaud* and then pulled out a guitar that was designated for communal use. Prior to his skiing career, Vallone had been a dedicated musician, having studied drums in college. He still played a few gigs every now and again down at the K2 Pub, but mainly his talents were put toward serenading the après scene.

Without removing his jacket, he began strumming the old acoustic guitar, which I could now see had a "Coombs" sticker stuck to it just behind the strings. Then, to my surprise, Vallone began to sing a ballad by Pink Floyd, "Wish You Were Here." Out the window, blackbirds floated in the opaque sky. The restaurant hushed to a murmur as he sang to his fallen friends.

As Vallone finished the song, a group of three people walked into the restaurant, two men and a woman. "Have you spoken to her yet?" Vallone nodded in their direction.

"Who?"

"Christina," he said. "Have you spoken to Christina Blomkvist?"

Ever since Spricenieks had informed me that Christina Blomkvist still lived in La Grave, she hadn't been far from my mind. Outside of Matt Farmer, she was the only person who could tell me what actually happened to Coombs and VanderHam on that fateful run. I found the circumstances around Doug Coombs's death both pristinely clear and maddeningly mysterious. Undeniable was the fact that Coombs was killed while trying to save VanderHam's life. Where the confusion entered was how exactly Coombs fell.

He was so surefooted in the mountains, so comfortable standing right on the edge, that the idea of him simply falling had seemed impossible to those closest to him. Instead, many thought that only an avalanche could claim the man that never fell, hence the initial report that an avalanche had taken him over the edge. To dispel this misinformation, Matt Farmer sat down the day of the accident and wrote a report. After detailing the technical specifics of Polichinelle, Farmer elaborated on the moments leading up to Coombs's fall:

> *Just as Christina entered the middle of the top of the third couloir, Doug yelled up that "Chad fell, come down with a rope." I traversed into the middle of the couloir to the point at which I could see down to Doug, who was sidestepping down a rock rib below and right of the constriction at the base of the couloir. Christina and I saw Doug yelling Chad's name while sidestepping down and attempting to see over the cliff to his right. We saw his skis slip on the rock and he fell out of view over the rib.*

Despite the succinct clarity of Farmer's account, it left a lot of room for interpretation, particularly about what caused Coombs's skis to slip when he was sidestepping down to the edge. Throughout my research, I heard various theories of what might have happened. Some believed that as Coombs was sidestepping down, he came to a band of ice that circled the entire mountain at that elevation, which caused him to slip off the edge. Along these lines, other people believed his skis just slipped out from beneath him as he was standing at the edge, while still others thought he slid for a period of time before falling over the side. Emily Coombs believed that when her husband began to slip, he actually pointed his skis over the edge and tried to jump the cliff. Finally, there was the theory that when Matt Farmer began skiing down with the rope, which Coombs had called for, Farmer's sluff caused Coombs to lose his footing and slip.

The last of these theories raised another question: Why had Coombs called for a rope when he already had one in his backpack? One possible explanation was that in calling for a rope, Coombs didn't mean for the rope to be skied down to him. Rather, he meant for Farmer to establish an anchor and then throw him down the anchored rope. This would have allowed Coombs to secure himself as he sidestepped down to the edge of the cliff. But given the fact that Farmer and Coombs didn't have a direct line of communication, this could have been lost in translation. Neither Farmer nor Blomkvist knew that Coombs had a rope in his backpack.

In grappling with all the different theories of what happened in those final moments of Coombs's life, I decided that the only accounts that mattered where those of Christina Blomkvist and Matt Farmer. They were the only ones there. Everyone else's interpretations were irrelevant, serving only as a basis for me to ask pointed questions.

"C'mon, I'll introduce you," Vallone said, putting aside his guitar.

A rush of fear and adrenaline pulsed through me as I trailed Vallone to Blomkvist's table. I stood there feeling intensely awkward as he introduced me.

"He's here working on a project about Doug," Vallone told them. The two men reluctantly extended their hands to shake mine, but Christina Blomkvist didn't even seem look up at me. Her eyes remained fixed on something outside the window. I repositioned myself around the table to catch her gaze, and she finally looked up and smiled briefly without a word. She had a pleasant, serene face.

"I'd love to speak with you some time," I said. She nodded, again without saying anything.

Uncertainty had defined every one of my days in La Grave, but I finally landed on something I felt absolutely sure of: Christina Blomkvist wanted nothing to do with me. She didn't want to talk to me. She didn't want to relive what had surely been the most traumatic experience of her life. At the same time, another certainty emerged: I was going to do everything I could to speak with her. I hadn't known it when I left the States, but she was the reason I was here. Blomkvist was the last person to see Coombs alive, the last person to try to keep him alive.

For the next three weeks, I did everything I could to get Blomkvist to warm up to me. Anytime I saw her with her friends at the restaurant, I would awkwardly ask to sit with them. I tried to be as cordial as humanly possible—not talking too much, buying rounds of drinks, listening and smiling. But nothing seemed to thaw her guardedness. I gathered that she was naturally shy, and during the handful of times that I mustered up the courage to sit with her, Blomkvist probably uttered a total of twenty words to me. At the end of each of these meetings, I'd always look her in the eyes and say, "I'd love to speak with you. Can we pick a time to meet?"

She would just smile lightly and nod as if to say, "Yes, but not now."

I WAS RUNNING OUT OF time to speak with Blomkvist. I was set to leave La Grave in a couple of days, and as I packed up my chalet, anxiety fluttered in my mind. *Am I really about to leave here without talking to her?* I needed to know what happened. I needed to hear her tell the story. I couldn't leave without it. I decided that the next day, my last day, I would stake out the top of the mountain for her, just as I had for Orlans when I first arrived.

I got to the mountain around ten, took the bin to the top, and then grabbed a table outside the restaurant, directly across from the lift station. Every time a set of bins arrived, I waited for Blomkvist to appear, but she never did. I waited for hours, sitting there in the sun, scribbling in my journal, keeping watch for her. Despair was beginning to set in. I kept thinking about how despite making this huge effort—moving to La Grave, being accepted by the community, skiing this terrifying mountain day in and day out—I was about to leave without the most important piece of information for my journey.

Around three, when I couldn't handle my restlessness anymore, I decided I would stretch my legs and take a run to the bottom, and then jump on the last lift back to the top. The entire run down, my mind was elsewhere. I'd come such a long way, committed so much of my life, battled through so much doubt and fear, and now I was about to leave without completing my final objective. The sense of failure was crushing. I climbed into the bin at the midmountain station and pulled off my helmet and goggles. I was alone. Without really thinking, I said out loud, "Make this happen. Make this happen. I've come all this way. Please, make this happen."

The bin mounted the top of the lift station, rattling in through the old machinery. The doors opened. I grabbed my skis and turned to the exit. And then, miraculously, there she was. Lit by the sun, Blomkvist was standing directly in the doorway. She was alone, the first time I'd ever seen her without her group of friends. Now was the time.

She went to sit at one of the picnic tables directly outside the lift station. I hastily leaned my skis up against the outside of the lift station and walked over to her. The sky was clear and sapphire blue. The mountain was awash in sunlight. The time was four o'clock.

"Hi," I said almost inaudibly, pulling off my helmet. She smiled. I shuffled in front of her a bit. "So," I began, "I'm . . . I'm leaving tomorrow. And you know why I'm here." I paused again. "I don't really have any questions to ask you, but if you have something you want to tell me, I'm here to listen."

I then sat next to her at the picnic table and gazed up at La Meije in silence, a silence that was neither awkward nor uncomfortable. I didn't know if she was going to say anything to me, but at this point it didn't really matter. I'd made my last stand.

Blomkvist began to speak. The words came as slowly as water melting off a glacier. She told me about her friendship with VanderHam. About the dinners they shared in Ventelon, of the soups he was famous for making. And then a minute passed in silence. She then told me about Coombs. What he was like around town, how he filled La Grave with such fun, amazing energy. Another minute of silence. She spoke slowly. Stopping and starting. Thinking and then beginning again. All the while, I listened intensely, more intensely than I'd ever listened to anything in my life.

In her own time, Blomkvist then went on to describe the last time she saw Coombs and VanderHam alive. She opened the door to a memory that I suspected she had tried to shut out but never could.

"We shouldn't have gone," Blomkvist said, explaining that she always hated the Polichinelle. "It's too exposed." When she heard Coombs yell up, "Chad fell, come down with a rope," she relayed the message to Farmer, who still hadn't entered the final couloir. Blomkvist didn't have a rope but knew Farmer did. After Farmer skied across the middle of couloir to Blomkvist, the two watched Coombs sidestepping down through the rocks, past the point where you would exit to safety during a normal run. Coombs looked to be making his way down a steep, rocky arête to the very edge of the cliff, craning his neck, trying to get a visual on VanderHam. He was screaming VanderHam's name, his usually calm and composed voice now overcome with emotion. Blomkvist had never heard him like that. Coombs descended more and more out of view, until he was abruptly out of sight. Blomkvist thought she saw Coombs's skis slip out from beneath him, but his disappearance was subtle. "It made no sense," she said. "It was so strange to see him fall." She told Farmer to continue down with the rope because he was a better skier than she was. Farmer set off, cautiously making his way down the couloir.

When Farmer reached the end of the couloir, instead of following Coombs's path directly down the rocky arête, he skied around the rocks and then sidestepped into a safe position where he could look down the cliff. One of VanderHam's skis was sticking up from snow some six feet from where Farmer was now standing. From this vantage point, Farmer could see VanderHam's body about five hundred feet from the base of the cliff, on the apron of snow below. Then he spotted Coombs sixty feet above VanderHam. Coombs was sliding slowly, bent at the waist. His body was limp and lifeless, and his skis were dragging in the snow. Farmer pulled out his phone and called the helicopter rescue.

Meanwhile, Blomkvist began carefully navigating her way down the final section of the couloir. Famer talked her down through the choke and then onto the couloir's exit to the left. He called Miles Smart and Pelle Lång and told them that Coombs and VanderHam had fallen before sidestepping and bootpacking back up and following Blomkvist down the rest of the couloir.

When they skied down below the cliff, Farmer and Blomkvist could see both Coombs's and VanderHam's bodies about seventy-five feet apart. Farmer reached Coombs first, who was lying on his right side, facing uphill and bent slightly at his waist. Coombs's eyes were open, and his pupils were fixed and dilated. Apart from a small cut below his chin, there were no obvious signs of trauma. But Coombs didn't have a pulse and wasn't breathing. His lips had turned yellow and one of his ears was purple. Farmer performed rescue breaths and CPR on Coombs for approximately two minutes. He worked hard on him, hoping to bring him back to life, but deep down, Farmer knew Coombs was dead.

Meanwhile, Blomkvist had skied down to VanderHam, who was facedown in the snow. She discovered that he was still breathing and alerted Farmer, who then left Coombs to help with VanderHam. Although he was nonresponsive and had some swelling in his face, VanderHam still had a strong heartbeat and was breathing deeply. As they waited for the rescue helicopter to arrive, Farmer worked on VanderHam, performing rescue breaths and trying to keep his air passage clear, while Blomkvist returned to Coombs. As the minutes ticked by, it became more and more difficult to keep VanderHam's airway open. The swelling in his face was becoming more severe. His eyes were now swollen shut, but Farmer sensed that he was still alive inside. VanderHam moaned slightly, and just before the rescue helicopter arrived, Farmer thought he felt him squeeze his hand.

When the rescue helicopter arrived, it lowered three medics with their supplies. They immediately went to Coombs and confirmed Farmer's initial assessment: he was beyond saving. The head medic declared him dead, and then they turned their full attention to VanderHam, administering an IV and placing an oral airway to help him breathe. As they loaded VanderHam onto a backboard, his breathing remained strong. Farmer was hopeful that he was going to make it when the helicopter took him away.

Blomkvist had remained undeterred by the medics' conclusion that Coombs was dead and continued to perform rescue breaths on him. "We needed to try," she said. With each breath, she listened to the air fill his lungs and expected him to wake up at any second. Farmer joined in her efforts. They continued performing CPR for thirty minutes, refusing to give up, until finally the helicopter returned and they were forced to give Coombs away to the medics. By the time Farmer and Blomkvist were flown back to La Grave, they had received word that Chad VanderHam had been declared dead at the hospital in Briançon. They would learn later that Coombs had been killed instantly by a broken neck.

Blomkvist came to a natural conclusion in her story. She wept softly, the tears rolling down her cheeks from behind her sunglasses. I felt deep anguish radiating off her. “I'm glad I was there,” she said, “so they didn't have to die alone.” We then sat there in silence, staring up at La Meije. The scene played over in my mind. It wasn't sluff that made Coombs fall. It wasn't ice. It was an accident, a freak accident that killed Coombs.

Blackbirds floated in the pristine blue sky—the souls of fallen skiers. I was mentally and emotionally wrecked. Doug Coombs was dead. He died of the injury doctors warned him of all those years ago. He died trying to save the life of a friend in the mountains. He died following his heart to the edge of that cliff, like he'd followed his heart throughout his life.

And yet in this moment, Doug Coombs didn't seem dead at all. From the tip of Tuckerman Ravine to the shadow of La Meije, the impact of his life clearly still reverberated off the people he touched and in the mountains that he made his home. Coombs proved that some people possess more energy than others. They stoke it into a roaring blaze during the course of their lives so that even when they're gone, even when their flames flicker out and the embers turn to ash, those they left behind still feel their warmth and see their light.

“Christina,” a voice called out. We turned to find one of her friends waving to her from the deck of the restaurant.

“I should go,” Blomkvist said, rubbing the streak of tears from her cheeks.

I thanked her, trying to express the depths of my gratitude through my gaze. She just smiled softly, then turned and walked away, leaving me alone staring at La Meije. The sun beamed down around the peak in bright warm rays, and it dawned on me that this was exactly how the day looked when Coombs and VanderHam were killed. In fact, they had set off on that run not far from where I was now sitting.

I leaned back and reflected on the journey that had delivered me to this rarified seat in the snow. All the fear and the doubt. All the moments of serendipity. How far I'd come from being a kid in my parents' basement watching scenes of Coombs in ski movies. Back then, these mountains were so completely foreign to me, and Coombs was nothing more than a stranger. And yet I was now in the grips of these wild peaks, guided by this man whom I felt I finally understood. As this thought settled in my mind, the swarm of blackbirds rushed back high into the sky. They climbed in front of La Meije, fluttered a bit, and then fixed their wings and floated down in a beautiful formation, arching before the ferocious peak and making it look easy.

EPILOGUE

THE LEGACY

Jackson Hole, Wyoming, 2015

The study in Emily Coombs's home no longer felt so much like a shrine to her late husband. The skis and boots that once protruded from the closet were gone. Many of the ski passes that had been propped up on the bureaus were now stowed in drawers. Coombs's backpack still hung on a hook in the room, but it no longer held all the contents from that fateful day—just a pair of his gloves, a hat, and the rope. Photos of him were still scattered throughout the room, but now they were accompanied by portraits of young children. The first things I noticed about these new photos were the smiles; they filled the frames with joy. The children in the photos were Hispanic, their hair olive black and their eyes wide and angelic.

"I'm coming up," Emily called from the stairway. She entered the room cradling two binders of 35-mm slides. "Going through these photos is a huge, *huge* job," she said, placing them next to me at a table by the window. She opened the first binder and began studying the old images of her and Coombs. "Oh, here are some classics from the Bozeman days," she said, eyeing a slide through the light from the windows.

"Look at us . . . how young we were." Emily handed me the slide. "You know, there was a time when I could never look at these photos."

Now, nearly ten years since the accident that claimed her husband's life, Emily had come a long way. Her relationship with Coombs had defined most of her life, and his sudden death had left her completely devastated. "It was like I had to become a different person just to deal with it," she said. "But now I'm back to how I used to be." She handed me an old photo of herself skiing through deep powder, her long red ponytail flying behind her. "Especially with what I'm doing now."

Around the time I first met Emily three years ago, she was in the process of launching a foundation in memory of her husband that would be dedicated to enabling children from low-income families to ski. Emily explained that 30 percent of the town's population was Hispanic, and almost none of them had ever stepped foot on the ski slopes that were right out their back doors. Parents of these families worked multiple jobs, which forced many of them to leave their children at home after school to watch television or play video games. Even if they did have the time to take them to the slopes, the majority of these families couldn't afford the exorbitant costs associated with skiing. Enter the Doug Coombs Foundation.

"You should see what skiing does for these kids," Emily said, her voice brimming with unmistakable passion. "It just changes them. All of a sudden they have this incredible confidence. And they're just so happy to be out there." The Doug Coombs Foundation now had well over a hundred children participating in the program, which provided them with skis, boots, gear, lift tickets, instructions, and perhaps most importantly, the opportunity to access the mountains that were previously so close and yet so far away. Much like she had done as a young girl mentoring kids in the inner city of Boston, Emily was now exposing these children to a whole new world.

"Some people have asked me why we're teaching these Latino kids to ski when they won't be able to afford to do it as adults," Emily said.

"But they're completely missing the point. We're trying to raise these children out of poverty. Skiing is just the tool that we're using to do it." Emily believes that the confidence these children develop through skiing combined with the good school system in town propels them into a more promising future. She wants to change the paradigm so that it isn't a matter of *if* these children will go to college, but *when*. I couldn't imagine a more fitting tribute to her husband, who in his life instilled confidence in his clients and peers, enabling them to achieve feats that they previously thought were impossible. Now Emily was doing the same for these children, and it was changing their lives dramatically. "Wait till you meet Jordan," she said. "You'll see what I'm talking about."

Ten-year-old Jordan Vargas had become one of the brightest stars of the Doug Coombs Foundation. Vargas was the son of two loving, hardworking parents. His father worked two jobs, seven days a week, while his mother worked full-time at the local hospital's employee and patient housing complex. Despite their tireless commitment to their family, the Vargases didn't earn enough money to support their son's budding interest in ski racing. That was when Emily swooped in. Now, through the Doug Coombs Foundation, Jordan and his younger sister Michelle were able to ski. I'd just traveled across the country to see Jordan in action.

The following day, I showed up at the base of Snow King Mountain in downtown Jackson around 2:45 p.m. to watch Jordan and the rest of the Jackson Hole Ski and Snowboard Club practice. Emily had arranged for me to ride the chairlift with Jordan as he skied laps with the rest of his team. Ambling around the parking lot, I watched as moms pulled up in Porsches and Land Rovers, and then unloaded their kids with their ski gear. A bus arrived, and another horde of young children poured onto the parking lot and then entered the locker room. Jackson Hole had become an enclave for the ultra wealthy, and the growing economic divide was evident just in this parking lot.

I snapped the buckles on my boots and made my way to the base of the lift to wait for Jordan. With all the kids dressed in identical jackets and helmets, I thought it was going to be impossible to pick him out from the crowd, but he made it easy. The ten-year-old skied right up to me and waved me along. "Come on," he said excitedly. "Follow me." We slid up to the lift attendant and then waited for the chair to swoop around.

"Do you want me to lower the safety bar?" I asked Jordan after we sat down.

"No, it's okay," he said. "So what do you want to know?"

Jordan sat poised, waiting with quiet confidence. He couldn't have been more than four feet tall, and yet he possessed that same heightened presence I'd witnessed in many of the guides I'd skied with over the last three years. He was like a taut spring loaded with energy.

"I heard you're quite the skier," I said. "You're skiing with the U-12 kids now, right?"

"Yeah, and I'm only ten."

"What's that like?" I asked.

"I like it," Jordan said quietly. "It's like . . . like I have a voice now. People listen to me."

"They didn't listen to you before?"

"No, kids used to pick on me because I was short. But now those kids are my friends. Like him, right there"—he pointed to a boy below us—"he used to make fun of me, but now he's my friend."

Jordan's self-assuredness suddenly made me feel like a sideline reporter. "So . . . where would you like to go with your skiing?" I asked.

"Alaska," he said without a moment's hesitation.

"Wow, really? Alaska, huh?"

"Yeah, I'd love to ski there," he said. "The mountains are so big, I heard, and there's also a husky dog race I want to see. I'm definitely going to go." Jordan stared up at me with big, optimistic eyes. He was absolutely sure of himself.

"Yes, you will," I agreed.

"So are you going to watch me ski?" Jordan asked as the chair reached the top and we prepared to unload.

"Yeah, I'll be watching from the side," I said, "but pretend I'm not here."

We slid off the chairlift, and Jordan rejoined his team while I continued along the cat track to the top of the run. The town of Jackson sprawled out below Snow King Mountain, which boasted the steepest north-facing FIS racecourse in the contiguous United States. I skied down halfway to a grove of trees to watch. The little racers peeled past me. All of them could have beaten me to the bottom, probably with seconds to spare.

Then I spotted Jordan about to drop in. He adjusted his goggles and pulled a balaclava up over his chin and then took off, lowering himself into a squat over his skis. He ripped each of his turns—*BAM BAM BAM*—and then scorched by me like a jet fighter. I watched him cruise all the way down until I lost him amid the other skiers collecting at the base.

Jordan was a damn good skier, that was for certain, but he didn't look all that different than many of the other kids on the hill. And that was exactly the point. Jordan's parents didn't drive a Porsche. He wasn't raised in ski boots. But with the opportunity given to him by the Doug Coombs Foundation, Jordan had become an equal. On this steep racecourse, it didn't matter what his parents did for work, or where he lived, or what color his skin was; the playing field was level. I could only guess where skiing would take Jordan in the years to come —like it had for Coombs. Like it had for me.

I turned my attention back to the top of the run. There was another skier I'd come to watch today.

Twelve-year-old David Coombs pulled up at the top of the slope. I recognized him by his height and his huge smile. He stood there laughing with his buddies, waiting for his turn to ski. When David shoved off down the slope, he looked loose and comfortable on his skis. He had a fluidity and style to his form. But what struck me most was David's smile—it never left his face. Watching him reminded me of something his father had said years ago when an interviewer asked him what he thought about being called the best skier in the world. "That's stupid," Coombs responded. "There is no best skier in the world." When the interviewer pressed him on it, Coombs said, "The best skier in the world is the one having the most fun."

By that measure, David Coombs looked to be the king of Snow King.

ACKNOWLEDGMENTS

Now, whenever I walk into a library or bookstore, I can't help but think, *Would you look at all these lives?* So many people go into the writing of a book beyond the person with the pen in his or her hand. Anyone who has been in my life during the last three years can be found somewhere between the lines of this book.

First and foremost, I must express my deepest gratitude to Emily Coombs and the whole Coombs family for entrusting me to tell Doug's story. This project has been the thrill of my life, and I will be forever grateful for this gift you have given me.

Thank you to my parents for your unwavering support of everything I've ever set my mind to. From the moment you dropped me off at the airport as I headed off into the wild unknown to pursue this project, you've believed in my every step. I love you.

Thank you to all of my family and friends, especially Jenny Johnson, Mark Cocuzzo, Michael Campbell, Joshua Simpson, Kit Noble, and Peter Sheppard. In moments of doubt, you were the ones to champion me forward to take the next step. I must also thank my buddies from my hometown, especially Walter Russell, Ryan O'Connor, Ryan Conlon, and Billy Regan, for keeping me connected to where the steps began.

Thank you to all those who helped me in the writing process, especially William O'Neill, Kirsten Colton, and the entire team at Mountaineers Books. Thank you to photographers Ace Kvale, Wade McKoy, and Larry Prosor for generously contributing images in honor of your friend Doug. I also owe a debt of gratitude to authors Ted Bell and Charles Graeber for their professional advice and insights. And, of course, thank you to Bruce Percelay and my team at *N Magazine* for truly making it possible for me to write this book.

Finally, thank you to the many people who helped me in tracking the wild Coomba. From Coombs's childhood friends, to his college buddies, to his fellow guides, former clients, and ski partners in Jackson Hole, Valdez, and La Grave, I sincerely appreciate all the intimate stories you shared about your friend.

And to all those pondering an idea for an adventure, remember what Doug Coombs would say: "You don't know if you don't go."

ABOUT THE AUTHOR

PHOTO BY KIT NOBLE

Robert Cocuzzo is a writer and editor. After studying English and history at the College of the Holy Cross and the University of St. Andrews, Cocuzzo became a US Coast Guard–certified charter boat captain and guided clients on the open Atlantic. He began his writing career during a winter-long backpacking trip in Patagonia. Shorty after returning, Cocuzzo became the editor of *N Magazine*, a lifestyle publication based on the island of Nantucket. Cocuzzo writes for a number of publications and splits his time between Nantucket, Boston, and the White Mountains of New Hampshire. His website is www.robcocuzzo.com.